EGYPTIAN POLITICS

EGYPTIAN POLITICS

The Dynamics of Authoritarian Rule

Maye Kassem

LYNNE
RIENNER
PUBLISHERS

BOULDER
LONDON

Published in the United States of America in 2004 by
Lynne Rienner Publishers, Inc.
1800 30th Street, Boulder, Colorado 80301
www.rienner.com

and in the United Kingdom by
Lynne Rienner Publishers, Inc.
3 Henrietta Street, Covent Garden, London WC2E 8LU

Library of Congress Cataloging-in-Publication Data
Kassem, Maye, 1966–
    Egyptian politics : the dynamics of authoritarian rule / Maye Kassem.
      p.   cm.
    Includes bibliographical references and index.
    ISBN 1-58826-222-7 (hc : alk. paper)
    ISBN 1-58826-247-2 (pb : alk. paper)
    1. Democracy—Egypt.   2. Authoritarianism—Egypt. 3. Egypt—
Politics and government.   I. Title.
    JQ3881.K37   2004
    320.962—dc22

                                           2003060297

British Cataloguing in Publication Data
A Cataloguing in Publication record for this book
is available from the British Library.

I don't believe the 1952 revolution had any positive features, since democracy is still missing. Even its social reforms led to the failure of our economy. The greatest failure of the revolution is the lack of democracy, which I believe led to our defeat in 1967. Egypt has never experienced a democratic government from 1952 up till now. Democracy has existed in some form in different stages, but its core is still missing. The press is not free in reality, otherwise Article 80(D) of the penal code would never exist. This article criminalizing "harming Egypt's image" in effect means no one can criticize the government, as in the old days when it was a crime to "dishonor the person of the king." It is this article that is disgraceful to Egypt and taints its status within the family of nations. The revolution embraced the slogan "raise your head, my brother, for the age of oppression is over," but it replaced it with the heavy foot of Abdel Nasser that kept people's heads down.

—*Reflections by Awad al-Mor,*
former chief justice of the Supreme Constitutional Court,
on the fiftieth anniversary of Egypt's 23 July 1952 revolution

Contents

Acknowledgments

I am indebted to many people without whom this book would not exist. First and foremost are those who allowed me to interview them and gain from their experience in political activism. Of course, I am responsible for all interpretations presented here.

I am also indebted to my senior colleague and good friend Enid Hill, who back in 1998 suggested the idea for this book and has since supported and encouraged me. I also thank Dan Tschirgi and Walid Kazziha for their constant academic support and friendship over the years. The capacity to nurture and encourage junior academics is second nature to Hill, Tschirgi, and Kazziha, and is something that makes me eternally grateful to them. The political science department at the American University in Cairo (AUC) is truly blessed to have such great people. The provost of AUC, Tim (Earl) Sullivan, is an institution in his own right, and his kindness and consideration for anyone who has ever sought his assistance makes me just one of numerous people who are grateful to him. I also thank the dean of the School of Humanities and Social Science, Nicholas Hopkins, for his kindness, support, and sense of humor over the years. Last, but by no means least, I would like to thank Ingy Kamel for being such a brilliant person and my anchor during what has been an exceptionally busy time at AUC.

I also extend my thanks to my colleagues and friends outside the realm of AUC. Raymond Hinnebusch, Diane Singerman, and Augustus Richard Norton are not only first-class scholars but first-class human beings. I am eternally grateful for their academic support and guidance on this project, as well as for their friendship, which means more to me than they can ever know. I also extend my gratitude to Sami Zubaida, Eberhard Kienle, Ann Lesch, and Lisa Anderson for their influence on my work and for being such great people. I remain indebted to my original mentor and good friend, Charles Tripp, whose academic influence on me remains as strong today as it was when I was his student many years ago.

My dearest friends, Dzidra Stipnieks and Conchita Anorve-Tschirgi, are an endless source of inspiration and love. I am lucky and blessed to have such wonderful girlfriends.

My immediate family provides support from both here in Cairo and from the United States. In the United States, I would like to extend my love and warmest gratitude to my in-laws, Kim and Marcia Stacher, and the rest of my wonderful "Amriky" tribe— Alexa, Grammy and Pappy Foutz, and Grammy Stacher. In Cairo, the unconditional love and support of my parents, "Popsy" and "Bata," makes it impossible to properly express my love and gratitude toward them. I dedicate this book to them and especially to my husband, Josh, whom I love and miss so very much.

1

Introduction

Since the military coup d'etat of 23 July 1952, the formal political structure in Egypt has changed considerably. The populist-socialist single-party system established under Nasser has been replaced by a political framework in which opposition parties have been legally functioning since 1976. Furthermore, the introduction of the *infitah* (the economic open-door policy) in 1974 and the adoption of an economic reform and structural adjustment program (ERSAP) in 1991 have reinforced the change of direction adopted by the post-1952 regime over the years. These trends, in turn, have caused some optimism among various academics and analysts, one of whom went so far as to conclude that "Egypt's democratization is functioning . . . [with Egypt being] a maturing rather than a mature democracy."[1]

It is clear, however, that this is not the case. Indeed, personal authoritarian rule in Egypt survives and has been maintained for more than five decades. Indicative of this, implementation of a multiparty arena has not affected the outcome of government. The formal branches of government remain subservient to the overwhelming domination of the executive, and the development of autonomous groupings and constituencies remains hindered and weak. In addition, the existence of Western and particularly U.S. support of the regime since the 1970s has allowed the political system in Egypt to adopt disparate liberal guises while in fact doing little to encourage genuine change with regard to the country's personal authoritarian system of rule. While the Nasser, Sadat, and Mubarak regimes have had their own distinct characteristics, the nature of personal authoritarian rule in the presidency has remained unchanged during all three eras. The purpose of this book is to examine why authoritarian rule is so resilient in contemporary Egypt—to explain why democracy is not developing in Egypt and why authoritarian regimes in general possess the ability to resist international pressures for democratization.

Democratization Trends in the International Arena

In what appeared to be a shift toward democratic transitions, more than 100 authoritarian regimes across the globe began moving toward political liberalization from the mid-1970s onward.[2] For its part, the Western democratic sphere and the United States in particular attempted to reactivate its role as a promoter of overseas democracy. The United States had already prominently pursued such a role following the successful wars of 1898, 1918, and 1945, when "international forces were in a position to overwhelm domestic political tendencies."[3] Economic and political incentives were subsequently extended in efforts to assist this so-called worldwide democratic revolution.[4] Yet as one study noted, democratization-linked incentives, as illustrated by those extended by the United States to Latin American countries, have "not been so stable, predictable, long-term and impersonal."[5] For example, it is commonly accepted that pressures for democratization on U.S.-allied authoritarian regimes are minimal in that "no precise criteria of what counts as 'democracy' are needed . . . [while] foreign governments that are not reliable allies of the U.S.A. as a global power . . . will find it hard to secure recognition in Washington as truly democratic, however liberal their electoral practices or their political philosophies."[6] In this regard, while international pressures for democratization may be vocal and at times linked to aid, in practice economic and security interests continue to take priority over genuine pressures to democratize.

This type of contradictory policy is most evident when assessing U.S. relations with the authoritarian regimes of the Middle East. Lisa Anderson put this very well when she raised the question of why the Middle East governments exhibit "uniform hostility to democracy."[7] As Anderson points out, it is partly U.S. foreign policy that has helped to shelter these regimes, since the United States is not only "supporting autocratic but compliant friends," but also "continues to collude with regimes in power, permitting fixed elections and human rights fakery . . . that allow it and its client regimes to continue in the game."[8] Though the international arena's interests can create indifference to genuine transformations from authoritarian rule, this is largely a secondary factor explaining the endurance and resilience of authoritarian regimes.

Indeed, it is the internal political dynamics and manipulative strategies of the authoritarian regimes themselves that predominantly determine their own survival. Most authoritarian regimes have, for their own benefit, allowed limited liberalization, but such concessions are based on concerns with self-preservation and were never intended to result in genuine democratization. Political liberalization, in other words, is not necessarily challenging to authoritarian rule because "even though there [are international and] societal pressures for reducing authoritarian controls, the process of political liberalization [is] state-induced, and the state retains a considerable degree of management over the process."[9] Thus, when an authoritarian regime embarks on a program of political liberalization, the process is generally well enough contained and controlled that it poses no threat to the regime's survival.

After all, one of the most fundamental aspects of authoritarianism is that "an arbitrary and usually a personal government uses law and the coercive instruments of the state to expedite its own purposes of monopolizing power and denies the political rights and opportunities of all other groups for that power."[10] Furthermore, enduring authoritarian regimes allow for limited pluralism (even under a single-party system) and do not depend on coercion as the predominant form of control (although, if necessary, there is little hesitation in resorting to it). Rather, as the case of Egypt illustrates, successful and enduring authoritarian regimes depend on a balanced use of patronage and skillful cooptation, the adoption of exclusionary laws, and the coercive apparatus of the state. The combination of these strategies allows for the existence of contained pluralism within an authoritarian regime and permits it to adopt images of liberalization/democratization without actually conceding to such measures.

Patronage and Cooptation

The significance of patronage and cooptation as mechanisms of containment and control within authoritarian regimes cannot be underestimated. True, all authoritarian leaders have resorted to coercion at some point during their tenure. However, in order to survive, they must seek the type of authority and power that extends beyond that produced by coercion and intimidation. Enduring authoritarian regimes, therefore, like all political systems, understand the necessity of expanding the basis of their political support. In this regard, most authoritarian rulers are aware that "acquiescence can perhaps be achieved solely by coercion, but support and acceptance cannot."[11] In the absence of democratic institutions, accountable representation, and a compelling and mobilizing ideology, authoritarian regimes depend on the distribution of patronage to establish a clientelist system that secures some form of stability. A clientelist system, or "clientelism," can be described as

> a system of patron-client ties that bind leaders and followers in relationships not only of mutual assistance and support, but also of recognized and accepted inequality between big man and lesser men. The ties usually extend from the center of a regime—that is from the ruler to his lieutenants, clients and other followers, and through them, their followers, and so on. The image of clientelism is one of extensive chains of patron-client ties.[12]

In all clientelist cases, "the interest in patronage resources is directed specifically at persons with power, positions and influence in the ruling councils of the state—that is at office holders in the cabinet, the party, the army, the civil service, and parastatal organizations."[13]

Authoritarian rulers inevitably provide their own parties with access to state resources, while denying such access to the legalized opposition. This was well illustrated in Suharto's Indonesia, where implementation of a three-party system was tightly controlled in favor of the president's Golkar Party. As Paul Brooker explains:

> The regime strengthened Golkar's competitive advantage by exploiting its status as the regime's official party. The civil service was mobilized to support Golkar and it became obligatory for civil servants to campaign as well as vote for the party. Officials' influence over rural society was particularly important, with the Department of Internal Affairs being used to create a rural vote-winning patronage machine for Golkar. In addition to various opportunities for using small-scale state patronage, public works projects, such as bringing electricity and clean water to the villages, provided opportunities for large-scale patronage.[14]

In the face of such tactics, the other two parties were so marginalized in the arena of electoral competition that it became difficult to maintain even an appearance of multiparty competition. In fact, "by the time of the 1987 elections the regime was actually becoming concerned about [the opposition parties'] weakness."[15]

Nevertheless, while clientelism clearly is an important source of opposition containment and control, it would be difficult for it to function as such without the safety net provided by restrictive exclusionary laws that formally ensure a regime's monopoly on power.

Exclusionary Laws:
The Legal-Constitutional Framework

Exclusionary laws can range from control over the appointment and dismissal of government officials to restrictions of the media, political contests, civil society, and policymaking. This encompasses virtually all the areas deemed important to the preservation of the political status quo. In other words, the law is used "virtually as a license of unrestrictive command."[16] Robert Jackson and Carl Rosberg explain this paradox in relation to former president Jomo Kenyatta of Kenya and other authoritarian rulers in Africa:

> An emphasis on legality has been characteristically strong in Kenya, where constitutional amendments and statutory provisions gave former President Jomo Kenyatta virtually a "blank cheque" to bring emergency powers into operation anywhere in the country and at any time. . . . Other African rulers have been granted similar discretionary powers. Both civilian and military rulers in contemporary Africa have employed law in a manner reminiscent of the royal use of edicts and decrees in absolutist Europe. . . . [This] has involved a degree of discretionary power that in some cases has added up to arbitrary rule.[17]

A legal-constitutional framework that provides authoritarian regimes with the right to exercise abundant powers is thus an additional tool that allows such regimes the necessary flexibility to change the outward appearance of the system while ensuring its survival. A good example of this is the case of Morocco under King Hassan in the 1960s. When, after the promulgation of a new constitution, the monarchical forces gained only 69 of 144 seats in a legislative election, the king "suspended the constitution and reverted to government through his ministry of interior, first under a state of emergency and later under a new fundamental law that legalized his absolute power."[18]

Similar tactics can be detected in other authoritarian regimes. For example, in Syria, a new constitution in 1973 was structured around the National Progressive Front (NPF), an alliance established in 1972 between President Hafez al-Asad's Ba'ath Arab Socialist Party (BASP) and four other legalized parties (the Union of Arab Socialists, the Socialist Unionist Organization, the Arab Socialist Movement, and the Syrian Communist Party).[19] Although such a venture indicated a democratic transition, in reality and decades later the "powers of the [Syrian] president remain, constitutionally and as a matter of fact, almost absolute. . . . According to the constitution, the president can rule by decree and without parliamentary participation, and if circumstances so demand, he can veto parliamentary laws and dissolve parliament."[20] Such a strategy meant that all the laws "that had been passed by parliament have been introduced by the executive."[21] The legal-constitutional framework allowed the fundamental nature of authoritarian rule to be preserved regardless of change to the system's outward appearance.

The use of the legal-constitutional framework to preserve the political status quo is particularly evident in the electoral arena. As Andreas Schedler points out:

> The electoral laws of post-revolutionary Mexico kept regional and religious parties as well as independent candidates out of the electoral arena. In Cote d'Ivoire, Kenya and Zambia incumbent presidents used custom-made "nationality clauses" to prevent their most serious competitors from running. In Gambia, coup-monger Yahya Jammeh pushed through a new constitution that shut the country's entire political elite out of the electoral game. In much of the Arab world, radical Islamist movements are either legally proscribed (as in Egypt, Tunisia, and Algeria) or admitted but tightly curbed (as in Yemen and Jordan).[22]

The legal apparatus in this regard is an instrument that not only empowers an authoritarian regime, but also provides it with the flexibility to move from a one-party to a multiparty structure (or to suspend such structures indefinitely) without being challenged in the process. Those individuals and groups who do challenge such unbalanced laws and rules are likely to unleash the state's coercive apparatus.

The Coercive Apparatus: Regime Protectors

In all systems of government, the state's military and police forces are important with regard to defending the country and ensuring that government policies are appropriately observed. In authoritarian systems, however, the role of the coercive apparatus extends into the political realm much more prominently. Apart from direct military interventions in the form of coups, the military (and police) performs an important political role in terms of supporting and even intervening to protect authoritarian regimes. In the absence of such support, it would be virtually impossible for an authoritarian regime to maintain its power. As Jason Brownlee recently argued, authoritarian regimes are more likely to be undermined if they are prevented from using repression "to stop opposition movements working for change."[23] Examples of regimes that were restrained from using the military during times of political unrest—primarily because of international pressure—and subsequently collapsed include the pre-1979 regime in Iran, as well as the regimes in the Philippines, Zaire, and Romania, to name but a few. The survivors, on the other hand, have been those that have not hesitated to repress political dissent, such as the regimes in Tunisia, Syria, Libya, and Iraq (until the U.S.-led 2003 war brought its downfall).[24]

Gaining and maintaining the support of the coercive apparatus entails the constant flow of state patronage, as well as strategic alliances within the highest levels of the security-apparatus hierarchy. The degree to which such controlling strategies assist in securing the support of the coercive apparatus is aptly reflected not only in the case of contemporary Egypt, as is discussed later in this book, but also in the case of contemporary Syria, among others. During the presidency of Hafez al-Asad (1970–2000), the senior military posts became reserved primarily for the president's "trusted Alawi kinsmen."[25] At the same time, "military expansion kept professional officers happy with promotions and equipment"[26] and their domestic role became incorporated in society to the degree that "in many villages, the military was a preferred prestige career . . . and local officers viewed as brokers with the state bureaucracy."[27] Corrupt behavior on the part of police and intelligence personnel was also tolerated by the regime.[28] As a result, the coercive apparatus in Syria safeguarded the Asad regime for more than thirty years and suppressed no less than three major antiregime uprisings (1973, 1980, and 1982) in the process.[29] The deaths of thousands in these uprisings undoubtedly acted "as a serious deterrent to violent opposition."[30]

* * *

A program of so-called political liberalization and the formal adoption of a democratic framework can hardly be perceived as threatening when autonomous political groupings are either extremely weak or entirely absent from the equation. When a multiparty arena is created in a contained and overtly controlled environment, the likelihood of participating groups developing into autonomous and potentially challenging entities remains slim. As Thomas Carothers notes, "It is . . . striking how often electoral competition does little to stimulate the renovation or development of political parties."[31] In fact, as long as an authoritarian regime maintains its manipulative and dominating strategies of rule, it can persist over a long period of time without actually conceding power. The very dynamics of authoritarian rule thus are useful for explaining the resilience of authoritarian regimes, indicating why, since the 1970s, less than 20 out of the 100 "transition" countries "are clearly en route to becoming successful, well-functioning democracies."[32]

Contemporary Egypt provides a good example in this regard since it remains one of the most embedded authoritarian systems in the Middle East. Although Egypt's political system has changed considerably over the second half of the twentieth century, the system of personal authoritarian rule created by Nasser has not only remained constant, but has also managed to incorporate those changes to further strengthen its own position.

Framework of Analysis

The chapters that follow illustrate why personalized authoritarian rule continues to survive in Egypt in the face of political changes and reforms. In Chapter 2, tracing the emergence of the presidency as the dominant power over the legislature and judiciary, I look at the balance of power that formally exists between these three branches of government and consider the political dynamic that renders the president the ultimate source of power and authority. This chapter provides insight into the nature and weaknesses of Egypt's political institutions and why such characteristics are important to the survival of the personal authoritarian rule that is embedded in the presidency.

Chapter 3 is devoted to party politics and electoral participation. Here, I discuss Nasser's, Sadat's, and Mubarak's perceptions of political parties and democracy, as well as the mechanisms that have been adopted over the decades to ensure that political parties and democracy fit within the framework envisaged by each president. I also analyze the patterns of participation that have emerged and the negative consequences of those patterns for political development in Egypt.

The nature of civil society and human rights in Egypt is the subject of Chapter 4. The examples of trade unions, professional associations, and human rights organizations illustrate how civil society and human rights are perceived by the regime, as well as the mechanisms adopted by the regime to contain and control developments in this arena. One point emphasized is that civil society groups in contemporary Egypt perform as they do because of the political system in which they function, and not because of the sociocultural environment in which they exist.

Chapter 5 examines the role of the opposition forces, for the most part political Islamists, which are legally and coercively excluded from the formally defined political arena in Egypt. The exclusionary nature of authoritarian systems means that potentially challenging groups are not recognized as legitimate players on the political scene. This, in turn, provides the regime with the legal authority to oppress these groups, thus maintaining the preeminent role of the presidency. A key question posed in this chapter is the degree to which such exclusion and oppression have shaped the nature of the Islamist parties in contemporary Egypt. A detailed examination of such moderate, popular groups as the Muslim Brotherhood, as well as the more extreme manifestations of Islamism, such as Al-Jama'a al-Islamiya and Jihad, supports the thesis that the rise of political Islam (especially in its extremist form) is directly linked to the exclusionary nature of the system and the occasionally brutal tactics it employs. The link between domestic regime tactics and the emergence of Islamic terrorism on the international, and in particular Western, front is also discussed.

Reassessing the main themes discussed in the book, I argue in Chapter 6 that the Egyptian political system is incredibly resilient due to the adaptable and flexible nature of its personal authoritarian system of rule—and point to the negative consequences of such systems both on the national level and in the international arena.

Notes

1. Korany, "Egypt," p. 65.
2. Carothers, "The End of the Transition Paradigm," p. 9.
3. O'Donnell, Schmitter, and Whitehead, *Transitions from Authoritarian Rule,* p. 8.
4. This term was adopted and regularly used by U.S. president Ronald Reagan and his senior officials in the mid-1980s. Carothers, "The End of the Transition Paradigm," p. 6.
5. O'Donnell, Schmitter, and Whitehead, *Transitions from Authoritarian Rule,* p. 23.
6. Ibid., p. 11.
7. Anderson, "Arab Democracy," p. 4.
8. Ibid., p. 13.
9. Monshipouri, *Democratization, Liberalization, and Human Rights in the Third World,* p. 14.
10. Jackson and Rosberg, *Personal Rule in Black Africa,* p. 23.
11. Ibid., p. 38.
12. Ibid., p. 39.
13. Ibid., p. 11.
14. Brooker, *Non-Democratic Regimes,* pp. 239–240.
15. Ibid., p. 240.
16. Jackson and Rosberg, *Personal Rule in Black Africa,* p. 24.
17. Ibid., p. 25.
18. Linz, *Totalitarian and Authoritarian Regimes,* p. 147.
19. Picard, "Syria Returns to Democracy," p. 132.
20. Perthes, "Economic Liberalization and the Prospects of Democratization," p. 252.
21. Ibid., p. 253.
22. Schedler, "Elections Without Democracy," p. 42.
23. Brownlee, ". . . And Yet They Persist," p. 57.
24. Ibid.
25. Hinnebusch, *Syria,* p. 86.
26. Ibid.
27. Ibid., p. 87.
28. Ibid., p. 85.
29. Ibid.
30. Ibid.
31. Carothers, "The End of the Transition Paradigm," p. 15.
32. Ibid., p. 9.

2

Governance from Nasser to Mubarak

In a recent study on legislative politics in the Arab world, the authors noted that, of the six countries studied, the Egyptian legislature since the 1990s performed "a less significant role than in the other five countries."[1] The reason is that the Egyptian legislature continues to find it difficult "to assert its influence against a powerful executive jealous of its prerogatives."[2] Consequently, the authors noted, "The balance of power between executive and legislative branches, which has always favored the former, tilted yet further in that direction in the 1990s."[3] This observation is not erroneous, because since Nasser ascended to the executive branch in June 1956, the presidency has developed and continues to be the most dominant force in contemporary Egyptian politics.

The main argument in this chapter is that the enormous powers that have accumulated in Nasser's, Sadat's, and Mubarak's presidencies have rendered the Egyptian political system one of the most resilient personal authoritarian systems in the world. Personal authoritarian rule, to borrow Robert Jackson and Carl Rosberg's definition, is a system of government whereby

> persons take precedence over rules, where the officeholder is not effectively bound by his office and is able to change its authority and powers to suit his own personal and political needs. In such a system of personal rule, the rulers and other leaders take precedence over the formal rules of the political game: the rules do not effectively regulate political behavior, and we therefore cannot predict or anticipate conduct from a knowledge of the rules. To put this in old fashioned, comparative government terms, the state is a government of men and not of laws.[4]

While the collapse of pan-Arabism and the socialist-populist ideologies by the late 1960s resulted in an ideological void, the presidency's extensive powers have remained intact. In this regard, Juan Linz's more contemporary concept of "neosultanistic regimes" can be applied to the understanding of Egypt's political system since Nasser's death in 1970. While a neosultanistic regime is a form of personal ruler, the system's underlying structure is that "loyalty to the ruler is motivated not by his embodying or articulating an ideology, nor by a unique personal mission, nor by any charismatic qualities, but by a mixture of fear and rewards to his collaborators."[5] In other words, "the ruler exercises his power without restraint, at his own discretion . . . unencumbered by rules" and without "any commitment to an ideology or value system."[6] This does not imply that such systems of rule are devoid of modern structures of government. Indeed, as Linz points out, "Such regimes can in many ways be modern . . . [but] what characterizes them is the weakness of traditional and legal-rational legitimization and the lack of ideological justification."[7]

In the case of contemporary Egypt, the emergence of personal authoritarian rule and its development were facilitated largely by the peculiar revolutionary fervor of the 1950s and 1960s. Thus it also includes Nasser's role, which was vital in Egypt's contemporary political development. To understand Egypt's system of government as it exists today, it is necessary to place it within the context of circumstances that allowed it to take shape.

Government Under Nasser: The Establishment of Personal Authoritarian Rule

Early indications that the July 1952 coup transformed Egypt's political scene were confirmed when the monarchy was formally abolished and Egypt was officially declared a republic in June 1953. While General Mohamad Nagib became the first president upon the declaration of the republic,[8] from the beginning Colonel Gamal Abdul Nasser had different views on the direction in which to steer the new republic. As P. J. Vatikiotis pointed out, the Revolutionary Command Council (RCC) suffered from splits due to the differences in opinion between Nagib and Nasser. As the author explains, "Although not an original or active member of the Free Officer movement, [Nagib's] eighteen months in office as Prime Minister . . . had earned him wide popularity in the country. Older than his RCC colleagues and a member of a military family . . . he was by temperament more inclined to favor a return to constitutional government."[9] Furthermore, he was also known to have "resented the RCC's dictation of policy, and criticized the summary sentences passed by the RCC on political leaders of the *ancien regime*."[10] By November 1954, Nagib had lost his political influence to Nasser. Under the pretext that the president had been collaborating with the Muslim Brotherhood, Nagib was tried and placed under house arrest, which cleared the way for Nasser to become president.

While Nasser's charisma did help pave the way for his personal domination of power, his legitimacy and position were enhanced by many factors. During his first ten years as president, Nasser was able to peacefully evict the British from Egyptian bases. The new leader embarked on a series of major changes, including agrarian reforms and nationalization of the Suez Canal Company and other major industries. Moreover, the implementation of popular laws such as that guaranteeing state employment for all university and high school graduates and the establishment of a national social insurance scheme all contributed to Nasser's heightening popularity in the eyes of the masses. These socioeconomic policies enhanced Nasser's personal power in that they created a new social contract between him and the masses. As Ray Bush points out, Nasser "promoted a modernization of the economy through the use of a large public sector, bureaucracy, and the mobilization of subordinate classes against the landed elites and private business elites."[11] This facilitated the establishment of a new social contract in which "the state delivered new economic rights and the working classes and peasantry submitted . . . to an authoritarian and unrepresentative new military and bureaucratic elite."[12] Put simply, Nasser not only headed but also dominated the new Egyptian elite.

Nasser's charismatic qualities, reinforced by his shrewd "populist" policies, left no doubt to the masses and the political elite that he was the ultimate source of power and authority. As Ali Wali, head of the then newly created General Petroleum Company (GPC) under Nasser, remarked, "Nasser was the most intelligent of the Free Officers. He did not talk much in meetings. He just listened, then he made the final decisions."[13] One such example of the personal nature of decisionmaking under Nasser is the manner in which the General

Petroleum Company was created, and the rise, fall, and reassent of Ali Wali within it.

The Case of the General Petroleum Company and Ali Wali

The establishment of Egypt's General Petroleum Company stemmed from an idea proposed to Nasser by Ali Wali in 1958.[14] Wali, the eldest of nine children, was born into a prominent family in Fayoum Governate (south of Cairo). His father was a judge and prominent politician as well as large landowner under the monarchy. As in the case of most of the landed elite, the post-1952 period resulted in the decline of the Wali family's fortunes. The agrarian reforms ensured that their estate, which comprised thousands of acres in Fayoum, dwindled to a few hundred. Ali Wali had graduated from what is now Cairo University with a degree in petroleum engineering in 1941. After graduation, he was employed with the British company Shell Petroleum and was posted in the mineral-rich Sinai desert until his resignation in 1958.

Wali became acquainted with Nasser due to several reasons. Most notably, it was the direct intervention of Aziz Sidki that boosted Wali's professional career. Sidki, a friend from college, was unexpectedly appointed by Nasser to the position of Egypt's first minister of industry in 1956. Sidki's appointment as minister is in itself an example of the personal nature of presidential decisionmaking that would come to be the most common feature of Egypt's post-1952 political system. As Raymond Baker points out, Sidki's appointment was based on the fact that he "had attracted Nasser's attention a year before his appointment by his professional competence when acting as a guide for the President in one of the agencies Nasser was visiting."[15] While the move to appoint an unknown person who had no personal links to the Free Officers might appear on the surface as a move away from personalism and control, this was not the case. Baker makes it clear that "before making his selection, Nasser had given himself a full year to determine Sidki's political loyalty."[16] Furthermore, Nasser made it clear to Sidki in private that his appointment was based on the regime's research. As Nasser reportedly told him, "I have selected you without knowing you. We talked only one time. . . . Since that time I have followed you."[17] This demonstrates that Nasser felt it prudent to clarify to Sidki that as a minister, he would be ultimately personally accountable to the president. As Nasser reportedly told him, "I will leave you considerable freedom but will ask for an account later."[18]

Once appointed minister of industry, Sidki approached former colleagues and friends, such as Wali, for various professional advice. It was not long afterward that Wali met Nasser in Cairo. Wali resigned from Shell and approached Nasser with the proposal to establish an Egyptian petroleum company. Until then, the petroleum companies in Egypt were foreign-owned, with Britain maintaining the dominant share. Nasser agreed to the proposal and the Egyptian General Petroleum Company was established in 1958 under Wali's supervision. The fact that Nasser agreed to the establishment of the GPC is not surprising in view of his increasing nationalistic tendencies and perceptions at the time. As in the case of Sidki, Wali's professional competence was not in doubt. He was one of only a small group of qualified Egyptian petroleum engineers at the time. Moreover, his long employment with Shell gave him the practical experience that was beneficial to his new position. Thus, primarily through Sidki, Wali became connected to the new regime.

The nationalization of major companies and industries in 1961 witnessed tremendous expansion of the GPC as foreign petroleum companies were nationalized and bought under the regime's umbrella. Wali soon felt that the nationalization of these companies was not necessarily beneficial to the development of Egypt's potential petroleum sector, as these companies were in the process of research at the time of their nationalization because no new petroleum resources had been discovered in Egypt. The GPC did not have the experience or the sufficient technological capability to take over in this capacity. As a result, Wali highlighted this predicament to Nasser. The only viable solution, Wali explained to Nasser, was for the GPC to enter a partnership with an experienced foreign petroleum research company that could provide the technological capabilities. While Nasser understood Wali's point of view, certain elements within his former Free Officers body viewed this proposal with suspicion. First, it contradicted the principles behind the nationalization of industries. Second, and potentially more serious, was the suspicion by certain individuals of Wali's personal motives. As Wali explains, "When I presented my case to Nasser, many of his men whispered accusations such as 'Ali knows where the oil is, he's just pretending he doesn't because he wants to take a bribe from a foreign company in return for letting them back in Egypt.'"[19] As the ultimate decisionmaker, Nasser eventually supported Wali's viewpoint. The president's justification: "So what if we bring in a foreign research company to find our petroleum? When they do find it, it is not like they can pack it up in a suitcase and run off with it."[20]

Nasser subsequently signed an agreement with a U.S. petroleum research company in 1964, which in 1966 located oil reserves in the Sinai. But the discovery of petroleum so soon after the signing of the deal led Nasser to believe that suspicion of Wali's ulterior motives was well founded. Wali was immediately fired and what remained of his family's estate in Fayoum, as well as his family's lesser properties, including their residential home in Cairo, were immediately confiscated by a presidential decree. The same decree also barred all Wali family members from any form of state employment, rendering them, at that particular point in Egypt's history, with almost no prospect of alternate viable employment. Luckily for the Wali family, Nasser gave personal instructions that the section of the decree that barred the family from government employment not be implemented. Regardless, the Wali family remained, on paper at least, formally barred from state employment.

In a twist of fate, Nasser recalled Wali in 1967 to rebuild the Egyptian oil sector following the military defeat that left the Sinai under Israeli occupation. While the Wali family was punished through no fault of their own in 1966, one year later the decree against them was abolished, their (postrevolutionary) properties were returned, and Wali was reinstated to his former position.

This case illustrates the dynamics and potential consequences of personal decisionmaking during Nasser's presidency. The establishment of the GPC, like other organizations and groupings that emerged in the new republic, was the result of Nasser's personal endorsement. The appointment of Ali Wali as head of the GPC was also based on the president's personal will. The GPC and Wali's role in it highlight the arbitrary nature of a system that is based on personal, unchecked rule as opposed to formal procedures and regulations. The absence of formal checks and balances on presidential decisionmaking is reflected when the political elite are unable to defend themselves and their families against the ruler. The fall and rise of the Wali fortunes between 1966 and 1967 is an apt illustration of this predicament and the partiality of personal rule. The fact that Nasser established himself as the ultimate decisionmaker was facilitated by various factors that linked his charismatic leadership qualities, the adoption of a populist-nationalist agenda, and a conducive political environment that was ready for change. The adoption of a legal-constitutional framework in favor of a dominant presidency reinforced and legalized the system of personal rule.

Legalizing Personal Rule

The provisional constitution of 1953 was followed by four more constitutions, in 1956, 1958, 1962, and 1964, all during Nasser's presidency. Each constitution was formulated to fit the president's political objectives and directions. In order to maintain overall unity between the Free Officers during their first years in power, the 1953 provisional constitution empowered the RCC with the responsibility of formulating national policy. The 1956 constitution, on the other hand, reflected the fact that Nasser had won the power struggle with Nagib and emphasized his elevated position among the other Free Officers. Most indicative, the 1956 constitution replaced a parliamentary system of government with "a presidential Republican system of government in which the President appoints and dismisses ministers."[21] This constitutional clause enabled Nasser, once he was elected president, to form a new government that replaced several Free Officers with civilians.[22] As Vatikiotis observes: "Whereas in 1954 Nasser used his closest associates to strengthen his position against Naguib . . . now with the consolidation of his position in 1956 after the elimination of his opponents he brought more civilians into the government. . . . Such alternation of personnel for his retention of power . . . was a trademark of Nasser's rule and political style throughout his Presidency."[23]

In addition, the 1956 constitution decreed the establishment of the National Union to replace the provisional government's Liberation Rally as the mass-mobilizing political organization. This newly established single party reinforced the president's powers. It also allowed for the reinstatement of the legislature for the first time since the military coup (under new electoral laws). Consequently, the National Union was a tool with which to "screen and select nominees for election to the National Assembly."[24] Indications that the new legislature was not intended to have any meaningful political role were evident both before and after the legislative elections took place. Over half the 2,500 candidates who applied to compete for the

350 legislative seats were disqualified through the screening process of the National Union's presidentially appointed National Executive Committee. Once elected, "the Assembly met from July 1957 to March 1958, but only as a dutiful audience for ministerial and presidential speeches."[25]

The dissolution of the legislature and the promulgation by decree of a new constitution in 1958 coincided with another of Nasser's political goals: the unification with Syria and the establishment of the United Arab Republic (UAR). Preserving the preeminent role of the Egyptian president, the UAR's provisional constitution replaced political parties in Syria with the National Union. With Nasser as president of the unified UAR, Raymond Hinnebusch points out, the UAR "began with a great fund of political capital, enormous mass adulation for Nasser in Syria. . . . But [it] turned out to be essentially bureaucratic rule from Cairo . . . with a charismatic leader at the top, legitimized by Arab nationalist ideology, and resting on a network of military and police control."[26] Due to the power imbalance between the countries, it is not surprising that a group of Syrian officers staged a military coup and regained Syria's political autonomy in 1961.

The failure of the UAR and the decline of Arab nationalism and socialism as a legitimizing ideology ensured that the 1964 constitution further consolidated the president's power. With the creation of the Arab Socialist Union (ASU) to replace the National Union following Syria's secession, the aspect of screening potential electoral candidates became redundant due to the fact that under the new stipulations, only ASU members were eligible to participate as electoral candidates. In other words, the screening process became more blatant and directed toward absolute conformity. This "lopsided" constitutional clause was intended to subordinate the legislature further, since the ASU, "itself a creation of the executive," became responsible for the selection of candidates.[27]

Equally important, two additional stipulations of the 1964 constitution sealed the powers of the president vis-à-vis the legislature. One was the requirement that half the legislature be composed of literate peasants and workers. This stipulation was significant because it "guaranteed executive control over those seats, since 'workers' were drawn from the civil service and public sector and thus were more or less nominated by the executive branch, whereas 'peasant' MPs were typically enmeshed in the government rural patronage network and hence beholden to it."[28] Connected to this was a second provision by which presidential election became replaced with popular referendum. In other words, the tightly controlled People's Assembly nominated the president, and his nomination could only be affirmed or opposed. The referendum was conducted under the watchful supervision of the Ministry of Interior so as to ensure the executive's desired result.

The 1964 constitution also authorized the establishment of state security courts (*mahakim 'amn al-daula*). As Enid Hill notes, these courts were created to "handle cases of treason and internal subversion, as well as 'political crimes' of lesser magnitude which are defined as coming under their jurisdiction."[29] Thus, having witnessed Syria slip from his grip, Nasser intended his 1964 constitution to ensure that this would not happen in Egypt.

Following the 1967 defeat and the economic, human, and political losses that incurred during the war of attrition, Nasser's political objectives can again be seen through the implementation of major laws. The most prominent related to the judiciary. The establishment of the Supreme Constitutional Court (SCC) by Law 81 of 1969 formally provided an independent judicial body to supervise the constitutionality of laws issued by the legislative and executive branches. Evidently, having created a weak legislature, the president needed to establish a new institution to help legitimize his personal monopoly over the policymaking process in the politically disillusioned post-1967 period. However, ensuring that the SCC did not become too independent, the new law stipulated that the SCC judges be appointed directly by the president. Additionally, in a blatant effort to propel the judiciary into direct executive control, known as the 1969 "massacre of judges," Nasser decreed that all judges must join the ASU and dismissed all those who refused.[30]

During his tenure, Nasser institutionalized a formal system of personal political control over individuals, groupings, and state institutions. This would have been impossible to sustain over a long period of time without his shrewd political acumen. One example of this is Baker's account. In 1966 the murder of a minor ASU official in the countryside led Ali Sabri, the ASU's first secretary, to launch a scathing attack on what he described as "rural feudalists." Sensing that Sabri was gaining popular following in the process, the president "acted quickly to undercut Sabri's drive. He established a special commission to investigate the rural feudalists and appointed Field

Marshal Amer to head it. Thus the prestige and popularity accruing
to Sabri was deflected to the military establishment. . . . One center
of power was played against another to protect Nasser's own position."[31] This political shrewdness, along with the immense formal
powers vested in the presidency, preserved the preeminent role of
Nasser until his death in September 1970. Nasser's successor, Anwar
Sadat, capitalized on these principles to ensure that his own presidential rule would be no less domineering.

Government Under Sadat: Reinforcing Personal Rule

The importance of political shrewdness for the survival of personal
rule could not have been more apparent to Sadat than during his first
year in office. When appointed vice president in 1969, the former
Free Officer and speaker of the People's Assembly did not raise suspicion among his colleagues. As with most elite positions, Nasser
rotated the position of the vice presidency on a regular basis.
Nasser's sudden and fatal heart attack on 30 September 1970 facilitated Sadat's formal acquirement, then through referendum, of the
presidency. Nasser's top men, such as Ali Sabri, did not attempt to
obstruct Sadat's elevation to the executive office because of two
main reasons. First, Sadat's public demeanor indicated an unthreat-
ening character, which meant they "regarded him as the man least
likely to disturb their privileged positions."[32] Second, they had
assumed that "as a veteran Free Officer, placed by Nasser to succeed
him, he would be an effective symbol of continuity."[33] Nasser's old
guard was confident that Sadat would maintain no more than a symbolic leadership role. For example, Mahmoud el-Sadani, a famous
political journalist, warned Sami Sharif, Nasser's former director of
personal security, that Sadat would put them all in prison within a
year. Sharif's response: "There is nothing to worry about, Sadat must
do as we say and if he does not, we will just dispose of him."[34]

On one level, Sadat had already started planning his consolidation of power by adopting the classic tactics of divide and rule. Over
the previous seven months in office, Sadat co-opted Mohamad
Ahmad Sadik, the army's chief of staff, and Lassi Nasif, commander
of the presidential guard, into his camp. Part of this strategy included
planting doubt of the intentions of his opponents. For instance, in the
case of Nasif, Sadat hinted that Sami Sharif was lobbying to post him

to London as Egypt's ambassador to Britain. Fearful of what was the equivalent of political exile for a man of his stature and power, it did not take Nasif long to reaffirm his loyalty to the new president.[35] The army's support, as reflected through Sadik, was not a difficult feat for Sadat to achieve either. As Baker notes: "Sadat apparently won this support of the military, despite defection of the minister of defense, with promises of a refurbishment of the military image and a reinstatement of the officers purged by Nasser after 1967. Lingering resentment of the ASU challenge in the post-1967 period was also probably a factor in swaying the military against the conspirators."[36]

The old guard's disregard for Sadat climaxed with the "corrective revolution" on 1 May 1971—Egypt's annual Labor Day. All official celebrations and posters for the Egyptian workers focused on Nasser's achievements in what appeared to be a deliberate snub to the new president. The following day Sadat placed Ali Sabri under house arrest. This potentially dangerous move could have had serious repercussions for Sadat had it not been for his ability to outwit his opponents—and their inability to retaliate. The fact that the Sabri incident did not produce a reaction from Sadat's opponents undoubtedly encouraged him to strike again.

At 4:00 P.M. on 13 May, when most police personnel had left work for the weekend, Sadat used the presidential guard to replace Sha'rawi Gom'a with his own man, Mamdoh Salim, as minister of interior. Two days later, with the start of the working week, Sadat's most prominent political opponents publicly announced their mass resignation.[37] The move was intended to publicly humiliate the president and shock the people into mass demonstrations. But they had overestimated their base of support and popularity, and no demonstrations materialized. This aspect led Sadat to comment, "I should put them on trial on charges of political stupidity."[38] The core group and their prominent supporters were arrested the same day. Their trial ended in the conviction of ninety-one senior officers and politicians in December 1971.[39]

Since personal rule is threatened by the presence of powerful individuals and groups who possess the potential to challenge the ruler, the survival of such a governance system is dependent on the elimination of these obstacles. The elimination of Nasser's old guard was a matter of survival for a president intending to maintain his predecessor's personal style of rule. One case, again involving Ali Wali, illustrates that Sadat's decisionmaking emerged as no less personal than under Nasser.

The Case of the Suez-Alexandria Pipeline and Ali Wali

The reinstatement of Ali Wali as the GPC's director in 1967 remained unaltered during Nasser's last years as president.[40] When Sadat assumed the presidency, Wali chose to ally himself with the new president, understanding well the potential perils of presidential power. To illustrate his loyalty, Wali organized a mass pro-Sadat rally comprising approximately 40,000 petroleum workers. The rally was held following the public resignation of Sadat's opponents on 15 May 1971. This decision, which was intended to counteract potential anti-Sadat sentiments, reaffirmed Wali's loyalty to the president. It also proved to be a successful gamble. The president, in traditional authoritarian custom, extended his patronage to his loyal political supporters. Two days later, the president issued a decree establishing a ministry for petroleum and appointed Wali as its first minister.

During his first months in office, Wali proposed the idea of constructing a major pipeline that could transport oil from the Gulf of Suez to Alexandria. Sadat accepted the proposal and encouraged Wali to seek its financing from the Suez Bank. The Suez Bank was established by France in 1958 to manage the reimbursements paid by Egypt for the nationalization of the Suez Canal. The bank also happened to be run by the powerful Rothschild banking family. Once Wali met with representatives of the bank, he discovered that they were more than willing to finance the project, but on harsh terms. The most important term was that all the profits from the pipeline would be taken by the bank and allocated toward the payment of Egypt's foreign debts. Although Sadat insisted that he must deal with the Rothschilds, Wali refused the conditions that they had set up. As a result, he was removed from office and placed under house arrest for most of 1973. Wali's tenure as Egypt's first minister of petroleum lasted less than a year and a half. In hindsight, Wali realizes that Sadat wanted to deal with the Rothschilds because, as a prominent Jewish dynasty, he had hoped they would act as intermediaries for potential peace negotiations between Egypt and Israel. However, Wali did not know that at the time.[41]

This case highlights two important characteristics of personal rule. First, while personal loyalty to the ruler is a prerequisite to the attainment of a high government position, it is subordination to the ruler's will that determines the length of one's career. Second, the fact that formal structures and positions of government exist does not imply that such entities share in, or at times are even aware of, the ruler's policies. The expulsion of the Soviets in 1972, the war with Israel in 1973, the adoption of an economic open-door (*infitah*) policy in 1974, the introduction of a multiparty system in 1976, and Sadat's historic visit to Jerusalem in 1977 were all the personal policy initiatives and decisions of the president. In this regard, Sadat's policies differed substantially from his predecessor's socialist orientation. Yet the fact that Sadat was in the position to personally redirect the policies does not imply that the fundamental dynamics of governance differed from those during the Nasser era. In fact, once Sadat undertook his "corrective revolution" and placed his own trusted men in office, he established a new legal-constitutional framework to encourage and legalize a system of personal rule similar to Nasser's.

Legalizing Personal Rule: The 1971 Constitution

The 1971 constitution, which remains in effect, provides an apt insight into the formal structure of government and the president's position in post-Nasser Egypt. One indication of the power imbalance between the three branches of government is the constitution's preoccupation with the president's role and functions in comparison to the legislative and judiciary branches. As one report highlights, out of the constitution's fifty-five articles, "the president is recognized by thirty-five articles (63 percent), the ministers by four (7 percent), the judiciary by four (7 percent) and the legislative branch with its two subdivisions by fourteen (25 percent)."[42]

As under the 1964 constitution, the president is officially instated by referendum. The legislature (People's Assembly) is responsible for this presidential nomination. Once nominated, the candidate must then obtain two-thirds of the votes of the People's Assembly before being "referred to the citizens for a plebiscite" (Article 76). The issue of referendum is significant for two reasons. First, since the assembly can only refer one person to a national plebiscite, the president does not compete for his position with other candidates. Second, and interrelated to the first, there are no sectors in society that formally support an opponent to the president. This means that formally the president acquires office not on majority-based support, but on near-unanimous support and thus absolute *legal* legitimacy. Once in office, the president under the 1971 constitution retains the authority to promulgate as well as object to laws (Article 112). The president's powers to rule by decree (Article 147), declare a state of emergency (Article 148), and appoint and dismiss the entire cabinet (Article 141) are also preserved. Furthermore, the powers to draft the budget of the state (Article 115) and formulate the state's general policy (Article 138) reinforce the formal powers of the president over the legislature. While the constitution empowers the legislature to query and dispute presidential authority, such powers are rendered ineffective by the president's authority to bypass them and call a referendum of the people (Article 152). Thus, for example, "if the Assembly decides to use its constitutional prerogative to withdraw its vote of confidence from the cabinet (Article 126), the president can refuse to endorse the decision (Article 127) and is legally entitled to take the matter to a public referendum."[43] Consequently, the fact that the legislature was little more of an independent lawmaking institution under Sadat than Nasser is reflected in the fact that in the 1970–1971 session, only 8 percent of the bills passed were initiated by the legislature.[44] In 1979, after almost a decade in power and following the introduction of a multiparty system, this ratio increased to barely 20 percent.[45]

The importance of the legislature for the president should not be underestimated. Controlling the legislature ensures that there are no formal competitors to the presidency. This control also ensures that the president's monopoly on policymaking remains unhindered. It is not surprising, therefore, that the 1971 constitution preserves the president's right to dissolve the People's Assembly if deemed "necessary" and "after a referendum of the people" (Article 136). This presidential safety valve carries enormous implications for the conduct of legislative members and the balance of power between members of parliament and the president. This means that should the legislature decide "to take on a bigger role than supporting and formalizing presidential legislation,"[46] the president can resort to referendum, dissolve it, and call for new elections. The nature of electoral competition, as examined in Chapter 3, ensures that the vast majority of opponents and independent-minded legislators are denied both entry and reentry to the assembly.[47]

The president's constitutional grip on other political and state institutions is also preserved through the implementation of several laws. Whereby the 1971 constitution guaranteed "the independence and immunity" of the judiciary (Article 65), the president was empowered with presiding over a supreme council that "shall supervise the affairs of the judiciary organization" (Article 173). Furthermore, the subsequent implementation of Law 46 of 1972 reinforces presidential control over the judiciary due to his powers of appointment and promotion. According to this law, the president's powers extend to the appointment and promotion of judges as well as the appointment of the public prosecutor. It should be noted as well that the president also determines the salaries and overall budget of the judiciary body.[48] Furthermore, as supreme commander of the armed forces (Article 150) and supreme chief of the police (Article 184), the president's powers of appointment and fiscal control remained as apparent within the military and police as under Nasser. In addition, the establishment of state security courts in the 1964 constitution is maintained in the 1971 constitution (Article 171), thus continuing to provide the president with an alternate judiciary body when required.

The 1971 constitution legally enshrines the preeminent position of the president over other government and state institutions in contemporary Egypt. It combines legal prerogatives with personal political judgment and enables the president to remain unchallenged at the apex of the governance structure. An example of such skills is well illustrated by Robert Springborg, who recounts Sadat's adopted tactics to depoliticize the military in his quest for peace and economic restructuring:

Before it became clear that Sadat intended to bring about fundamental strategic changes, he had already displayed his willingness and ability to purge those who opposed him. He jailed the Minister of War Muhammad Fawzi in 1971, after having previously secured the support of General Muhammad Sadiq, who then replaced Fawzi. A year later Sadiq was himself placed under house arrest after Sadat had ensured the loyalty of Chief of Staff Saad al-Din Shazli, who in turn was chased into exile once Sadat was assured the loyalty of Minister of War Ahmed Ismail and Shazli's replacement, General Abd al-Ghani Gamasi. Gamasi, who took over as Minister of Defense after the death of General Ismail in 1974, and Gamasi's Chief of Staff Muhammad Ali were then replaced in 1978 as a result of the former's opposition to Sadat's seeking a peace treaty with Israel and the latter's dissatisfaction with the

downgrading of the military and the redirection of its mission away
from the eastern front. . . . Any potential reaction within the ranks
against the removal of Gamasi and Fahmi was preempted by
Sadat's relationship with Husni Mubarak, whom he promoted from
Commander of the Air Force to Vice President.[49]

Sadat applied these political skills ingeniously and, as a consequence, successfully reinforced a personal system of rule until his
assassination in 1981.[50] However, it is Hosni Mubarak, as Egypt's
longest serving president, who best utilized and built upon his predecessors' system of governance.

Government Under Mubarak

As vice president at the time of Sadat's assassination, Mubarak
ascended to the presidency straightforwardly. In contrast to his predecessors, the new president was not confronted with any particular
power struggle at the start of his tenure in office. What Mubarak
faced, however, was arguably something more challenging to the
system of personal rule. Namely, there was the existence of ideological, socioeconomic, and political disillusionment in Egypt. The 1967
war, which ended with Israel's occupation of Egyptian, Syrian, and
Jordanian territories, ended the illusion of Arab power, nationalism,
and unity. Sadat's peace treaty with Israel reinforced this and consequently isolated Egypt from the rest of the Arab world as well as created voices of dissent within the country. Nasser's socialist experiment with a centrally planned economy left the country in debt.
Sadat's attempt at economic restructuring (*infitah*) did little to help
address the problem.[51] Rather, the *infitah* produced a consumption
boom that failed to stimulate investment in productive or export-ori-
ented industries. Furthermore, the president inherited a newly constructed multiparty arena that could potentially challenge the existence of the personal authoritarian system.

On the surface, Mubarak was not particularly concerned at the
prospect of the latter. During his first few in years in power, the new
president portrayed himself as a prominent advocate of democracy.
Stating that "democracy is the best guarantee of our future" and that
he "had no wish to monopolize decision-making," the president went
as far as to declare his disapproval of long-term presidential rule.[52]

As he stated in 1984, "I do not conceal from you the fact that I believe that the assumption of the office of the president by any one of us should not exceed two terms." Furthermore, he went on to pledge, "I will be the first President to whom this rule shall apply."[53]

Sadat had also initially proclaimed his disdain for long-term presidential rule. He even went as far as to implement a two-term limitation in Article 77 of the 1971 constitution, although this was duly amended in 1980 so that he could enter his third term.[54] As in the case of his predecessor, Mubarak went on to exceed two terms and is currently serving his fourth term in office. Moreover, the president's views on democracy soon changed. As he argued in 1987, democracy cannot be achieved "overnight."[55] The president's revised argument was based on the view that as a developing country, Egypt's priority was economic development. As he stated, "If we cease economic activity and grant freedom . . . we consequently place people in an unstable state."[56] In this regard, Mubarak's change of views indicates that he projected the image of being an advocate of democracy in order to legitimize his position and consolidate his power, as illustrated by the dynamics of governance within the formal institutional framework under his presidency.

The Cabinet

The president's constitutional power to appoint "the Prime Minister, his deputies, the Ministers and their deputies and relieve them of their posts" (Article 141) means that the president's authority over the cabinet is intact. Nevertheless, in order to maintain personal rule, two factors are crucial. First, there is the issue of loyalty to the ruler, in the absence of which the prospect of potential challenges to authority becomes a serious reality at this high political level. Second, the issue of loyalty accommodates subservience to the ruler's policies. Consequently, personal decisionmaking is less likely to be questioned, let alone challenged. The personal qualities of those appointed to executive office are also an important consideration. While it is necessary to appoint a minister with some degree of professional competence, it is the ruler who must appear the most competent of all his ministerial elite. The degrees to which these factors are taken into account during the recruitment of ministerial elite are indications of the ruler's preservation of personal power. Nasser's and Sadat's high turnovers of ministerial elite reflected this predicament and their respective attempts to overcome it.

In the case of Mubarak, the turnover of ministerial elite has been much more stable. Some political figures, such as Zakaria Azmi and Kamal al-Shazli, have held their elite positions since the early 1980s. In some instances there have been no circulations of elite positions since Mubarak's ascent to power. Osama al-Baz, senior political adviser to the president, Safwat al-Sharif, minister of information, and Yosif Wali, minister of agriculture, have held the same portfolios since 1981. Furthermore, the government of 'Atif Sidqi (1986–1996) was Egypt's longest-serving cabinet since the establishment of the country's first modern cabinet in 1914. However, the long-term tenure of Mubarak's ministerial elite cannot be viewed as a shift from the underlying principles of his predecessors as much as a shift in tactics to maintain the same objectives. Those who have success-fully maintained long-term positions within the executive realm either have maintained a very low-key public persona (such as Zakaria Azmi and Yosif Wali), or lack charismatic and popular quali-ties that would pose a challenge on the mass level (such as Safwat al-Sharif and Kamal al-Shazli). The abrupt removal from office of pop-ular and potentially challenging individuals remains a dominant feature of Mubarak's rule. One example of this is the case of Abd al-Halim Abu Ghazala.

Abu Ghazala was appointed minister of defense in 1980 follow-ing the death of his predecessor, Ahmed Badawi, in a helicopter crash. After Sadat's assassination, Mubarak not only assumed the presidency, but assumed Sadat's appointed ministers, including Abu Ghazala. As a popular and charismatic leader who managed to estab-lish a sprawling patronage system within the armed forces, Abu Ghazala posed a threat to Mubarak from the beginning of his presi-dency. Furthermore, as a former military attaché to Washington, Abu Ghazala's political connections and his public anticommunist posi-tion further elevated his status within the inner circles of U.S. policy-makers. In fact, as one author noted, Abu Ghazala had reached a position during the first few years of Mubarak's rule that made it "very difficult for anyone to undermine his authority."[57] After slowly consolidating his position of power, Mubarak abruptly removed Abu Ghazala in 1989 and replaced him with the less charismatic Hussein al-Tantawi. While Abu Ghazala has been confined to political exile, al-Tantawi's less challenging persona has allowed him to maintain his position to this day.

More recently, a similar situation occurred with the minister of foreign affairs, Amr Mosa. As a Ministry of Foreign Affairs official and a client of senior presidential adviser Osama al-Baz, Mosa was appointed minister of foreign affairs in May 1991. Mosa's appointment was based primarily on the personal recommendation of al-Baz. As an eloquent and charismatic individual, Mosa's mass popularity peaked in 2000 when the popular Egyptian singer Sha'ban Abd al-Rahim released a highly popular song, "I Hate Israel and I Love Amr Mosa." The song, which reinforced Mosa's esteem on the mass level, became almost a national anthem. That a popular singer declared his love for the foreign minister was not wholly unexpected. Over the years, Mosa's articulate and controversial views in regard to the Palestinian-Israeli conflict had made him a highly criticized figure in the Israeli press and elevated him as a highly respected politician on the domestic level. Indeed, as one report noted, the Egyptian masses "began to believe that Mosa and his ministry possessed a voice independent of the presidency."[58] In March 2001, Mosa was unexpectedly replaced by the obscure and less controversial former ambassador Ahmed Maher. As in the case of his predecessors, this indicates that the appearance of being independent of the presidency remains unacceptable under Mubarak's rule.

The Legislature

Indications that the role of the People's Assembly remained restricted can be seen early in the Mubarak presidency, when, following the introduction of the 1983 electoral law, then–prime minister Fo'ad Mohyi al-Din admitted that "one of the clauses—which outlawed independent candidates—was intended to limit access to the legislature of individuals who might not be 'known' to the regime."[59] The concern here is to assess the degree to which legislators are contained and controlled within the assembly.

One of the most prominent indications that the legislature is a weak entity under the Mubarak leadership is the discrepancy in the number of executive-initiated laws in comparison to its own members. For example, following the first (1984) legislative elections of Mubarak's rule, the number of bills and international agreements initiated by the executive totaled 427 while the members of parliament initiated a meager 27 bills. Following the premature legislative elections of 1987, the discrepancy was even starker as the executive initiated 659 bills in comparison to 10 from legislators.[60]

The president's initial support for democracy appeared genuine as opposition parties in the 1984 and 1987 elections acquired a respectable number of parliamentary seats that has not been matched since.[61] In the elections that have followed in 1990, 1995, and 2000, the "erosion of political participation and liberties" and hence the "political deliberalization"[62] that occurred resulted in a smaller minority of opposition intake by the assembly. However, the ratio of bills initiated via the two branches did not change substantially. For example, in the 1996–1997 parliamentary session, the executive initiated thirty-six bills while none came from the legislature.[63] In percentage terms it means that at the height of "multiparty" participation in 1987, the executive initiated 98.5 percent of legislative bills. Ten years later in the "deliberalization" period, the executive's share rose 1.5 percent to complete a total 100 percent of the initiated bills. This illustrates that while signs of "liberalization" were evident in the 1980s, the fundamental structure of the system was in reality unchanged.

The dynamics of executive domination within the legislature can be understood on three main levels. On one level is the actual process of legislation and the measures that are adopted to help facilitate a swift and positive outcome for presidentially endorsed bills. One such example is the frequent adoption of Article 153 of the rules of procedure of the People's Assembly. According to routine procedure, the legislative process entails three consecutive steps. The first step is submitting the bill to the relevant standing committees, of which there are eighteen. The committee, in turn, reports the bill to the legislature, which must consider and discuss the bill. The last step is the voting by the legislature on the bill. According to formal procedure, "A bill cannot be put to a final vote before the lapse of at least four days after deliberations." However, "in urgent cases and with the approval of the Assembly a bill may be put to a final vote at the same sitting in which it has been approved."[64] The executive's reliance on this clause cannot be overlooked. As one report notes, Article 153 was used to quickly pass the thirty-six executive-initiated bills in the 1996–1997 parliamentary session, "most of [them] as urgent cases without reasonable grounds."[65] One such example of this is the continuity of Law 29 of 1972. The law, which enables the president "to sign confidential military agreements for the sake of national security,"[66] was presented to the legislature more as an ultimatum than as a bill for deliberation. As one report noted, "This important piece of legislation was debated in one meeting which was not enough. . . . [Only] ten members participated in the debates . . . [and] the Assembly approved the bill as an urgent case despite the rejection of 12 [out of 13 total] members of the opposition parties."[67]

Another example of an "urgent" bill was that aimed at amending Law 27 of 1994 regarding arbitration in the area of trade, economy, and tax policy. The aim of the bill was to "speed the settlement of disputes in the commercial and industrial sector."[68] The significance of such a bill for Egypt's developing economy cannot be overlooked. However, it could not possibly warrant the fact that "the Assembly approved it urgently at the same meeting"[69] without much thought or deliberation on the part of the legislators. An even more mundane bill concerning practicing pharmacists was also "approved without any amendment, urgently and in one meeting" and reinforces the executive's abuse of Article 153 to curtail the legislative process. In this context, it is not surprising to find one report noting that during the 1997–1998 legislative session, Article 153 was used to pass 55.7 percent of all bills enacted into law that year.[70]

On a second level, efforts to facilitate the passing of executive-endorsed bills have entailed the manipulation of schedules. This maneuver tends be adopted when the executive wants to pass a highly controversial bill in parliament discreetly. The implementation of press restrictions embodied in Law 93 of 1995 is an apt example of such a tactic. The inevitable publicity that was anticipated by the passing of a press law that "provides harsh penalties, including prison sentences, for the publication of false or malicious news"[71] was overcome by scheduling it on a Saturday (when most legislators are absent) and failing to place it on the day's parliamentary agenda.[72] Law 153 of 1999, concerning nongovernmental organizations, is another example for which this tactic was used. This executive-initiated law caused enough governmental concern that it was rushed through without the formal procedures usually required for a law of this significance. Because this law fell into the category of being "complementary to the constitution," it should have been, according to Article 175 of the constitution, reviewed by the Shura Council before being passed by the People's Assembly.[73] While the government eventually backed down due to the Supreme Constitutional Court's declaration of the law as unconstitutional because of procedural errors of its presentation, a carbon copy of the law was passed in June 2002. Similar tactics were applied as the government, "in time-honored fashion," intentionally kept it on hold until summer "hoping that the deputies' high absentee rate during this time of the year will translate into a speedier passing" of the bill.[74]

A third level of legislative dynamics relates to the issue of immunity. According to Article 99 of the constitution, "Except in cases of *flagrante delicato,* no member of the People's Assembly shall be subject to a criminal prosecution without the permission of the Assembly." This means that in order to carry out their roles unhindered, members of the legislature enjoy parliamentary immunity from criminal and noncivil procedures unless the assembly authorizes its removal. While in some cases the assembly has found genuine justification to lift a legislator's immunity, the motivations for doing so can also be clearly political. One example of the dubious manner in which the lifting of immunity has been applied is the case of Ali Sayid Fath al-Bab. As the sole "Islamist" to enter parliament in the 1995–2000 term and a member of the Islamist-oriented Labor Party, al-Bab found himself being accused in 1997 of "participating in illegal [i.e., Islamist] activities."[75] As al-Bab was an Islamist politician, the accusations were not necessarily ungrounded. However, the skepticism of the case rested in the procedure in which his immunity was lifted. According to Article 360 of the rules of procedure, the request for the lifting of immunity must be accompanied by documents of the case from the minister of justice. This condition was ignored and the documents enclosed were found to be state security investigation files highlighting al-Bab's "opposition to the normalization of relations with Israel, [and] his organizing meetings in mosques, syndicates and his party's headquarters."[76] In the absence of the necessary documents from the minister of justice, the request to lift immunity was unanimously rejected by the assembly except for one National Democratic Party (NDP) member. What emerged was that the chairman of the committee, who had presented al-Bab's case to the legislature, "asked the report to be returned for further study. The committee convened the same day to take a decision to lift [al-Bab's] immunity after ten minutes only."[77] This decision violated Article 73 of the rules of procedure since the committee returned to the assembly with a decision without giving assembly members the opportunity to hear the government's viewpoint.[78] The committee members themselves, who had initially refused the request to lift al-Bab's immunity, "quickly changed this refusal into an immediate approval" during their short meeting.[79] Although al-Bab had his immunity lifted, it was reinstated a few months after the charges against him were dropped. In some cases, however, the lifting of immunity can result in more problematic predicaments.

The case of Ramy Lakah is one example. As one of Egypt's most successful and prominent businessmen, Lakah declared his intention in summer 2000 to enter the November legislative elections as an independent candidate in the Cairene working-class area of Al-Izbakaya. On the surface, the news was not particularly exceptional. Prominent individuals such as Mohamad Abu al-Anian and Ahmad 'Izz have occupied the dual role of prominent businessmen and legislators successfully. As NDP members, individuals of this nature are co-opted into the ruling party and their presence in the legislature is not a cause of governmental concern. Lakah, on the other hand, does not fit into this category. Rather, Lakah was a close childhood friend of Ayman Nor, an outspoken independent who was formerly a member of the opposition party Al-Wafd. Nor was one of the most charismatic and astute politicians in the 1990s.

Financially independent, Nor entered the People's Assembly at the age of thirty in 1995 representing the working-class constituency of Bab al-Sharqiya in Cairo. According to Nor, senior NDP officials approached him more than once during 1997–1998 to convince him to join the NDP.[80] Having refused governmental co-optation, Nor went on to convince Lakah to enter the arena of political competition. Apart from choosing Lakah's electoral constituency (next to Nor's) and helping him with electoral strategies during the campaign, Nor convinced his politically naive friend that "like Talaat Harb [an Egyptian nationalist figure of the early twentieth century], decent businessmen should have integrity and not join the NDP."[81] Lakah acquiesced and won a majority as an independent candidate in the elections.

Since summer 2000, when he declared his intention to run for elections as an independent candidate, Lakah began facing financial problems in his multimillion-pound empire. Apart from claims that Lakah owed over U.S.$2 million to prominent businessmen and government allies Hossam Abol Fotoh and Montasir Abo Ghali, the chairman of the Bank of Cairo, Ahmed al-Bardai, called in Lakah's U.S.$140 million business debt.[82] A major part of Lakah's business empire focused around the construction industry. Furthermore, much of this construction took the form of state contracts for the building of schools and hospitals around the country. While his main creditor, the Bank of Cairo, decided to call in his debts, Lakah was not in the position to pay because he could not recoup payments from his state contracts. As one of the country's top ten businessmen and employer of approximately 8,000 people, Lakah did not have problems acquiring loans from the Bank of Cairo over the years, particularly as he held major contracts with the state.

Indeed, Lakah's connection to the political elite was so strong that a couple of years earlier he had argued that he did not see the relevance of business associations in Egypt. As he stated in 1998, "I am not a member of any [business] association. These channels are not necessary to get through to government. If there is a problem, it is better to go directly to government, to one of the ministers or the prime minister. He is accessible so there is no need for organization [interference]."[83] In fact, it was assumed that with such close ties to the government, Lakah would join the NDP before even declaring his intention to run in the elections. The fact that he did not and, more important, given his close association with one of the most charismatic opponents of the regime, raises much suspicion on the timing of the bank's loan recall and his alleged dues to the other businessmen.

While Lakah won his seat, regardless of the debt distractions, his new role as a parliamentarian was short-lived. The deputy speaker of the assembly, invoking the rights as accorded in Article 99 of the constitution, used the 2001 summer recess to revoke Lakah's parliamentary immunity. Fathi Soror, a senior NDP official and speaker of the assembly, stated that he came to this decision after he "received three requests from Lakah's creditors for permission to sue to recover debts."[84] At the same time, the Higher Administrative Court upheld a previous Court of Cassation ruling that dual-nationality citizens are ineligible for membership in the assembly. As a dual Egyptian-French national, Lakah was expelled from the assembly at the start of the fall 2001 session. In regard to the ruling, Mohamad Mosa, chairman of the assembly's Constitutional and Legislative Affairs Committee, claimed that "the rulings issued by the Supreme Administrative Court are final and cannot be appealed. They must be respected by parliament."[85] While rules and regulations should be respected, it is the selective nature in which these rules are applied that reinforces their use as mechanisms of political control. After all, while unconfirmed reports suggest the existence of other dual-nationality parliamentarians including senior NDP figures such as Yosif Botros Ghali (Egyptian-American, the minister of economy), Ibrahim Soliman (Egyptian-Canadian, the minister of housing), and Mohamad Abol 'Anian (Egyptian-Italian, a prominent businessman),[86] none have faced formal investigation. Furthermore, the fact that the legislature chose to "respect" the court ruling in Lakah's case is contradictory to its general pattern—"a habit of openly ignoring judicial rulings against its members, claiming that only the legislative body itself had the authority to police its rank."[87] With Lakah out of parliament and his business empire in ruins, the regime showed the various mechanisms of parliamentarian control at its disposal.[88] As Nor concluded, "We frightened the regime—the combination of money and independent political thought could lead to power and this made them scared."[89]

In view of such stringent control over legislators, those who do manage to overcome the imposed electoral impediments tend to play passive roles within the legislature. In fact, the phenomenon of the "silent majority" has led one parliamentary report to note that in the 1996–1997 parliamentary session, "250 members [out of 454] did not participate in the legislative process in any way."[90] The same situation was confirmed in a 1997–1998 parliamentary report that found that only 53.3 percent of legislators participated in the discussion of that year's government-proposed bills. It is also noted that the vast majority of those who did participate (85 percent) "welcomed and approved them."[91] As if to further confirm their loyalty and subservience to the executive, the few parliamentarians who did use their right to request information did so in the most inappropriate manner. For example, of the sixty-eight requests for information in the 1997 parliamentary session, "90 percent . . . were of little importance and were confined to thanks and showing appreciation of political leaders."[92] On this basis, the majority of legislators are aware of the role expected of them and are aware that the system is constructed to ensure that they abide by it. If legislators in Mubarak's Egypt do have a role in addition to formalizing presidential policies, it is limited to the directing of state resources into their local constituencies. While this parochial role may enhance their future reelection prospects, it also reinforces their dependence on the government via its distribution of patronage.[93] Consequently, the legislature remains, in general, a weak and dependent institution in Mubarak's Egypt, as it was during the Nasser and Sadat eras.

The Judiciary

According to Law 46 of 1972, which remains in effect, the president is responsible for appointing and promoting judges. Furthermore and according to the same law, the president is also responsible for the appointment of the public prosecutor, attorney generals, and Court of Cassation judges.[94] The president's powers of appointment extend to the appointment of Supreme Constitutional Court judges. The state council courts that specialize in the settling of "administrative disputes and disciplinary cases" are also, according to the constitution, "presided over by the President of the Republic" (Article 173). The intertwined relationship of the president with the judiciary is as prominent a feature under Mubarak. In this regard, it is difficult to determine the degree of political influence that affects political and constitutional rulings. Indeed, the SCC has made some important rulings that were unsupportive of the government. For example, the opposition's decision to challenge the constitutionality of the government-imposed party-list system resulted in two simultaneous victories for the opposition parties. The SCC upheld the opposition's view and declared unconstitutional Law 114 (an electoral law of 1983) in 1987 and the amended Law 188 (an electoral law of 1986) in 1990. While these rulings resulted in the premature dissolution of the People's Assembly in 1984 and 1987, the SCC made it clear that the annulment of the assembly in both rulings "would not result in annulling the laws and decisions made by them."[95] This contradiction indicates that rather than being truly independent, the judiciary is forced to maintain a fine balance between its rulings and their political implications.

Nevertheless, the judiciary does attempt to preserve its independence in the face of governmental constraints. For example, in 1984 the Supreme State Security Court of Cairo "acquitted several people of having participated in the assassination of President Sadat. And in the 1990s the alleged assassins of the former speaker of the People's Assembly, Rif'at Mahjub, were acquitted for similar reasons, which pertained to the abuses of power, including the use of torture, by the investigating authorities."[96] While the judiciary maintains a code of ethics, the fact that the president is in a position to circumvent rulings perceived as obstructive to regime objectives renders the judiciary's role in the political sphere limited. Indicative of this is the case of the 1986 rail workers strike. As Eberhard Kienle points out:

> The Supreme State Security Court in Cairo . . . which was supposed to sentence the leaders of the railway workers strike of 1986, did not meet the regime's expectations. It ruled the strike legal because Egypt was a party to the International Covenant on Economic, Social and Cultural Rights. As was permitted under the law on the state of emergency, President Mubarak refused to ratify this verdict.[97]

As in the case of his predecessors, the law on the state of emergency has proved enormously beneficial to the maintenance of personal authoritarian rule under Mubarak. Emergency law, however, as Enid Hill clarifies, "is not martial law as is usually understood—the Constitution is not suspended and the civil courts have not ceased to function."[98] Under a state of emergency, its application for the main tenance of political control is prominent. For example, emergency law allows for censorship over political activity that can range from the monitoring of political activity to the limiting of political expression. Furthermore, "individuals can be arrested solely on the basis of suspicion of political crimes, and the gathering of five or more people or the distribution of any political literature without government authorization gives the government the right to arrest all those involved."[99]

In regard to the judiciary, the imposition of a state of emergency proves useful to the regime in that it limits judiciary intervention due to several reasons. On one level, under a state of emergency "the 45 days limit on holding an accused person in custody for questioning can be extended indefinitely without a formal court hearing."[100] More important, the role of the judiciary can be completely overlooked as a consequence of a 1966 military judiciary law stating that "the President of the Republic has the right to refer to the military judiciary any crime which is punishable under the Penal Code or under any other law."[101] This means that the president is given a virtual carte blanche "to detain and prosecute civilians in military courts regardless of whether their activity endangers fundamental interests."[102] It is worth noting that once a military court has passed its

verdict, there is no appeal, even in the case where a civilian is condemned to death. This is in direct contradiction to standard judiciary
procedure, whereby a civilian is permitted to appeal to Egypt's
Supreme Court of Appeals.

The prevalence of emergency rule is overtly significant because
it limits the role of the judiciary and further contributes in the consolidation of authoritarian power. According to Article 148 of the constitution, the president can declare a state of emergency for a "limited period" and upon the approval of the People's Assembly. Since
the assassination of Sadat, Egypt has remained under a "state of
emergency," as Mubarak requests (and is granted) an extension every
three years to combat the threats of violence and terrorism. Based on
this view, the official argument for the most recent extension was
that emergency rule acts as "an indispensable deterrent . . . and guard
. . . against the criminal forces who are still intent on seizing all possible opportunities to incite unrest and hit national interests."[103] The
fact that emergency law is utilized for political as opposed to security
reasons is evident on several levels.

On one level, the application of emergency law has made it difficult if not impossible for political parties to function and interact outside of their own offices. It allows the security forces to arrest individuals who plan to partake in legitimate activities such as legislative
or syndicate elections. Indicative of this, prior to the 1995 legislative
elections the security services arrested fifty-four prominent Muslim
Brotherhood leaders to preempt their electoral participation in legislative elections. Placed in front of a military court, the fifty-four
men were sentenced to between three and five years in prison with
hard labor. Largely as a consequence, only one Islamist-oriented par-
ticipant, Ali Sayid Fath al-Bab, won a parliamentary seat in 1995.

A similar pattern emerged before the 2000 elections. A new
group of twenty Islamists were arrested and accused in 1999 with
"working to revive the outlawed Muslim Brotherhood."[104] As in the
case of the earlier group, these Brotherhood-affiliated individuals
consisted of prominent professional figures in the legal, medical,
engineering, and academic spheres. In November 2000 the military
tribunal had passed sentences of between three and five years'
imprisonment for fifteen of the accused. As one reporter noted,
"Mass Brotherhood trials have become something of an election-year
tradition in Egypt."[105] While these cases involved Islamists, the timing of the arrests and the fact they were not charged with terrorist-

related or violent acts reflect the political benefits the regime concurs in the application of emergency rule. As one report noted with regard to the 2000 case:

> The trial . . . at times descend[ed] into near comic absurdity. Audio and videotapes of the allegedly subversive meeting at the Maadi Engineering Union headquarters were key pieces of the prosecution's case. But the defense attorneys argued that the transcripts of the three-hour audio tapes had more than 1500 instances where the tape was unclear or indecipherable. The videotape was meant to show the suspects entering the union headquarters for the incriminating meeting . . . and in the end it became apparent that the police had, in fact, videotaped the entrance to the wrong building . . . [O]n allegedly subversive pro-Brotherhood materials and books confiscated from the defendants' homes defense attorneys took on a nearly mocking tone in pointing out that many of the same books can be purchased by the general public in any bookstore.[106]

By applying emergency rule and using military courts to try civilians, the regime has become further empowered at the expense of the judiciary and has increased the government's reliance on the coercive apparatus.

The Coercive Apparatus

On the surface, the military and security forces perform a less political role under Mubarak in comparison to Nasser and Sadat. While all Egypt's presidents have been of military origin, the political prominence of the military was overtly evident between 1952 and the formation of the last government under Nasser in October 1968. During that period the military maintained control over the numerous single-party political organizations that had been formed at the time. It provided a recruiting pool that ensured that all of the vice presidents and prime ministers under both Nagib and Nasser came from military backgrounds. In fact, during this period military officers occupied 33.6 percent of the cabinet.[107] That the military maintained a prominent role in the Nasser era is understandable because the new republic emerged from a military coup.

As a former Free Officer himself, Sadat did not continue the recruitment of military personnel into high government positions with the same vigor as his predecessor. As a consequence, only 20 percent of all cabinet positions during his tenure were occupied by military officers.[108] More recently, the occupation of military officers in ministerial positions is even less evident, with no more than 10 percent held by military personnel at any one time under Mubarak.[109]

This does not imply that the military and the security apparatus play a less important role in Mubarak's rule. Rather, the role of both the military and the security apparatus as the defenders of the regime has been preserved. Indicative of this is the role of both the military and the police in the containment and control of political activities. In regard to the military, arguably its most prominent political role in the Mubarak era is the use of its courts to try civilians. According to one study, during the 1992–2000 period 1,033 civilians were tried in military courts. Of this number, 92 received death sentences and 644 were sentenced to prison.[110] Furthermore, as in the case of his predecessors, when the military in Mubarak's Egypt has been called upon to contain mass riots and demonstrations such as in 1968[111] and 1977,[112] it has never refused the president's call for assistance, even when it meant quelling their own conscripts, as was the case in the 1986 uprisings.[113]

As in the case of the army, the president presides over the police. As its commander in chief, Mubarak depends on and has expanded the powers of the police in the fight against the opposition challenge in general, and the Islamist challenge in particular. The dependence on emergency law has seen the power of the police expand considerably as they are granted a virtual carte blanche to arrest and detain suspected political activists, regardless of whether or not they fit the description of a "terrorist."[114] Furthermore, amendments of Laws 109 (of 1971) to 116 (of 1981) expanded police responsibility from "safeguarding public security" to include the vaguely termed "public order."[115] Backed by such powers, it is not surprising to find that there exist an estimated 12,000–15,000 political prisoners currently lingering in Egyptian prisons.[116] The regime's dependence on the police in regard to the Islamist threat is not based on counterterrorism tactics, but on "counterinsurgency warfare."[117] While the theme of Islamist activism will be examined later, the major role of the police has expanded in their quest to protect the regime against its challengers, and fatal casualties have increased dramatically as a result. Indicative of this is that while the number of police killed as a direct result of their confrontations with Islamists was 62 in 1992, that number doubled the next year as 120 policemen lost their lives.

In fact, the number of police deaths was higher than the number of Islamist deaths (111) in 1993.[118] Nevertheless, the number of individuals arrested on the basis of alleged Islamist activities rose from 3,600 in 1992 to 17,000 in 1993.[119] Such an increase in the number of politically motivated arrests illustrates their expanding political role under Mubarak.

The police forces have maintained a prominent role in supervision of voting and ballot counting in legislative and local elections (and since 1980 Shura elections), as well as presidential referendum results. While the Ministry of Interior maintained such a role under both Nasser and Sadat, it has more significance under Mubarak due to the prevalence of the newly established multiparty arena he inherited in 1981. In this regard, the police have not only ensured that presidential referendums have resulted in consecutive unanimous "yes" votes for the president, but have also ensured that his party has obtained no less than 75 percent of national votes in multiparty elections.[120] As one Egyptian newspaper columnist sarcastically noted in regard to the 1987 legislative election results:

> The computer in charge of the law on election by party lists is well behaved. It speaks when we want it to speak and shuts up when we tell it to. At first it announced the election of Khaled Muhyi al-Din, leader of the NPUP [National Progressive Unionist Party], but an official glared at it, whereupon it announced the failure of Mr. Muhyi al-Din after he had won. The computer remembered that it is an official of the Ministry of Interior and announced all candidates of the National Democratic Party had won and all opposition candidates had lost.[121]

Indeed, the role of the police in maintaining the regime's electoral success can be seen in the 2000 legislative elections. In this instance, and as a consequence of judiciary supervision, the police prevented voter entry to polling stations in constituencies and areas that had popular opposition candidates. This, in addition to its role of arresting potentially popular opposition leaders, reflects the degree of the police-backed interference and bias toward the regime.

On closer inspection, it is not surprising that both the military and the police maintain a vested interest in the preservation of the political status quo. While military and police personnel do not maintain an overtly public political role under Mubarak, the security forces do benefit. The establishment of a multiparty arena was followed by a ban on military and police personnel joining political parties or voting.[122] However, their exclusion from conspicuous political participation has been compensated for through additional material benefits for officers and their families.

Such forms of indirect patronage include state-financed study-abroad programs for police and military officers, subsidized housing, cars, electrical appliances, groceries, medical care, and leisure facilities. In addition, the tradition started by Nasser to reserve the presidentially appointed posts for retired police and military officers as provincial governors has been preserved by Sadat and Mubarak. The patronage of presidential appointments in regard to the military has also expanded due to the implementation of Law 32 of 1979. The implementation of this law led to the establishment of the Civil Service Authority (CSA), whose role has been "to implement projects in a number of sectors that, prior to its establishment, had been run entirely by civilians."[123] Not only have the projects of the CSA increased under Mubarak to include "a number of huge projects in the field of development of human resources and infrastructure,"[124] but it also runs a large number of endeavors that include hotel and tourist resorts[125] as well as various military-industrial complexes.[126] This permits the hiring of "thousands of retired officers [and consequently also satisfies] one fifth of the demands of the internal markets."[127] Moreover, such economic enterprises are not included in the formal annual military budget expenditure, which itself amounted to approximately U.S.$4.04 billion in 1999–2000,[128] nor are they supervised by any civilian authority. In 1990 "military production industries produced about £E1 billion worth of military products and £E622 million of civilian commodities [in addition to] 12,000 tons of meat and almost 11,000 tons of dairy products [as well as managing to produce] over 60 percent of military consumables [such as] uniforms, food, footwear etc."[129] As one author notes, in efforts to "ensure the loyalty of and obedience of the officers, [the regime provides] opportunities for commissions . . . so that wealth is spread among a reasonable number of the general officers corps. Military attaché positions in London, Paris, and Washington are the top plums, and hence are rotated on a biannual basis, about twice the turnover rate for equivalent foreign ministry positions."[130]

Under the Mubarak regime, the coercive apparatus of the state remains embedded in presidential patronage and political control. As a consequence, while the political system under Mubarak was "demilitarized" within the formal governmental sphere, it remains the most important backer of the Mubarak regime. Also, and more important, it gives the regime the stability it needs to maintain a system of personal rule.

Conclusion

It would be difficult to argue that the formal structure of government in the Mubarak era has changed dramatically since the declaration of the republic in 1954. While the formal structure of government has changed—especially in regard to the less conspicuous role of the military in politics, Egypt's post-Nasser Western and particularly U.S. alliance, as well as the implementation of a multiparty arena— the fundamental nature of the system has not. The presidency during Mubarak's tenure remains the ultimate source of power and authority, as was the case with his predecessors. Advantageous laws and an extensive patronage system, combined effectively, have not only hindered the balance of power within the formal governmental branches, but also ensured the preservation of personal authoritarian rule for Egyptian presidents for over half a century. The next chapter examines the survival of personal authoritarian rule in the face of party politics.

Notes

1. Baaklini, Denoeux, and Springborg, *Legislative Politics in the Arab World,* p. 3.
2. Ibid.
3. Ibid.
4. Jackson and Rosberg, *Personal Rule in Black Africa,* p. 10.
5. Chehabi and Linz, *Sultanistic Regimes,* p. 7.
6. Ibid.
7. Ibid.
8. Although General Nagib was not actually a Free Officer, he was chosen as a figurehead to represent the military coup. The reason, as Nasser later explained, was because he feared that the British would try to pit the young thirty-something Free Officers against each other, so his view was that, "if we had had the sense to let an older man like Nagib be the figurehead, we would retain our unity." Baker, *Egypt's Uncertain Revolution,* p. 32.

9. Vatikiotis, *The History of Modern Egypt,* p. 384.

10. Ibid.

11. Bush, *Economic Crisis and the Politics of Reform in Egypt,* p. 15.

12. Ibid.

13. Ali Wali, former minister of petroleum (1971–1972), interview by author, 6 April 2002, Cairo.

14. This section is based on personal interviews by the author with Ali Wali, former head of the General Petroleum Company and former minister of petroleum, 6 April 2002 and 13 April 2002, unless otherwise indicated.

15. Baker, *Egypt's Uncertain Revolution,* p. 178.

16. Ibid., p. 179.

17. Ibid.

18. Ibid.

19. Wali interview, 6 April 2002.

20. Ibid.

21. Vatikiotis, *The History of Modern Egypt,* p. 387.

22. At that time, Free Officers Gamal Salim, Anwar al-Sadat, and Hasan Ibrahim were dropped. Vatikiotis, *The History of Modern Egypt,* p. 388.

23. Ibid.

24. Ibid.

25. Ibid.

26. Hinnebusch, *Syria,* pp. 42–43.

27. Baaklini, Denoeux, and Springborg, *Legislative Politics in the Arab World,* p. 224.

28. Ibid.

29. Hill, *Mahkama!* p. 35.

30. A couple years later, the new president, Anwar Sadat, publicly apologized on behalf of his predecessor and reinstated the judges. Ibid., pp. 35–36.

31. Baker, *Egypt's Uncertain Revolution,* p. 112.

32. Ibid., p. 124.

33. Ibid., p. 125.

34. Wali interview, 13 April 2002.

35. Ibid.

36. Baker, *Egypt's Uncertain Revolution,* p. 126.

37. This included the resignations of Gom'a (even though he was effectively under house arrest at the time), Sami Sharif, Mohammed Fawzi, Mohamad Fayik, Hilmi Said (minister of electricity), Adel Abu al-Nor (minister of agriculture), and Lagib Shokir (speaker of the assembly).

38. Wali interview, 13 April 2002.

39. Baker, *Egypt's Uncertain Revolution,* p. 126.

40. This section is based on personal interviews with Ali Wali unless otherwise indicated.

41. The Suez Bank deal fell through because of the 1973 Egyptian-Israeli war. Saudi Arabia, Qatar, Kuwait, and Iran financed the pipeline project in 1976 with the more favorable conditions of 50 percent profit to Egypt and 50 percent to be distributed among the investors. Interview with Ali

Wali, 13 April 2002.

42. Ouda, el-Borai, and Saada, *A Door Onto the Desert*, p. 21. The legislative branch acquired a second house, the Shura (Consultative) Council in 1980, which was added to the constitution during the 1980 amendments. There have been no further amendments to the constitution.

43. Kassem, *In the Guise of Democracy*, p. 38.

44. Baaklini, Denoeux, and Springborg, *Legislative Politics in the Arab World*, p. 226.

45. el-Mikawy, *The Building of Consensus*, p. 103.

46. Kassem, *In the Guise of Democracy*, p. 39.

47. A second legislative house, the Consultative (Shura) Council was constitutionally established in 1980.

48. Ouda, el-Borai, and Saada, *A Door Onto the Desert*, pp. 30–31.

49. Springborg, *Mubarak's Egypt*, p. 97.

50. For more details on this, see Chapter 5.

51. When Sadat became president, he inherited a debt calculated at U.S.$5 billion. With the introduction of the *infitah*, this number multiplied by a factor of six to U.S.$30 billion in 1981. See Ibrahim, *Islam, Democracy, and Egypt*, p. 141.

52. Public address, April 1982, cited in "Egypt: A Decade of Peace, Development, and Democracy, 1981–1991," 1991.

53. British Broadcasting Corporation, "Summary of World Broadcasts," 26 June 1984.

54. There has been no formal limitation on presidential terms since 1980.

55. Mubarak interview, cited in Owen, "Socio-Economic Change and Political Mobilization," p. 189.

56. British Broadcasting Corporation, "Summary of World Broadcasts," 15 February 1987.

57. Springborg, *Mubarak's Egypt*, p. 124. Also see pp. 118–123 for in-depth analysis of Abu Ghazala under Mubarak.

58. Okasha, "In With the New."

59. Kassem, *In the Guise of Democracy*, p. 60.

60. el-Mikawy, *The Building of Consensus*, p. 103.

61. The opposition obtained 50 seats in 1984, while the president's party (the NDP) obtained 390. In 1987 the opposition gained 100 seats compared to the still-dominant NDP with 339 seats.

62. Kienle, "More Than a Response to Islamism," p. 219.

63. It should be noted that seventeen legislators submitted motions for a bill, of which only two were approved by the assembly. The thirty-six executive-endorsed bills, however, were all approved. Radwan, Ibrahim, et al., "Evaluation of the People's Assembly's Performance," pp. 31, 38, 67.

64. Abdel-Magid, "Assessment of the Performance of the People's Assembly," p. 32.

65. Radwan, Ibrahim, et al., "Evaluation of the People's Assembly's Performance," p. 67.

66. Ibid., p. 36.

67. Ibid. It is worth noting here that in the 1995–2000 legislative term,

in which this bill was passed, the total number of opposition members was thirteen.

68. Radwan, Ibrahim, et al., "Evaluation of the People's Assembly's Performance," p. 33.

69. Ibid.

70. Abdel-Magid, "Assessment of the Performance of the People's Assembly," p. 32.

71. Kassem, *In the Guise of Democracy,* p. 63.

72. See "Strangling the Press."

73. Apiku, "Notorious NGO Law Thrown Out."

74. el-Ghobashy, "With All Deliberate Speed."

75. Mohama Mursi, journalist on Egyptian parliamentary affairs, interview by author, 10 June 2002, Cairo.

76. Radwan, Ibrahim, et al., "Evaluation of the People's Assembly's Performance," pp. 48–49.

77. Ibid., p. 49.

78. Article 73 of the rules of procedure states: "The Assembly shall take its decision to have a report referred back to the committee after hearing the committee chairman's viewpoint . . . as well as the government's." Ibid.

79. Radwan, Ibrahim, et al., "Evaluation of the People's Assembly's Performance," p. 49.

80. Ayman Nor, member of parliament, interview by author, 28 March 2002, Cairo.

81. Ibid.

82. Essam al-Din, "Lakah Hard Times."

83. Ramy Lakah, prominent businessman and member of parliament (2000–2001), interview by author, 17 November 1998, Cairo.

84. Farag and Mursi, "Requiem for a Heavyweight."

85. Essam al-Din, "Lakah Hard Times."

86. For a list of more individuals alleged to be in the same predicament, see ibid.

87. Farag and Mursi, "Requiem for a Heavyweight." The People's Assembly is infamous for invoking its constitutional right (Article 93) to ignore court rulings that invalidate the electoral results of its members (the NDP).

88. Since his dismissal from parliament, Lakah has been living in London and Paris while he continues to fight the legal battles relating to his business empire. Nor was expelled from his party, Al-Wafd. He believes his expulsion by the chairman of the party, Noman Gom'a, was based on interference from the government. Furthermore, Nor found himself at the center of controversy in July 2001 when the state-owned *Al-Ahram al-Riyadi* published a copy of a 2 million Egyptian pound check in the name of Nor and claimed it was U.S. Central Intelligence Agency money. It turned out that the account in Paris from which the check had been issued was opened by "a junior police officer" from Egypt. The government, it seems, was trying to trump up charges with serious political implications. Ayman Nor, independent member of parliament (1995–present), interview by the author, 28

March 2002, Cairo. For an in-depth assessment of the Nor case, see Stacher, "Parties Over?"

89. Nor interview, 28 March 2002.

90. Radwan, Ibrahim, et al., "Evaluation of the People's Assembly's Performance," p. 37.

91. Abdel-Magid, "Assessment of the Performance of the People's Assembly," p. 33.

92. Radwan, Ibrahim, et al., "Evaluation of the People's Assembly's Performance," p. 42.

93. For in-depth study on patronage and clientelist control in Egypt, see Kassem, *In the Guise of Democracy.*

94. Ouda, el-Borai, and Saada, *A Door Onto the Desert,* p. 30.

95. Ibid., p. 28.

96. Kienle, *A Grand Delusion,* 47.

97. Ibid., pp. 47–48.

98. Hill, *Muhkama!* p. 36.

99. Kassem, *In the Guise of Democracy,* p. 58.

100. Ibid.

101. *Military Courts in Egypt.*

102. Kassem, *In the Guise of Democracy,* pp. 58–59.

103. Memorandum presented to the People's Assembly by Habib El-Adli, the minister of interior, justifying the extension of emergency rule until May 2003; see Essam al-Din, "Three More Years of Emergency." It is worth noting that still another three-year extension on emergency rule was approved in April 2003.

104. Khalil, "Case Closed."

105. Ibid.

106. Ibid.

107. Ouda, el-Borai, and Saada, *A Door Onto the Desert,* p. 24.

108. Ayubi, *The State and Public Policies in Egypt Since Sadat,* p. 92.

109. Ouda, el-Borai, and Saada, *A Door Onto the Desert,* p. 24.

110. Ibid.

111. Nasser resorted to the army to maintain order when in 1968 public anger erupted in mass demonstrations against the system in the wake of the 1967 defeat.

112. The 1977 food riots erupted when Sadat attempted to balance the budget via the removal of basic food subsidies that had been implemented under Nasser. While the army was called in to help maintain order, it was Sadat's decision to keep the subsidies intact that ultimately calmed the people.

113. The army proved indispensable for Mubarak when thousands of conscripts in the Central Security Forces wreaked havoc in Cairo upon hearing rumors that their military service might be extended in 1986.

114. Journalists, student activists, and even innocent civilians have been the victims of such police roundups. For example, see al-Kabanni, "Behind Walls of Oblivion."

115. Ouda, el-Borai, and Saada, *A Door Onto the Desert,* p. 25.

116. al-Kabbani, "Behind Walls of Oblivion," p. 5; and U.S. Department of State, "1999 Country Reports on Human Rights Practices: Egypt."

117. Cassandra, "The Impending Crisis in Egypt," p. 21.

118. Ibrahim, *Islam, Democracy, and Egypt,* p. 73.

119. Cassandra, "The Impending Crisis in Egypt," p. 20.

120. It is worth noting here that during Mubarak's 1981 presidential referendum, the percentage of "yes" votes was declared by the Ministry of Interior to be an astounding 98.46 percent. In 1987 the percentage of "yes" votes for the president's second term was also highly favorable, at 97.12 percent. In 1993 again, according to the Ministry of Interior, the president acquired 96 percent. In 1999, the start of his current term in office, the president remained as popular as ever, acquiring 93.79 percent of "yes" votes according to official records.

121. Springborg, *Mubarak's Egypt,* p. 190.

122. Kassem, *In the Guise of Democracy,* p. 46.

123. Ouda, el-Borai, and Saada, *A Door Onto the Desert,* p. 24.

124. Ibid.

125. Ibid.

126. On military-industrial complexes, see Bill and Springborg, *Politics in the Middle East,* pp. 264–269; and Ayubi, *Overstating the Arab State,* pp. 273–276.

127. Ouda, el-Borai, and Saada, *A Door Onto the Desert,* p. 24.

128. "Egypt: 2001."

129. Cassandra, "The Impending Crisis in Egypt," p. 23.

130. Ibid., p. 22.

3

Political Parties and Participation

There is little doubt that the political system in contemporary Egypt is characterized by the prevalence of weak institutions and organizations. As stressed previously, certain tactics and policies adopted by the state over the years have been aimed largely at ensuring that this characteristic is preserved, especially within the realm of potentially challenging civil groupings and organizations. This chapter assesses the formal and informal boundaries that govern the participation of political parties in contemporary Egypt and examines how the nature and dynamics of multiparty legislative elections are affected as a consequence.

Political parties are important organizations because their establishment and effectiveness help, among other things, to structure "the participation of new groups in politics."[1] Moreover, political parties do not simply structure and "organize political participation" but also "affect the rate at which participation expands."[2] Thus, due to their role in the integration and assimilation of the various social forces in a society, political parties can be viewed as instrumental tools with which to achieve political development and stability.[3]

Moreover, in contrast to all other organizations and groupings found in civil society, the role of political parties extends, through electoral competition, to efforts at placing their own "representatives in the government."[4] This latter role, however, can only function effectively in the context of a competitive multiparty system. As a consequence, it is logical that authoritarian systems of rule view the establishment of a competitive multiparty system with overt caution.

Indeed, in the case of most developing and newly independent nations of the 1950s and 1960s, the adoption of a single-party system was the norm rather than the exception. As one author points out in regard to his study on postindependence West African states: "With few exceptions the trend has been for one man in each state to be elevated to a position of great power. . . . Often the constitution reflects this domination of the state not only by a single party, but within that party, by a single man." In this regard, it is understandable to find that the nature of such a party is overly influenced by a "populist" theme that is more "a style of leadership rather than ideology."[5] What this implies, therefore, is that the populist-based party

> seeks to mobilize people regardless of class by denying the significance of class and of any class-based ideology. Populism tries to mobilize all interests under a single conception of the national interest. . . . Society is presented as "cellularized" into factions whose common interests outweigh their particular and possibly conflicting interests as illiterates or intellectuals, young or old, producers or consumers. . . . Populism is thus a way of presenting a view of society that stresses homogeneity rather than diversity. . . . Leaders specifically aim to prevent the development of a consciousness of conflicting interests. The methods used include building support on the basis of rewards rather than ideological conviction. . . . Populism is inevitably conservative, since it seeks to prevent alternative perspectives to the status quo developing.[6]

In the case of Egypt, the post-1952 regime's adoption of a single-party system is embedded within the context of such populism. Indicative of this was the new regime's decision to suspend the pre-1952 form of parliamentary government and abolish political parties that were "regarded as a disruptive force, a source of disunity."[7] President Nasser himself acknowledged his disregard for political parties and the democracy they are intended to entail. As he publicly stated:

> Can I ask you a question: what is democracy? We were supposed to have a democratic system during the period 1923 to 1953. But what good was this democracy to our people? I will tell you. Landowners and Pasha . . . used this kind of democracy as an easy tool for the benefits of a feudal system . . . the peasants would cast their votes according to the instructions of their masters. . . . I want to liberate the peasants and workers both socially and economically. . . . I want the peasants and workers to say "yes" and "no" with-

out any of this affecting their livelihood or their daily bread. This in my view is the basis of freedom and democracy.[8]

Indeed, following the abolition of the multiparty system, the Revolutionary Command Council (RCC), and in particular Nasser, emphasized that the establishment of the single, all-encompassing Liberation Rally (1952–1956) was not intended to serve as a political party. Rather, the new regime's perception was that "Egypt needed all the energy of its leaders and it would therefore be unwise to dissipate this energy in parliamentary debates."[9] The Liberation Rally, under the motto of "Unity, Order, and Work," was intended simply "to create a popular base for the new regime, to mobilize and unite people around the new elite and to confront and neutralize former politicians."[10]

The establishment of a new constitution following the three-year transitional period imposed by the regime coincided with the establishment of the National Union (1956–1962) to replace the Liberation Rally. Similarly, the National Union was replaced by the Arab Socialist Union (ASU, 1962–1976) six years later. This move was justified by President Nasser on the basis that several shortcomings were linked to the National Union, namely that "the Union lacked authority and autonomy, and was overly dominated by the government. In addition, the 'instant' membership of it permitted infiltration by the enemies of the revolution, and further, there has been a lack of adequate ideology."[11] Nevertheless, the ASU did not manage to fill the shortcomings of its predecessor. As in the case of the two previous organizations, the ASU "was still plagued by the same problems—lack of ideology, lack of autonomy."[12] In short, the Liberation Rally, the National Union, and the Arab Socialist Union were "all . . . conceived as mass organizations with a monopoly of legitimate political activity."[13] Equally significant are the choices of names for these organizations. As one author points out, "In each case the word 'party' was deliberately avoided, given its powerful connotations of division and lack of national purpose."[14] Therefore, the single party in Egypt was "never meant to be an active institution with decision-making powers, but was conceived basically as a civic association to mobilize the people. . . . Indeed, it was viewed more as a means of mobilizing political participation than as a vehicle for popular participation."[15] Thus, arguably to avoid potential challenges to his personal consolidation of power, Nasser's hesitation to encour-

age the institutionalization of any of the three single-party organizations facilitated his successor's multiparty initiative. Most reflective
of this predicament was the apparent ease through which President
Sadat was able to take the personal initiative of dismantling the ASU
and begin the transition to a multiparty system.

The Multiparty System Under Sadat

President Sadat's 1976 decision to move to a multiparty system initially began with the announcement that the ASU was to be split into
three ideological platforms representing the ideological orientations
of the left, center, and right. In 1977 the president conferred upon
these bodies the official status of fully fledged political parties and a
year later decided to create his own party, the National Democratic
Party (NDP). Indeed, the degree to which such a move was based on
the president's personal political orientation can be detected in his
own words. As he explained at the time:

> When I became convinced of the necessity of debating different
> opinions publicly, I suggested to the people the establishment of
> forums within the unique political organization: the Arab Socialist
> Union. . . . The consensus that emerged indicated the necessity of
> establishing three such forums: one each for the Right, the Left,
> and the Center. . . . Elections for the forums started in 1976. I fol-
> lowed the election campaign very closely, and I was surprised. The
> campaign's conduct overlooked the existence of the Arab Socialist
> Union and adopted instead a truly multi-party-style. . . . On the
> basis of this experience, many decisions were taken. I said to
> myself: why do we not call these things by their real names? I thus
> went to the inaugural session of the People's Assembly, as is my
> habit. I declared the abolition of the forum concept and the estab-
> lishment instead of the multi-party system.[16]

To further illustrate the weakness of the party as an institutionalized political organization, President Sadat's announcement of the
decision to create his own party produced a new situation such that
"within a matter of days the membership of the existing Government
party resigned almost to a man and joined the new one."[17] As a consequence, the old party was dissolved. The adoption of a multiparty system, however, was part of the president's wider reorientation of the
Egyptian political arena. Prior to formalizing the multiparty system,

the president took several other major initiatives including the expulsion of Soviet advisers in 1972 and the liberalization of the economy (*infitah*) in 1974. In addition, a visit to Israel in 1977 and the start of formal peace negotiations at Camp David the following year led to the signing of a peace treaty between the two countries in 1979. In this context, the multiparty transition was part of a wider effort by Sadat to establish his own authority independent of his predecessor and his powerful cronies as well as to attract Western aid and investment for Egypt's ailing economy. As one author aptly points out:

> In the early seventies the Sadatist regime managed (especially with the "Corrective Revolution" of May 1971) to rid itself of leaders of the Nasserist trend. . . . The war of October 1973 enabled the new leadership to silence the main sources of popular and nationalist discontent. . . . [T]his allowed them on one hand to declare the Infitah laws . . . and on the other to introduce some daring changes . . . by dismantling its ties with the socialist countries and consolidating links with the United States and the West.[18]

The aim of political liberalization was "to encourage foreign capital investment in Egypt, and to rearrange ties and alliances in order to form the broadest possible front for the encirclement of Nasserist and socialist trends."[19] Thus the point here is that Sadat's motives for liberalizing the political system were influenced by economic and political priorities other than a desire for genuine democratization. This assumption is further reinforced by the nature of Law 40 of 1977, governing political parties. According to this law, political parties can only be established if their goals, principles, and programs do not conflict with either *sharia* principles, national unity, or public order. Equally important is that "the programs, policies and goals of every party should be distinct from those of other parties" and that political parties and party leaders are forbidden to have any "connection with organizations abroad" and to ensure that their finances are made public.[20] As will be illustrated later, the main implications of this law have resulted from the broad manner in which it was written. Such vagueness has left it open to interpretation and much controversy in regard to applications for party licenses and activities. As one author notes, in the law governing political parties, "most of the programmatic conditions were so vague and general it was easy to reject almost any demand for the creation of a new party by pointing to one section or another of its manifesto."[21]

In addition, to further ensure state control, a Committee for the Affairs of Political Parties—commonly known as the Political Parties Committee (PPC)—was established to regulate party activities as well as license new parties within the guidelines of Law 40. The PPC, which remains unaltered under the Mubarak presidency, comprises six regime-linked individuals: the minister of interior, the minister of justice, the state minister for affairs of the People's Assembly, and three judicial figures appointed by the president's ministers. These individuals tend to be former chairmen, deputies, or representatives of a judicial body. The speaker of the Shura Council chairs the PPC. Hence the point here is that having created a multiparty arena from above, and having imposed stringent conditions aimed at preventing the emergence of popular and potentially challenging groupings, Sadat's objective was to ensure a transition from a weak single-party system to an equally weak multiparty system.[22] It is worth mentioning that by September 1981 Sadat believed that the "democracy" he had created was becoming too vocal in its opposition to his policies—namely the peace treaty with Israel and the issue of food subsidies. Hence his reaction was to round up and imprison approximately 1,500 political thinkers and activists. The warning was the same as that expressed during the crackdown that followed the 1977 bread riots, namely that people should "understand that democracy has its own teeth. The next time I'm going to be ten times as ruthless."[23] While Sadat's assassination in October 1981 meant there would be no "next time," the preservation of the weak multiparty system has been reinforced over the last two decades by his successor, Hosni Mubarak.

The Multiparty System Under Mubarak

Shortly after acquiring the presidency, Mubarak, the former vice president, publicly hinted at his vision of building upon the new multiparty system inherited from his predecessor in order to create a democratic system of rule. As he declared shortly after assuming power: "I believe democracy is the best guarantee of our future. . . . I totally oppose the centralization of power and I have no wish to monopolize the decision-making because the country belongs to all of us and we all share a responsibility for it."[24] Five years later, however, the president, having consolidated his power, was less enthusiastic about the suitability of democracy for Egypt, arguing: "We are providing democracy in doses in proportion to our ability to absorb them . . . but we need time for our democracy to fully develop."[25] Indeed, the establishment of a democratic multiparty system is not straightforward under any circumstances. Nevertheless, the adoption of various policies over the last two decades of Mubarak's rule has contributed more to the containment rather than the development of Egypt's multiparty arena. This appears to be a common phenomenon in personal authoritarian regimes. As Robert Jackson and Carl Rosberg explain:

> In institutionalized systems personal political calculations are made, but in terms of the universally accepted rules and require-ments of the political game; in personal systems such calculations are not mediated by reference to rules agreed to by all leaders and factions. Thus for example, while a governing party and its rivals in a constitutional democracy will go to great lengths to win elec-tions, they will not seek to abolish elections to stay in power or manipulate electoral rules or their supervision to the point where they no longer are basically fair. By contrast, such manipulation is precisely what we should expect in personal, authoritarian regimes.[26]

As will be examined, such manipulation, as reflected in the preva-lence of systematic constraints aimed at undermining the rules of the game, is a prominent feature of multiparty dynamics in Mubarak's Egypt. This is most prominently reflected by the regime's application of emergency rule.

The continuous renewal of emergency rule every three years since Sadat's assassination in 1981 provides the government with the legal right to control every level of political activity, including that within the confines of the formally defined political arena. Under emergency rule, for example, the government is entitled to censor activities including freedom of expression and freedom of assembly. As one report explains, emergency law allows the government "the right to censor, seize, or confiscate letters, newspapers, newsletters, publications, and all other means of expression and advertising before they are published."[27] It also provides the government with "broad powers to disregard the provisions set forth in the Criminal Procedure Code regarding those accused [as well as allowing for] the immediate arrest of those who disobey the orders issued according to the emergency law or those who commit any of the crimes described by it."[28] While President Mubarak has argued that the renewal of emergency rule is necessary "in order to confront terrorism [and] protect democracy and stability,"[29] the law is used to contain and control not just terrorism but also legitimate political activities. Indicative of this is the manner in which the restrictions on freedom of expression and assembly are applied during legislative election campaigns. Campaign gatherings cannot take place under emergency rule without prior permission from the Ministry of Interior. Hence, when a candidate intends to hold a public gathering, he is formally required to submit an application to the local police station stating details such as date, location, and estimated size of the gathering. This application is forwarded to the Ministry of Interior, where a decision is made.

While government-supported NDP candidates are never refused permission, and indeed are provided with access to prime premises such as state-owned youth and sports clubs, the situation is different for those outside the NDP's circle. In other words, independent and opposition candidates are for the most part refused formal permission to hold election gatherings. Consequently, the majority of these candidates do not bother to apply for permission and subsequently take the risk of being arrested as a result. The few who are given permission are notified at very short notice—usually the day of the intended gathering—thus finding themselves with little time to prepare and publicize their gathering. In addition, the right of the Ministry of Interior to select the location where the gathering will be held, by virtue of Article 7 of Law 14 of 1923,[30] which concerns the prevention of meetings and demonstrations, means that in contrast to NDP candidates, opposition candidates have little choice in the location venue of their intended gathering. Hence it is not unusual for the few opposition candidates who are given permission to hold their gatherings, to find themselves located in small alleyways at distant and relatively inaccessible areas of their respective constituencies.[31] The right of the police to subsequently attend and dissolve a meeting in session due to Article 7 of Law 14 places further constraint on non-NDP participants. While NDP candidates in their prime locations and well-attended election rallies can praise the achievements of the government to their heart's content, their political opponents find it difficult to either challenge or compete with the claims of their government-supported rivals. It is difficult for an opposition candidate to make the same claims as an NDP candidate who promises workers in the predominantly industrial area of Helwan, for example, that "we will be giving a pay rise for all our workers in Helwan . . . in gratitude for all the hard work."[32] Neither can an opposition candidate challenge his NDP counterpart when the latter reminds his less than affluent audience that "you must remember that your interest lies in the government party, the [NDP]. . . . I will not forget, and you must not forget, that the NDP, headed by President Mubarak, has paid for all your services."[33]

Indeed, should an opposition candidate make a critical or challenging remark toward the government during an electoral campaign, the candidate faces not only the risk of having the gathering dissolved by the police, but also arrest and imprisonment under Articles 98b, 102, 102b, and 174 of the penal code. These articles authorize imprisonment for "anyone in Egypt who advocates, in any way, the changing of basic principles of the constitution"[34] as well as for "anyone who shouts or sings in public with the purpose of inciting dissent"[35] and disseminating "false or instigating news, information, or rumors that disturb the public peace, frighten people, or harm the public interest."[36] In addition, penalties of imprisonment are also reserved for "anyone inciting the overthrow of the ruling regime in Egypt, or expressing hatred or contempt."[37] As these articles are very broadly written, they allow the government much room for interpretation and leave political opponents with participatory constraints.

In addition to the stringent rules defining the limits of political participation, the regime's control over the PPC has meant that for the eleven political parties legalized under Mubarak's rule, ten obtained their legal status as a consequence of a Higher Administrative Court ruling. Indeed, of approximately fifty applications for the establishment of prospective political parties, only one party (the National Accord, established in 2000) was approved by the PPC under the Mubarak presidency.

The expansion in number of formal political parties due to court rulings means that significant resources, energy, and time are used in the process. For example, the Nasserist Party applied for party status in 1988 and was refused by the PPC under the pretext that its platform was not sufficiently different from that of existing parties. It was not until it appealed to the Higher Administrative Court, which ruled in its favor, that the Nasserist Party gained legal status in 1991.

The Wasat (Center) Party provides another example of a group's struggle to gain legal recognition in the face of PPC rejection. The

Wasat Party comprises largely former Muslim Brotherhood members who for various reasons decided to split from the organization and form their own legal political party.[38] The Wasat Party's first application for party status in January 1996 was rejected by the PPC in May the same year on the basis that it did not comply with the stipulation of Law 40 of 1977 requiring a potential party to have at least fifty members. The Wasat Party subsequently appealed to the PPC after expanding its membership list but was again rejected in May 1998 on the basis of another stipulation of Law 40, namely that it "failed to add to existing parties."[39] The members, having amended their platform, decided to submit a new application to the PPC a few days after losing the appeal. In September 1998 the PPC rejected its new application again on the premise that it "failed to add to existing parties."[40] In addition, the Wasat Party's appeal to the PPC was also rejected in June 1999. Following the last rejection, the group then applied to the Ministry of Social Affairs for status as a nongovernmental organization (NGO). In April 2000, having acquired permission to function as an NGO, the group, now called "Egypt: For Culture and Dialogue," held its first conference, ironically titled "The Right to Expression," in May 2001. The PPC's tactics achieve the objectives of discouraging potential parties from applying for legal status and as a consequence can lead to proposed parties eventually deciding to redirect their energies to the less challenging and more controllable NGO arena. While in some cases the PPC finds its decisions challenged in court, the fact that only ten parties in a period of over twenty years won such court cases indicates that the PPC continues to function as a powerful barrier to the formation of political parties in Egypt.

While hesitant to approve new party applications, the PPC is less hesitant to issue decisions to suspend opposition parties. Indeed, the PPC has been responsible for the suspension of seven political parties since 1998. These decisions are aimed primarily at containing political parties that are deemed as challenging to stability. Indicative of this is the case of the Labor Party. Since its alliance with the Muslim Brotherhood during the 1987 legislative elections, the Labor Party has maintained its links with the formally outlawed organization. As a consequence, it has adopted an increasingly Islamist orientation that led to its formal change of name from the Socialist Labor Party to the Labor Party in 1990. On 20 May 2001 the PPC issued a decision to freeze the Labor Party and suspend publication of its biweekly newspaper, *Al-Sha'b*. The PPC cited "party in-fighting and disputes over leadership of the party" as the main justification for its decision.[41] It is convenient that the decision to freeze Labor Party activity coincided with the party using its newspaper to publicly discredit the minister of culture, Farouk Hosni, for his role in authorizing the reprinting in Egypt of the novel *A Banquet for Seaweed,* authored by the Syrian writer Haydir Haydir. Indeed, claims by the party via its mouthpiece that the book was a sacrilegious novel sparked violent riots at the religiously based university Al-Azhar, resulting in the injury of approximately fifty-five students and the arrest of many more.[42] The timing, it should be noted, was not lost on the Labor Party. As the late Adel Hussein, the party's outspoken secretary-general, remarked at the time: "The Government realized that we were capable of mobilizing popular support against its policies. This is an act of a serious opposition and they resent us for that."[43]

Following the freeze on its activity, the Labor Party was unable to mobilize popular support on its own behalf against the PPC's decision. This reflects the important point that while a political party in Egypt may potentially be capable of provoking demonstrations and unrest, as the Haydir novel proved, this type of mobilization does not emerge on behalf of the party. Indeed, the various tactics adopted by the government are intended to ensure that political parties do not develop to a level whereby their grassroots links would enable them to mobilize widespread support on their own behalf. An examination of the nature of electoral laws under Mubarak further reinforces this assumption.

Rules of the Game: Electoral Laws

Prior to the first legislative elections under Mubarak's rule, a controversial electoral law was implemented. According to Law 114 of 1983, the electoral system was to change from the previous individual-candidacy or "first past the post" system to that of a party-list or "proportional representation" system. The number of constituencies was also changed, from 176 to 48. Furthermore, a party would need to gain a minimum of 8 percent of the nationwide vote in order for its representatives to enter the People's Assembly. Should a party not achieve this minimum percentage, its votes would automatically be credited to the largest party, or the NDP. In view of the fact that Egypt's multiparty arena was a relatively new entity and opposition parties did not have sufficient experience in electoral competition, the 8 percent barrier was potentially unattainable for the majority of opposition parties. Moreover, the new law was also aimed at excluding independent candidates just in case their political affiliations might not be known to the regime. As one author noted, "The then prime minister, Fouad Mohieddin, put into private conversation, he did not want 'new men' to be able to stand for election when 'we' [the government] don't know them."[44] The stringent electoral rules excluded not only independent candidates but also all the legalized opposition parties apart from Neo-Wafd, which formed an electoral alliance with the Muslim Brotherhood to gain a combined total of fifty-eight parliamentary seats. Not surprisingly, therefore, the 1983 law was challenged by political opponents at the Supreme Constitutional Court (SCC). The argument presented was that the 1983 electoral law prevented individuals from nominating themselves in elections and was a breach of public right, equality, and opportunity as enshrined in Articles 8, 40, and 62 of the constitution. Interestingly, the president decided at the end of 1986 to approve the amendment of the existing electoral law, dissolve the People's Assembly, and set a premature election date of April 1987.[45]

The amended electoral law did not differ much from the original. Independents were allocated one seat in each of the forty-eight constituencies, with the condition being that the overall winner should gain no less than 20 percent of total votes cast in the constituency. However, this new feature did little to assist independent candidates. In fact, following the 1987 elections, only nine of the forty-eight independent seats were acquired by genuine independents. Individuals identified as NDP members won thirty-eight of the seats.[46] The remaining constituency representatives under the amended electoral law were to be elected under the old party-list system, the minor change being that the votes of those who did not obtain the 8 percent vote requirement would have their votes distributed among all the successful parties in direct proportion to their scores in the elections. It should be noted that opposition entry to the People's Assembly peaked following the 1987 elections. Neo-Wafd campaigned alone and won thirty-six seats. The Muslim Brotherhood created an electoral alliance with the Socialist Labor Party and the Liberal Party (Al-Ahrar) to gain a combined total of sixty-two seats in the legislature. Nevertheless, the opposition returned to the SCC questioning the constitutionality of the 1986 electoral law based on the same arguments presented against the 1983 electoral law. The SCC declared the electoral law unconstitutional in May 1990. The ruling pressured President Mubarak to issue a decree abolishing the party-list system and announcing a return to an individual-candidacy system by absolute majority for the premature 1990 legislative elections. In addition to the abolishment of the party-list system, the size and number of constituencies were also altered, from 48 to 222, thus allowing for two representatives per constituency.

The president's decision to abolish the party-list system was very much a political tactic. By abiding by the court decision the president was highlighting his respect for the rule of law, an aspect he has strenuously attempted to utilize as a legitimization platform for his rule. The opposition's apparent unity under the party-list law, as reflected in electoral alliances, as well as the court challenges and condemnation of the government-imposed rules, all indicate that Mubarak realized that the party-list system was not as conducive to containing political opponents as originally intended.

The return to individual candidacy for the premature 1990 legislative elections did little to encourage opposition confidence in the system. Rather, the opposition continued to object to the prevalence of emergency law and its hindrance on political participation. Equally contentious was the Ministry of Interior's tradition of supervising polling stations and the ballot count. In this regard the change in electoral laws was not seen as a sufficient guarantee for fair and free elections. Excluding the Tagammu' Party, the other main opposition parties decided to boycott the 1990 legislative elections. If the aim was to pressure the government into concession on the basis of these contentious issues, the boycott did not succeed. Rather, it would seem that the participation of Tagammu' helped to prevent the boycott from appearing as a wholesale rejection of the system. Arguably a consequence of its decision to participate, Tagammu' won five parliamentary seats—its first electoral gains under the Mubarak presidency. The opposition boycott lost some of its impact due to the national and international preoccupation with the events unfolding prior to the Gulf War (1990–1991). Either way, the opposition found itself defeated by its actions. Hence, by the time the People's Assembly had completed its first full five-year term, it decided to voluntarily reenter electoral competition. As the Labor Party explained in its newspaper, *Al-Sha'b:*

> We boycotted the last elections to pressurize the government into allowing free and fair elections. The government however ignored us. This time we are participating with no illusions. . . . [W]e are aware that this time round government malpractice will be even more intense. However, we decided, in spite of their careless and shortsighted approach, not to continue the boycott. This is because we care about the constitution and the stability of the nation and we do not want to leave the government with a free rein in these elections. This can only be achieved with our participation.[47]

One of the most prominent features of the 1995 elections was the opposition's poor electoral gains in comparison to their achievements during the 1980s. While Tagammu' managed to maintain five seats, Neo-Wafd gained only six. The Nasserists, the Liberals, and the Muslim Brotherhood all gained one seat each. The Labor Party did not obtain any seats. The lack of opposition success in the 1995 elections "can be accounted for . . . by the fact that the legal opposition parties were so closely tied to the government (via their support for its campaign against the Muslim militants) that their programs were hardly distinguishable from that of the NDP."[48] Indicative of this was the fact that throughout its electoral campaign Tagammu' adopted the campaign slogan "*al-din lillah wa al-witan lil jami'*" ("religion is for God and the nation is for all"). Neo-Wafd adopted similar tactics; its campaign posters depicted an imam and priest in their respective religious garb alongside a peasant at work under the slogan "*al-Wafd al-jaded: hizb al-wihda al-wataniya*" ("the Neo-Wafd: the party of national unity").[49] Most revealing of the opposition parties distancing themselves from the Islamists is a point reflected in the comments of Abd al-'Aziz Muhammad, a senior Neo-Wafd member who declared: "It is not in our interest to co-operate [in the 1995 elections] with an organization [the Muslim Brotherhood] that is targeted by the authorities."[50]

The main opposition parties were not necessarily unanimous in support of the regime's wholesale anti-Islamist campaign. The Labor Party continued to maintain its increasingly Islamic overtones and cooperation with the Muslim Brotherhood, to the degree that the

Muslim Brotherhood's slogan *"Al-Islam howa al-hal"* ("Islam is the solution") was used on the campaign pamphlets of the party's secretary-general, Adel Hussein.[51] On a less involved level, the Nasserist Party questioned the logic of excluding the Muslim Brotherhood from legitimate political participation. As a senior member of the Nasserist Party, 'Abd al-Halim Qandil, stated: "The general feeling in the party at the moment is not only that there should be more solidarity with the Islamists, but that the Muslim Brotherhood should be allowed to operate as a political party."[52] While opposition parties such as Tagammu' and Neo-Wafd incurred electoral losses in the 1995 elections due to the adoption of platforms similar to that of the government, the lack of electoral success for Labor and the Nasserists is linked to their encouragement of Islamist views. Indeed, prior to the elections the minister of information, Safwat al-Sharif, made clear the regime's position by stating that "there will be no room [in the 1995 elections] for political groups who use religion as their platform."[53] As the 1995 election results indicate, the government's ability to put its words into action was by no means a difficult feat. As in the case of the 1990 elections, the 1995 elections were followed by a complete five-year legislative term. However, while emergency rule remains intact, an SCC ruling provided hope of a potentially advantageous electoral procedure for the opposition prior to the 2000 legislative elections.

The 2000 Legislative Elections: The Court Ruling

Egypt's Supreme Constitutional Court declared on 8 July 2000 that Article 88 of the 1971 constitution, which calls for complete judicial supervision of legislative elections, must be implemented according to the law. The SCC ruled that Article 24.2 of Law 73 of 1956, on the exercise of political rights, was unconstitutional because it allowed for nonjudiciary members to share the supervision of elections with the judiciary. The ruling is based on the judicial acknowledgment that Article 24.2 directly violated various articles of the constitution "which pertain to the monitoring by the judiciary of parliamentary elections."[54] The Supreme Constitutional Court sided with the views of political opponents who for years have been claiming that free elections in Egypt can be better realized if full judicial supervision is implemented. Indeed, the main reason for the opposition's boycott in the 1990 legislative elections was the government's refusal to allow for full judicial supervision.

During the decade of legal wrangling between the government and opposition over this issue, the government has defended its position on the basis of the practical considerations involved, namely "that there were not enough judges to oversee the balloting process in all polling stations and, secondly, that judiciary monitoring was a formal supervisory capacity that did not require the actual presence of judges at the polling stations."[55] In response to the government's argument, the SCC justified its ruling by noting that the judiciary's supervision of the election process is necessary because the judiciary is an impartial entity. Moreover, it added that judicial "supervision must be substantive rather than merely formal or professed" if citizens are to "choose their representatives in a safe and confident environment."[56] As a consequence, "Any excuse on the grounds that practical considerations stand against the application of the constitution's provisions is not acceptable, because constitutional requirements cannot be parleyed by excuses."[57] In regard to such a verdict and the equally powerful comments of the SCC, the government was left with little room for maneuver. Ignoring the verdict of the nation's highest court would have undermined respect for the rule of law, which has been the main legitimization tool for the president's authority. As constitutional law professor Mohammed Merghani points out, "The government complied with the Constitutional Court's decision and saved itself from any embarrassment that might have arose from other options."[58] Interestingly, following the 2000 elections the president stated, "I took steps to place the electoral process under the supervision of the judiciary after listening for many years to opinions on how to promote confidence in the voting process and freedom of choice."[59] Yet contrary to producing "confidence in the voting process and freedom of choice," the implementation of new electoral rules expanding the role of the judiciary produced new forms of constraining tactics previously unfamiliar to the majority of Egyptian voters. Early indications that the new electoral framework was to face disparate resistance are detected in view of the Ministry of Interior's increasingly prominent role during the elections. On one level, the fact that the Ministry of Interior maintained its customary control over registered voter lists meant that certain obstructions and disruptions continued. The obstruction of an independent or opposition candidate's access to their constituency's voter list, for example, remained a common occurrence. The case of Hisham Kassem, an independent candidate participating in the Cairo constituency of Kasr al-Aini, reflects the frustrating nature of such obstructions.

Absurd Obstructions: The Case of the Photocopier

As the publisher of an independent English-language newspaper, Hisham Kassem decided to nominate himself in the Kasr al-Aini constituency, where his weekly's office is based.[60] Adopting a realistic approach, Kassem was aware that as it was his first time to participate in legislative elections, his networks within the community and the resources at his disposal were limited in comparison to those of his more veteran competitors.[61] Consequently, he was aware that his chances of success were marginal. In this regard, it is illogical that the police assumed such a candidate to be a serious electoral threat to his NDP opponent or any of the other participating candidates. However, upon registering his candidacy, Kassem arrived at the local police station to request a copy of the registered voter list—a legal right for any registered candidate. The response of the officials was that this would not be possible because apart from the master copy, no additional copies were available. Undeterred, Kassem inquired as to when copies would be available, to which he was told that in the absence of a photocopier, it would be best if he simply looked at the master copy on the premises. Arguing that this would be impractical, the candidate asked if it would be possible to borrow the master copy in order to photocopy it somewhere else. Again, the request was refused on the justification that the master copy could be "misused" if it were taken from the premises. After a few days, Kassem did manage to obtain a copy of the constituency's voter list, but this entailed the candidate personally leasing a Xerox machine and bringing it into the police station to copy the list on the premises.

This incident reflects a petty form of disruption that can hinder a candidate's electoral campaign for a few days. A less familiar candidate may simply give up and participate in an electoral campaign in the absence of the guidance of the constituency's registered voter list. While it is difficult to measure the prevalence of such covert forms of obstruction, overt actions by the police are more evident.

Overt Obstructions: Arresting Assistants and Turning Away Voters

The presence of members of the judiciary in polling stations during the 2000 elections implies that the rigging of ballot papers on election days became a more difficult process in comparison to the previous elections. It is in this context that the Ministry of Interior increased its obstructive tactics outside polling locations, thus preventing voters from entering while the bewildered judges sat inside empty stations. In one reported case a judge presiding over the elections in the Qalyoubian village of Nay left the polling station to see why, with so much noise outside, there were no voters inside. Having discovered that the police, who officially were placed outside to protect the polling station, were serving an additional role of blocking voter entry, the judge demanded that they move aside so that voters could enter. The reply of the officer in charge was that "judges were only responsible for the ballot box inside and had no authority outside the polling station."[62] Indeed, the Egyptian Organization for Human Rights (EOHR) noted in its 2000 electoral report the prevailing "pattern of preventing voters from casting their ballots," focusing in particular on the constituencies of Maadi and Basatin, regarding which it noted that "only buses packed with NDP supporters were permitted to reach the polling stations."[63] Preventing voters from entering polling stations is a blatant form of obstruction and abuse of the electoral process in itself. However, the violent clashes that emerged as a consequence of such tactics between the security apparatus and the voters contributed an additional dimension to the 2000 elections that in previous elections may have also existed, but on a less widespread scale.

Coercive Tactics: The Urban Areas

The clashes between security forces and the voters being barred from casting their ballots took two main forms in urban areas. On one level, a more covert approach was adopted in which plainclothes individuals posing as voters started arguments or fights with legitimate voters. In provoking trouble, the intention was aimed at either intimidating citizens into leaving or, if this proved unsuccessful, providing the security forces with a reason to dispel the crowd using less diplomatic means. In the Cairo constituency of Shubra, the absence of a majority vote for either the minister of foreign trade, Yousif Boutros-Ghali, or his main rival, Medhat Abdel Hadi, a former NDP member turned independent candidate, led to the adoption of such tactics during the runoff day. Arguably apprehensive that an incumbent minister could lose the election, black-clad riot police were observed outside the polling station at Shubra secondary school "cordoning off the streets around the school [as] crowds of voters looked on in disbelief."[64] One schoolteacher, Farid Seghawi, recounted that when he arrived at 8:00 A.M. to vote, the guards responded, "What are you doing here? Go away!"[65]

Less fortunate were those who encountered "plainclothesmen" throwing pepper sauce into voters' eyes. Moreover, according to one witness, "Police stood by doing nothing while women were pulled to the ground by their hair by state security plainclothesmen."[66] Apparently, such tactics were not confined to this particular station; it is reported that the security forces surrounded at least eight polling stations in Shubra in efforts to prevent supporters of the trade minister's opponent from voting. Not surprisingly, Boutros-Ghali won the election.

Another example of the use of coercive tactics took place in the Doqqi constituency of Cairo, where Amal Osman, a former long-serving minister and senior member of the NDP, competed against Ma'moon al-Hodabi, a senior member of the Muslim Brotherhood and its official spokesman. In this case the voters, a majority of them apparently Muslim Brotherhood supporters, were "surrounded by policemen armed with rifles and tear gas canisters, [who] refused icily and with indifference" to allow voters entrance to the polling station.[67] When one female voter, accompanied by her young son, asked an officer to allow her inside, his response was: "The place is very crowded. Wait a while."[68] In the meantime, a journalist observing the events noticed that "as the number of voters blocked from the station swelled, hired thugs (of both sexes) attacked voters. . . . Amid the clamor [the same female voter] was hit on the head by a stone, then nearly pushed to the ground by one of the female thugs. She quickly lifted her child and ran away."[69] Interestingly however, as the same observer noted, "A few minutes later, the situation calmed down slightly and a bus loaded with voters and bearing a picture of the NDP candidate arrived. After a brief conversation with the same police officer, roadblocks were removed and the bus was allowed into the courtyard with its precious cargo."[70]

Norbert Schiller, an American photographer, was also present at this polling station. In regard to the buses containing NDP supporters, Schiller noted that one of his colleagues had managed to interview some of these voters who admitted "that they had been picked up from different areas around Doqqi and were here to cast ballots."[71] In other words, these individuals were not genuine supporters of the NDP candidates and their presence was the consequence of some form of incitement. As in the case of his colleague, whose tape recorder was "snatched by an unidentified 'thief'" following this particular interview, Schiller didn't fare much better. Rather, he could not gain entry to the polling station with Hodabi's entourage because the police had sealed off the perimeter of the compound. Hence they decided to try entering through the exit by way of the back gate. However, as they waited for the back gate to open, dozens of people started crowding around them. More chilling was Schiller's account of what happened next:

> As soon as the gate swung open, the women grabbed my cameras and as I was fighting to pull them free a gang of thugs drew their knives. With that I let go, watching as they smashed all my equipment into the ground. As I tried a second time to recover some of the pieces the thugs began threatening me with knives again. I turned to the police who were standing directly behind me but none of them made a move to help.[72]

When Schiller started yelling loudly, "Is this what you call democracy?" a plainclothes police officer approached him and said, "They're thieves—go and report it to the police," to which the angry photographer pointed out, "Do thieves smash cameras they steal?"[73] Indeed, Schiller did find his way to the Doqqi police station and upon reporting this incident, the officer in charge attempted to justify it by arguing that the thugs had probably mistaken him for "a member of a political party." Moreover, the officer explained that the "police don't like to interfere in such matters because it looks as if they are meddling with the political process." The officer tellingly added that this was "a sign of democracy."[74]

The significance of the Doqqi case is twofold. On one level, a senior Brotherhood member competing against a senior NDP member is a sensitive issue for the government. After all, it would be highly embarrassing if the Doqqi voters were to give preference to a senior Brotherhood leader over a competitor of equal seniority in the ruling party, particularly given that Hodabi was a popular candidate. Hodabi's popularity may not have been simply a consequence of the political support he derived from the Muslim Brotherhood, but also a consequence of his Doqqi family origins and hence presumably his status as a "local son" (*ibn al-hay*). Indeed, Hodabi competed and won the seat in the 1987 elections. However, having abstained from the 1990 elections due to the opposition boycott, he returned to recontest his seat in the 1995 elections to find that Osman, then incumbent minister of social affairs had been nominated by the NDP to stand against him.

While Osman won both the 1995 and 2000 elections, the manner in which the former minister won the seat in the 2000 elections reflects a difference in tactics adopted by the state in 1995. In 1995 the voters faced few obstacles, as most irregularities were targeted directly at the opposition candidate. Hodabi was heavily monitored by security forces during that election campaign and in one instance they dispatched five fully manned police vans to the mosque where he was performing Friday prayers to ensure that he did nothing but pray.[75] This is not to imply that the monitoring of the opposition candidate was less stringently enforced this time around.

The presence of state security to restrain a candidate's campaign movements and control the voting process meant that prior to the 2000 elections, the blatant tactic of physically preventing voter entry to the polling station was largely a secondary option. More disturbing is that this tactic was not limited to urban areas in which prominent personalities were competing, but also detected in the more obscure rural areas.

Coercive Tactics: The Rural Areas

The adoption of coercive tactics aimed at preventing opposition supporters from gaining entry to vote gained considerable prominence in the rural Delta town of Ashmoun, Menoufiya. Ashraf Badreddin, a Muslim Brotherhood member, was considered the town's favorite candidate. Consequently, when the town's voters turned up at the polling station on election day, they were "blocked from the polls, their ID cards were torn up, and they were threatened, beaten, teargassed and even shot at as parts of efforts to alter the outcome of parliamentary elections in the town."[76]

Ironically, one innocent passerby, Gamal Abdel Yousif, was shot and killed as he made his way home from work at the local primary school where he was a teacher. The stray bullet came from police who opened fire on frustrated voters who had begun throwing rocks after being denied entry to vote. Although many other voters were injured, "the fear of being arrested or further harassed by police" meant that less than sixty were admitted to the local hospital and city hospitals.[77] One local doctor who treated some of the injured noted:

> The police opened fire in all directions. They had orders to do it. And they had high orders to prevent people from voting. All the time [the government talks] about democracy. Where is it? People go out of their houses to die and be injured. . . . I saw two hundred and fifty people shot with my own eyes. I did what I could. I advised them not to go to the hospital. They will be taken away by the police.[78]

This incident can be discarded as an exceptional case in that being a member of the Muslim Brotherhood, an illegal opposition party, the town's popular candidate may have caused some concern for the government. However, that such violent tactics were adopted by the state in situations where the popular candidate was not associated with any legal opposition party, let alone the Muslim Brotherhood, indicates the prevalence of this trend. The case of the rural village of Al-Ammar, Qalubiya, provides an apt example.[79]

The inhabitants of Al-Ammar, an agricultural village of 45,000 inhabitants, 12,000 of whom are registered voters, woke up to the sound of state security trucks making their way through the village on 14 October 2000. The excitement of the villagers at this sight was ironically linked to their belief that the government had sent state security forces to protect them and ensure their safety during the electoral runoff of Omar Amir Mitwali and Mansour Amir—both independent candidates. As the voters made their way to one of the four polling stations located in the village, they discovered to their dismay that barriers had been erected and police were forbidding entrance to the stations. In an effort to break the villagers' morale, the security forces began ordering the inhabitants to alternately sit down and stand up—treating the villagers as soldiers in training rather than as civilians waiting to vote.

Failing to sufficiently demoralize the voters into leaving, the security forces allegedly began pushing and harassing them. At approximately 1:45 P.M., Fathi al-Hajj, a thirty-four-year-old herb merchant from the village, was helping to reorganize the long queues when he saw a police officer kick a female villager. Al-Hajj approached the officer and said to him, "Would you do that if she was your sister?"[80] to which the officer responded by slapping al-Hajj across the face. In the space of a few seconds, al-Hajj retaliated by pushing the officer and quickly running away. The officer subsequently ordered the shooting of al-Hajj, who died immediately of his wound.

In a frenzy of panic and anger, the villagers began shouting and attempted to break down the school gates while the police responded with further shootings and tear gas. In addition to approximately eighty people being injured, two inhabitants were shot dead and a four-month-old baby died as a result of the tear gas. According to the villagers, the only reason they had turned up en masse to vote was because they had encouraged Mitwali, a highly respected local man, to run for election after retiring as a civil servant for the Ministry of Transport. As one inhabitant explained: "During his forty years tenure at the Ministry, Mitwali had helped over one thousand villagers acquire state employment. We felt if he entered parliament he would do even more for us. The presence of judiciary supervision as well gave us hope that he could win. This is why we encouraged him to compete and this is why we all turned up to vote."[81] According to the villagers, Mitwali's opponent, Mansour Amir, a highly successful businessman with significant political connections, allegedly used his position to block Mitwali's supporters, resulting in the use of blatantly coercive tactics by the security forces. Since Al-Ammar villagers did not get the opportunity to vote, Mansour won the elections and subsequently joined the NDP upon entering the People's Assembly. This was not an unexpected move considering the high unlikelihood that state security would intervene to support a candidate who could not be co-opted into the system. Yet state-directed coercion can also backfire, as in the case of Kafr al-Mikdam, which highlights the unpredictable and fragile nature of political participation in Egypt.

The Case of Kafr al-Mikdam

Kafr al-Mikdam is a small rural village on the outskirts of Mit Khamer (electoral constituency of Atmeda) with a population of less

than 20,000. This unassuming, conservative village came to prominence during the 2000 legislative elections, when it confronted the
state over a misunderstanding and won. Mortada Mansour, a prominent and popular lawyer, had secured the support of Kafr al-Mikdam
during his campaign as an independent candidate. Part of his appeal
to the villagers was his apparent independence from the government.
He maintained that he played a prominent role in the fall of the former minister of interior, Zaki Badr, and had published a book based
on his claims. More important, his position as lawyer to several
Egyptian movie stars rendered Mansour a very wealthy man; he
spent over 2 million Egyptian pounds (U.S.$570,000) on his cam-
paign. As one villager stated, Kafr al-Mikdam supported Mansour in
his quest for office because "he paid money to the village."[82]

Mansour's main rival in the elections was the NDP's official
candidate, Abdel Rahman Barakah, an incumbent representative of
Atmeda since 1990. In addition to being the official NDP candidate
and a relative of Mustapha Said, a former minister, this retired bank
manager was also a "local son," or *ibn al-hay,* of the neighboring village, Sintemay. In the absence of ties linking candidates to voters on
the basis of party platform or ideology, the villagers of Sintemay
were supporting their *ibn al-hay* on the assumption that, when in
office, he would continue channeling much-needed state resources
into his hometown. In this regard, both villages were supporting the
competing candidates largely in return for short-term material
rewards.

On election day, residents of both villages went to cast their
votes at their respective polling stations. In the case of Sintemay, the
villagers were facing little difficulty entering the station to cast their
votes since their candidate was also the official NDP candidate.
However, at the middle school polling station in Kafr al-Mikdam, the
situation was different. Because of the existence of judiciary supervision inside the polling station, and the fact that the villagers were
intending to cast their votes for the NDP's main rival, the security
forces adopted what had become a common tactic throughout the
2000 elections—preventing voters from entering the station. As one
villager observed: "The police barracked the school. Every time the
judge came out to ask why there were no voters inside the station,
the police would reply that they were just organizing the crowds first
and then they would send in the few Barakah supporters to keep the
judge occupied."[83]

Although the security forces were armed and were telling people that they "had orders from above to send everyone home," the villagers were not intimidated and refused to leave. In the midst of the shoving and pushing, a thirty-three-year-old villager, Sayyed Mohammed al-Salkh, had a fatal heart attack. The crowd started screaming "*al-hukoma mawetto*" ("the government killed him"), and before long the rumor that the victim had been murdered by the security forces spread across Kafr al-Mikdam and into the neighboring villages. In truth, the young man had suffered from heart problems all his life and the security forces were not directly responsible for his death. What is of particular significance are the events that immediately followed.

The head of police (*al-Ma'mur*), located in Mit Khamer, authorized the immediate issue of a death certificate for al-Salkh. Within an hour of reaching the local hospital, the formalities were completed and al-Salkh was ready for burial.[84] On the way to the burial, the villagers decided to take the route past the polling station, though there were two other routes to the village graveyard.[85] Their intention was to provoke the police into a confrontation. While screaming that the government had killed al-Salkh, the villagers began filling their pockets with bricks belonging to an unfortunate villager who was in the process of building a house. As expected, the police tried to reroute the funeral procession. When the villagers began throwing their accumulated bricks at the police, the latter retaliated by firing rubber bullets—a tactic that provoked further anger and violence from the villagers. Eventually the police exhausted the supply of rubber bullets and started throwing tear gas canisters to dispel the crowd. This too backfired, because, as one villager explained, "The young men have all watched the Palestinian intifada on television so they started imitating what they've seen and picking up the canisters and throwing them back at the police."[86] A few tear gas canisters found their way into nearby houses. Believing their homes to be on fire, given the smoke emerging from them, the villagers escalated their violent confrontation with the police. In addition to their accusation that the government had killed al-Salkh, they began screaming that the government was burning down their houses. The police, having now exhausted their supply of tear gas as well, began firing live ammunition. At this point, groups of about ten villagers each began to surround and separate the police officers in order to overpower them. The tactic worked and the villagers found themselves in the dominant position.

The fact that the security forces were unable to find immediate backup, due to their election-day dispersal throughout the various constituencies, undoubtedly played an important role in the outcome of events. In the case of Kafr al-Mikdam, the confrontations fortunately did not result in any fatalities. Furthermore, al-Salkh was eventually buried that day, even though the few villagers who had managed to sneak the coffin to the graveyard temporarily had to set the coffin aside as they fought with police. In regard to the electoral outcome, Mansour won over his NDP rival, because the distorted news that had emerged from Kafr al-Mikdam regarding government brutality led voters from the other villages, including Barakah's own, to retaliate by casting their ballots for the NDP's main opponent. As one villager explained:

> When the news spread to the other villages about what was happening [in Kafr al-Mikdam], many switched their allegiances and voted for Mansour out of spite for the government. . . . In fact the vote counting went on until early next morning. All along, Barakah was slightly in the lead and all that was left was the vote-count from his own village [Sintemay] which he assumed he had won. However he soon discovered that his village voted for Mansour against *ibn al-hay* to spite the government. . . . [T]he presence of judges during vote counting meant that the government could not do anything about it. That was a big surprise for the government because they thought they had blocked all the villages which did not support its candidate.[87]

The point is that hindering political competition and choice does not necessarily strengthen the bonds between the state and society. Indeed, as the Kafr al-Mikdam case illustrates, even in instances where the government has not committed the accused crime, it still emerges as the prime suspect in the eyes of its people. In its refusal to share power, the government becomes unable to share the blame.

Reassessing the 2000 Elections

The implementation of full judiciary supervision in the 2000 legislative elections brought revived hope for both contestants and voters in regard to Egypt's ailing twenty-year democratic experiment. One prominent opposition member initially declared the SCC ruling on judicial supervision as "a pleasant surprise" that was "in the interest of democracy and, consequently in the interest of the opposition."[88] The Al-Ammar villagers, as in the case of many other optimists, had high hopes for the amended electoral system. As one villager explained, "We were sure these elections would be clean. We had such high hopes; the re-run gave us even more hope. We've never had a 'son of the village' (*ibn al-hay*) in parliament before."[89]

The prevalence of coercive tactics aimed at voters simply dashed such hopes. More important, such tactics had sown seeds of resentment in diverse sections of the population who previously regarded the state as their protector. This frustration toward the state can be detected on two levels. First, resentment and anger vented by citizens against the government was reflected in their attempts to destroy state-owned property. In the case of Ashmoun, the violence and death that ensued at the hands of the police led inhabitants to stone local NDP offices and set fire to several buses after their failed attempts to set fire to the local hospital and police station. On another level are the psychological aspects of voter anger and frustration, which in the long term are more threatening to the political stability of the country. While the inhabitants of Al-Ammar did not retaliate against the state's violence, their psychological scars are evident. Feeling betrayed and angry over what is perceived as a gross injustice, one villager explained:

> We have never been a political village. Now we are angry at what the government did to us. We feel helpless at the injustice that happened to us. We used to respect the state (*al-dawla*) and thought that these terrorists were mad people who deserved to die. Now we secretly feel so happy when we hear of terrorism against the state. We can never go back to our normal lives again—they took away our old life. Why didn't they just leave us to vote and rig the election results afterwards as they used to do. We wouldn't have cared; we're used to that. Why did they have to kill us this time. . . . Injustice breeds hatred.[90]

Indeed, the electoral death toll of less than ten people in the 2000 elections is lower than that of the 1995 elections, which witnessed fifty-one nationwide deaths. However, the difference is the cause of the deaths. In the 1995 elections, most of the electoral fatalities were largely a consequence of "feuds within the confines of personality-based politics which are more easily begun and harder to contain."[91]

In other words, electoral violence before the 2000 elections was predominantly confined to conflict between competing candidates and their personal groups of supporters. This is a pattern that is not unusual in developing systems in which political parties are weak. The 2000 legislative elections brought state-directed violence in which the most blatant tactics were used to target and confront citizens. This fact is confirmed by one independent report that noted that while "violence between their candidates and supporters decreased, the violence from security forces against voters increased."[92] Indeed, "Approximately 80% of the killings and injuries resulted from bullets or tear gas fired by security forces and not through rival fighting."[93]

Sameh Ashour, a member of the Nasserist opposition party, commented prior to the elections that the court ruling could be considered a step forward toward achieving fair elections. However, he predicted that attempts by the government to avoid the application of the new ruling in the elections would lead "to a catastrophe that would endanger the stability of the state and society."[94] In hindsight, the new tactics adopted by the regime to complement the new rules of the SCC have touched upon these fears. The latest ruling and the indirect restrictions that have emerged as a consequence have further contributed to reinforcing regime domination in the face of potential progress within the arena of political participation.

Effects of Electoral Rules on Political Participation

With the various constraints imposed on party formation and participation, political parties in contemporary Egypt remain weak and underdeveloped entities. As a consequence, it is not uncommon to find them referred to as "parties of pressure."[95] In other words, due to the fact that multiparty participation does profoundly impact the political arena, such as affecting the outcome of government, political parties remain excluded from the realms of the policymaking process. Rather, the "pressure" role in the case of the NDP stems from the fact that "its parliamentary caucus has assumed considerable authority over lesser matters: it is the source of a constant stream of initiatives and responses to government meant to defend and promote the interest of its largely bourgeois constituency."[96] However, what this means is that although the NDP does not actually concede any accountability to the bourgeoisie, it "provides enough privileged access to keep them satisfied."[97] In the case of opposition parties, the "pressure" factor can be detected in their attempt to "articulate the interests and values of sectors of the population ignored by the dominant party."[98] This has entailed attempts at high-lighting various socioeconomic concerns, as during a debate in parliament in summer 2001, when opposition forces united in vocal protest regarding the negative consequences of the government's proposed mortgage law on low-income groups. While such opposition did not deter the government from proceeding with the scheme, it pressured the state into delaying the passing of the bill for a month until it was revised and modified to incorporate some benefits for the low-income sectors of society. As Raymond Hinnebusch points out, "A party of pressure may also act as an interest group advocating particular interests in elite circles or promoting the fortunes of aspirant politicians hoping for co-optation."[99] In view of the disparate constraints imposed on Egypt's multiparty arena, this latter characteristic is an overtly prominent feature of the current nature of Egypt's political parties.

It can be detected in the individualistic, personality-dominated, intra- and interparty rivalry that exists. Indicative of the personal nature of interparty rivalries is the case of the Tagammu' Party's decision to break the opposition boycott and participate in the 1990 legislative elections. The opposition decided to boycott those elections to press the government to concede to its demands. While initially united, Tagammu' broke ranks on the basis that the boycott would merely isolate the parties from the electorate. Underneath this formal argument was a more trivial motivation for Tagammu's actions, namely that Khalid Mohyi al-Din, the party's leader, resented the fact that Neo-Wafd leader Fouad Sarag al-Din had assumed the role of opposition spokesman. Sarag al-Din had taken the initiative of approaching the government with the final decision to boycott without informing the rest of the opposition leaders beforehand. Having set a meeting with the Tagammu' committee, Mohyi al-Din informed his party seniors of the decision to participate in the elections. Some members of the committee viewed this decision as a betrayal to the other opposition party and a sign of weakness in their confrontation with the government. However, Mohyi al-Din was adamant, arguing that the party was an independent entity and "not a branch of the Neo-Wafd, and that Sarag al-Din had no right to inform the authorities of a final decision which involved other parties than his own without their prior knowledge and consent."[100] As this episode illustrates, the personal rivalry between two party leaders resulted in the division of what was a valid and potentially effective opposition protest. In turn, the fact that party leaders are in the position to make and implement important party decisions on the basis of personal inclinations highlights the weak and underdeveloped nature of political parties. In addition, the prevalence of individualistic intraparty rivalry further reinforces this predicament.

Indicative of the personality cliques that currently continue to shape the nature of political parties in Egypt is the fact that political parties have difficulty remaining unified in the absence of their "founders." The death of Al-Ahrar leader Mustapha Kamel Murad in 1998, and the death of Neo-Wafd leader Fouad Sarag al-Din in 2000, have both highlighted this aspect. The succession process for Al-Ahrar leadership proved to be a battle of personalities threatening the existence of the party rather than a formal and orderly routine procedure. The leadership struggle that ensued between Hamza Dabas and his pro-Islamist camp and Mohammed Farid Zakariya and his pronationalist camp led not only to a war of words and accusations, but also to physical confrontations and injuries.[101] The internal disputes provided the Political Parties Committee with the opportunity to freeze party activity for sixty days on the condition that Al-Ahrar settle its internal disputes, "call for a party congress and elect a new leader without causing further trouble."[102] It is worth noting that, including Dabas and Zakariya, a total of seventy-nine party members subsequently applied for the leadership position.[103] The disputes have yet to be settled and hence years after the death of Murad, party activity remains formally frozen.

Due to the relatively smooth leadership elections in September 2000, which resulted in a win for No'man Gom'a with over 78 percent of the vote, Neo-Wafd was able to avoid the fate of Al-Ahrar. Nevertheless, by early March 2000, Gom'a had expelled three of his party's seven incumbent parliamentarians. The reasons stem from an assassination attempt on one of the parliamentarians, Farid Hassanain, while he was making the rounds in his home constituency of Tukh. While the incident received coverage in the party's newspaper, *Al-Wafd,* Hassanain urged the paper's editors to condemn the government, which he believed was taking the assassination attempt too lightly, "for its harassment and their lack of investigation."[104]

According to one report, Hassanain wanted to call a press conference on the matter, but Gom'a rejected the initiative. As a consequence "more than 70 supporters of Hassanain and Ayman Nor—who threw his lot in with his fellow MP—crowded the party headquarters. In the wake of the incident Gom'a expelled both Nor and Hassanain from the party and asked for police protection."[105]

That Gom'a expelled two parliamentarians from the party stems from personally based inclinations. First, the new leader did not appreciate that Hassanain and Nor challenged his authority in the form of protest at the party's headquarters, so he expelled them immediately. Second, this protest could have been avoided had Gom'a allowed the requested press conference to take place. In addition, the decision to refuse permission for a press conference that would portray the government's role in the incident reflects a willingness on the part of Gom'a to sacrifice the interests of his own party members rather than challenge the conduct of the government and its alleged interference. The damage to the party is most evident in the fact that, given the nature of voter participation, Neo-Wafd lost not only three parliamentarians but their respective constituencies. This is not an insignificant aspect in view of the political dynamics that exist in such a constrained and noncompetitive multiparty arena. As one author noted:

> Under a competitive party system, it makes sense for citizens to pay attention to a candidate's stand on those issues affecting the entire national political system. For if a candidate is committed to a party, then [that party's] success could conceivably affect national policy. . . . [Under a noncompetitive party system,] if successful, a candidate . . . would . . . have little impact upon national policies. . . . [V]oters behaving rationally . . . therefore tend to pay more attention to the ability of candidates to do things of immediate, local value than to their stands on national issues.[106]

At the grassroots level, the noncompetitive nature of the multiparty system in contemporary Egypt has not been lost on the voters. Contrary to President Mubarak's view that democracy in Egypt is provided in "doses . . . in proportion to our ability to absorb them,"[107] a rare public opinion survey conducted in Egypt suggested otherwise. In this survey, 86 percent of those interviewed regarded a democratic multiparty system as beneficial to Egypt. Moreover, a minority of 36 percent regarded Egypt's current multiparty system as beneficial.[108] Indeed, Egyptian citizens are aware of what a multiparty system entails and understand that Egypt's multiparty system does not fit within that framework. In this context, Egyptian voters apply the parochially oriented rationale to political participation. In other words, the noncompetitive nature of Egypt's multiparty arena encourages voters to support electoral candidates on the basis of a personal, patron-client nature rather than on the basis of party programs or policies that have little effect on national policies. In the words of one prominent political opponent, "My party connection is of no help at all. Actually it is not popular in Port Said [where his constituency of Hay al-'Arab is located]. . . . I am proud of being a member of the Tagammu' and everyone knows I am a member of that party. But in reality, they vote for me because I am able to help them in their everyday problems."[109]

The dominant power of the presidency means that support for NDP candidates, as well, has patron-client characteristics. As one veteran NDP member complained, "I have competed in legislative elections eight times. . . . The voters have specific expectations. . . . 'I'll get you the water, the school, the electricity' is all I say in my election campaign. Nobody cares what my political orientation is. Nobody bothers to ask me."[110] In this regard, the NDP, like the opposition parties, tends to choose candidates "who have a good local reputation. Sometimes that person with a good local reputation might not be the best man for the job. But he is usually the most popular person with a lot of family support and recognition from the local people."[111] The weak ties bonding voters to political parties accentuate the significance of individual politicians within the realms of their own parties, because these individuals enter their respective parties with their followers and supporters in tow. In turn, should they leave, they also leave with these same clients in tow, as in the case of the Neo-Wafd parliamentarians.

Indeed, the imposed constraints discussed in this chapter make it very difficult for political parties to expand and develop a broad base of support at the grassroots level so as to marginalize the existing clientelist structure. Rather, constraints on the activities of political parties marginalize their role as organized political entities, leaving them to resemble little more than a conglomerate of personalities possessing their personal networks of supporters. It is not uncommon for party members to switch political affiliation to suit their personal

interests or compete against each other in elections. As one prominent analyst commented following the sharp increase in violent feuds
during the 1995 legislative elections:

> It is hard to explain how, after claiming so many victims, the elec-
> toral battle ended in such a sweeping victory for one party. No one
> can believe that these casualties were the result of one party which
> won over 90 per cent of the votes and 14 opposition parties which
> together managed to win only 14 seats! They are seen rather as
> reflecting the vicious in-fighting among the candidates of the
> National Democratic Party (NDP) itself, or among its candidates
> and defectors from the NDP who ran as "independents" when not
> nominated by the party and who, on being elected, returned to its
> ranks.[112]

A similar pattern of intraparty competition can be detected during the
2000 legislative elections, aptly illustrated in the fact that NDP-nom-
inated candidates were elected to only 172 of the 444 elected seats in
the People's Assembly. As one electoral report points out,
"Following the elections, the NDP added to its ranks 217 parliamentary members who ran as independents, giving it a majority of
87.8%."[113] While the imposed participatory constraints encourage
individualistic and parochially oriented forms of political participation, the constraints are less challenging to the political status quo.
Such patterns of political participation are also more fragile and
unstable than those within an institutionalized, competitive, multiparty system.

Conclusion

This chapter has highlighted several aspects in regard to the nature of
Egypt's multiparty arena, which although reinstated over twenty-five
years ago, remains a fragile and weak entity. This is directly linked
to the manner in which the law, combined with patronage and coercion, is utilized by the regime to preserve its monopoly on power.
Such tactics are advantageous to a regime intent on controlling and
containing autonomous political groupings and constituencies. Yet
by hindering the development of multiparty participation, the regime
is not preserving or gaining a broad base of support in the process.
Rather, what has emerged in Egypt, as with any government whose

institutions are weak, are rules that are "defied or ignored" because "they appear artificial and without meaning."[114] Because "the rulers and other leaders take precedence over the formal rules of the political game," the result is that "the rules do not effectively regulate political participation."[115] As a consequence, it is difficult to "predict or anticipate conduct from a knowledge of the rules."[116] In this context, the characteristics of personal authoritarian rule as exemplified under Nasser and Sadat are preserved under Mubarak, albeit under the guise of a multiparty system. Personal authoritarian rule is "usually a personal government that uses law and the coercive instruments of the state to expedite its own purposes of monopolizing power and denies the political rights and opportunities for all other groups to compete for that power,"[117] a description that aptly circumscribes the structure of political participation in contemporary Egypt. The next chapter examines how such efforts to reinforce the domination and continuity of personal authoritarian rule hinder the development of civil society.

Notes

1. Huntington, *Political Order in Changing Societies,* p. 401.
2. Ibid.
3. Ibid.
4. Lawson, *The Human Polity,* p. 164.
5. Smith, *Understanding Third World Politics,* p. 202.
6. Ibid., pp. 202–203.
7. Dessouki, "Democracy in Egypt," p. 12.
8. Quoted in British Broadcasting Corporation, 12 March 1957, in Owen, *State, Power, and Politics,* p. 149.
9. Ibid., p. 11.
10. Ibid.
11. Ibid., p. 13.
12. Ibid., p. 15.
13. Ibid., p. 150.
14. Ibid., p. 150.
15. Dessouki, "Democracy in Egypt," p. 15.
16. President Sadat as quoted in the newspaper *Mayo,* 4 May 1981, cited in Korany, Brynen, and Noble, *Political Liberalization and Democratization in the Arab World,* pp. 46–47.
17. Hill, "Parties, Elections, and the Law," p. 26.
18. Ayubi, *The State and Public Policies in Egypt Since Sadat,* p. 223.
19. Ibid.

20. See Law 40 of 1977, *The Constitution of the Arab Republic of Egypt.*

21. Kienle, *A Grand Delusion,* p. 29.

22. It is worth pointing out here that prior to formalizing the multiparty arena, Sadat allowed the ideological "platforms" to participate in the 1976 legislative elections. Competition in the 175 two-member districts resulted in "his" centrally oriented Nationalist Socialist Rally gaining 280 seats in comparison to 12 seats gained by the Liberal Socialists and 2 seats gained by the National Progressives. The overwhelming victory of Sadat's platform gave him the confidence to pursue the transition to a formal multiparty system that he could control.

23. Bill and Springborg, *Politics in the Middle East,* p. 224.

24. Presidential public address, April 1982, cited in "Egypt: A Decade of Peace, Development, and Democracy, 1981–1991," 1991.

25. Owen, "Socio-Economic Change and Political Mobilization," p. 189.

26. Jackson and Rosberg, *Personal Rule in Black Africa,* pp. 11–12.

27. Ouda, el-Borai, and Saada, *A Door Onto the Desert,* p. 36.

28. Ibid.

29. "Presidential Public Address," 1 May 1998.

30. Ouda, el-Borai, and Saada, *A Door Onto the Desert,* p. 36.

31. Based on author interviews and observations during the 1995 and 2000 legislative elections.

32. 'Atef 'Obayd, then minister of public enterprises, speech at NDP election rally, 25 November 1995, Helwan.

33. Hamdi Al-Sayyed, NDP veteran, speech recorded during his electoral gathering, Hickstep, Nozha, 18 November 1995.

34. Article 98b of the penal code, cited in Ouda, el-Borai, and Saada, *A Door Onto the Desert,* p. 40.

35. Article 102 of the penal code, cited in ibid.

36. Article 102b of the penal code, cited in ibid.

37. Article 174 of the penal code, cited in ibid.

38. For an in-depth study on the Wasat Party, see Stacher, "Moderate Political Islamism."

39. Ibid., p. 128.

40. Ibid.

41. Apiku, "Egypt Cracks Down on Islamist Party."

42. Ibid.

43. Ibid.

44. Owen, *State, Power, and Politics,* p. 152.

45. Kassem, *In the Guise of Democracy,* p. 99.

46. "Egypt," *Middle East Contemporary Survey,* vol. 11, p. 328. The remaining seat was won by a Muslim Brotherhood member.

47. *Al-Sha'b* (29 September 1995).

48. Owen, *State, Power, and Politics,* p. 154.

49. For more details, see Kassem, *In the Guise of Democracy,* pp. 108–121.

50. *Al-Ahali* (4 October 1995).

51. Author observation on 13 November 1995, during Adel Hussein's electoral campaign

52. *Middle East Times* (10–16 December 1995).

53. Ibid.

54. Abdel-Fattah, "A Time to Judge."

55. Farahat, "Courting Constitutionality."

56. Abdel-Fattah, "A Time to Judge."

57. Ibid.

58. Shehab, "Missing the Point."

59. Khalil, "Setting the Standard."

60. Hisham Kassem, owner of the *Cairo Times,* interview by author, 7 November 2000, Cairo.

61. Kassem's main competitor was Hisham Badrawi, an NDP candidate familiar to the constituency and a very wealthy man who owns numerous private hospitals. Badrawi spent several million Egyptian pounds on his campaign in comparison to Kassem's 35,000 Egyptian pounds. Kassem interview, 7 November 2000.

62. Dawoud, "Necessary Precautions."

63. Howeidy, "Registering the Aftershocks."

64. Elamrani, "Divide and Rule."

65. Ibid.

66. Ibid.

67. Dawoud, "Necessary Precautions."

68. Ibid.

69. Ibid.

70. Ibid.

71. Schiller, "Beaten at the Polls."

72. Ibid.

73. Ibid.

74. Ibid.

75. Senior member of the Muslim Brotherhood, interview by author, 11 November 1995, Cairo.

76. Gazzar, "The Ballot and the Bullet."

77. Ibid.

78. Ibid.

79. This case example is derived from personal interviews by the author with villagers and victims, 5 January 2001, Al-Ammar.

80. Al-Ammar eyewitness, interview by the author, 5 January 2001, Al-Ammar.

81. Ibid.

82. Kafr al-Mikdam villagers and eyewitnesses, interview by author, 19 May 2001, Cairo.

83. Ibid.

84. In hindsight, the villagers believe that *al-Ma'mur* was concerned that police brutality may have been the cause of death and authorized the immediate death certificate to avoid a postmortem.

85. Islamic custom advocates the burial of the dead as soon as possible.

86. Kafr al-Mikdam villagers and eyewitnesses interview, 19 May 2001.

87. Ibid.

88. Ayman Nor, former Wafd member and incumbent parliamentarian in Bab al-Sharqiya (Cairo), cited in Abou al-Maged, "Tempered Jubilation."

89. Al-Ammar villager interview, 5 January 2001.

90. Ibid.

91. C. H. Lande, cited in Kassem, *In the Guise of Democracy,* p. 171.

92. Ouda, el-Borai, and Saada, *A Door Onto the Desert,* p. 75.

93. Ibid.

94. Abou al-Maged, "Tempered Jubilation."

95. See Hinnebusch, "Formation of the Contemporary Egyptian State."

96. Ibid., p. 199.

97. Ibid.

98. Ibid.

99. Ibid., p. 201.

100. Kassem, *In the Guise of Democracy,* p. 104.

101. Apiku, "Ahrar Evicts Renegades in Further Squabbles."

102. Apiku, "Political Parties Committee Spares Ahrar."

103. Apiku, "Ahrar Crisis Gets More Intricate."

104. Apiku, "The Plot Thickens."

105. Ibid.

106. Bates, *Beyond the Miracle of the Market,* p. 92.

107. Presidential speech at Alexandria University, 18 July 1992, British Broadcasting Corporation, "Summary of World Broadcasts," ME/1438, A/2-3 (21 July 1992), cited in Owen, "Socio-Economic Change and Political Mobilization," p. 189.

108. al-Fergany, "Yes to Pluralism, No to Violence."

109. Al-Badri Farghali, member of the Tagammu' Party and member of parliament, interview by author, 31 December 1994, Cairo.

110. Hamdi al-Sayyed, speaking during a conference on elections at the Research Center for Human Rights, 25 December 1995, Cairo.

111. Hamdi al-Sayyed, NDP veteran, interview by author, 1 January 1995, Cairo.

112. Sid 'Ahmad, *Al-Ahram Weekly* (14–20 December 1995).

113. Ouda, el-Borai, and Saada, *A Door Onto the Desert,* p. 51.

114. Jackson and Rosberg, *Personal Rule in Black Africa,* 10.

115. Ibid.

116. Ibid.

117. Ibid., p. 23.

4

Civil Society

Civil society can be broadly defined as a formal "mélange of asso-ciations, clubs, guilds, syndicates, unions, parties and groups come together to provide a buffer between state and citizen."[1] Civil society is intended to represent the various and at times competing interests, views, and values of the people. In this regard, civil society represents the pragmatic, class-based interests of specific sectors in society via trade unions, professional associations, and business associations. Civil society also represents the competing ideologies and quest for power of political parties and the idealist concerns of society at large through human rights advocacy groups. The underlying core of civil society is "the peaceful management of differences among individuals and collectivities sharing the same public space—i.e., the polity."[2] The state apparatus, theoretically, is the neutral arena in which civil society functions. However, this is rarely the case in reality. As Saad Ibrahim notes:

> The positioning of the relationship between state and society in "zero-sum" terms may be a misleading dichotomy. A strong state may not necessarily imply a weak civil society or vice-versa. In fact, most stable Western democracies represent cases of a strong civil society and a strong state. Similarly . . . in the Arab World, a more common case is that of weak civil societies and weak states.[3]

The weakness of civil society in the Arab world in general, and Egypt in particular, is intrinsically linked to the authoritarian nature of the political systems that exist. After all, as Augustus Norton points out, "Civil society is sometimes credited for thwarting authoritarian designs and challenging arbitrary rule."[4] With such an erroneous view in mind, authoritarian regimes attempt to maintain a tight rein over civil society, and ensure that it does not topple regimes even though it is "internal corruption and hollow claims for legitimacy" that cause regimes to eventually crumble.[5]

The point is that there is much to be understood about the nature and objectives of a regime based on its relationship with civil society. This relationship, in turn, contributes to the development and character of any given civil society. As will be argued in this chapter, the development of Egypt's civil society has been hindered to a large degree as a consequence of the enduringly persistent authoritarian political system since 1952. To illustrate this predicament, trade unions, professional associations, and human rights organizations are used as case examples. Based on these case studies, the chapter examines the regime's disparate perceptions of these groups and the variation in containment tactics it applies to them. The aim is to illustrate the flexibility and survival tactics of a political system intent on preserving its monopoly on power, as well as how such tactics hinder the development of Egypt's civil society.

Civil Society Under Nasser

Egyptian civil society in its most basic form can be described as having been incorporated and almost extinguished under the populist policies of Nasser. In addition to the banning of political parties, the regime established Law 32, regarding civil association, in 1964. According to this law, civil associations in Egypt could not function without first being registered with the Ministry of Social Affairs. Furthermore, this law stipulated that in order to register, the organization in question was required to adhere to the condition that it not engage in any "political activities."[6] However, because "the term 'political activity' is a rather ambiguous term, this allows the ministry to utilize the law to intimidate . . . societies by threatening to suspend their activities if they continued certain actions or if their elected leaders were not approved by security agencies."[7]

Equally important is the manner in which Law 32 was intended to formally prevent civil associations from gaining legal status. In addition to the broad definition of what constituted political activity, there was also an additional stipulation (Article 12) that gave the government the right to reject an association if its "founding is not in accord with security measures; or for the unsuitability of the place health-wise or socially." More important, this same article provided the authorities the right to reject the founding of an organization "if the environment has no need for the services of another association."[8] This particular stipulation, which was formally intended to prevent a redundancy in civil associations, can be interpreted as a mechanism that empowered the Ministry of Social Affairs to exclude unwanted organizations from civil participation. There are no official figures pertaining to the number of civil associations registered under the Ministry of Social Affairs during this period. However, one report notes that in the mid-1960s less than 20,000 existed in the entire Arab region.[9] This figure is not surprising since in Egypt alone, civil associations were almost extinguished under the Nasser presidency. Apart from Law 32, it is also noted that "bureaucratic tutelage over society since 1952 put a halt on traditions of private funding of civil associations . . . [while] on the other hand the complete take-over of the *Waqf* (Islamic public and private endowments) by the state was not compensated by the setting up of a new functional structure for private funding of civil activities and purposes."[10]

In this regard, the domination of most civil associations was rather straightforward. With limited resources and membership, they simply could not compete with the state. As a consequence, associations found themselves incorporated into the formal state structure, dissolved, or rendered obsolete. However, in the case of two main groups—trade unions and professional associations—the post-1952 regime could not obliterate them, so it focused on containing and controlling their development.

Trade Unions

The post-1952 regime inherited a conglomerate of trade unions numbering nearly 500 with a registered membership base of 150,000 workers.[11] Less than a month after the coup in early August, members of the new military establishment visited Kafr al-Dawar, a textile center south of Alexandria. The officers were confronted by workers who had been demonstrating for pay increases and better work conditions. An unknown assailant, presumably from the disgruntled workers, fired a bullet and injured one of the army person-

nel. The official reaction was swift and ruthless. Two activist workers known for their communist tendencies, Mostapha Khamis and
Mohamad al-Bakari, were arrested, tried by military court, and executed on 7 September 1952. This incident proved significant on two
levels. First, the demonstrations illustrated the potentially disruptive
capabilities of the Egyptian workers for the new regime. Second, the
executions signaled the new regime's intolerance to unruly behavior
from workers. While the executions were swiftly implemented, the
new regime took the precaution of implementing favorable new laws
for the workers two days later. In what appeared to be an effort to
counteract demonstrations and strikes by workers in protest against
the executions, the regime implemented on 9 September three new
labor laws: 317, 318, and 319. These new laws permitted the right of
agricultural workers to join a union (317), the right to be represented
on the executive boards of their companies (318), and the right to
turn to the judiciary in regard to work-related grievances (318).
Furthermore, in addition to pay increases and other benefits, the hiring and firing of workers was established in favor of the workers
(319). The favorable labor laws undoubtedly acted as a buffer to the
September 1952 executions. However, they also came at a price in
that "an unspoken bargain was struck: no strikes in exchange for no
dismissals without cause."[12] That workers accepted such rules, while
overlooking the September executions, indicated a weakening of
class-consciousness in Egypt. This assumption is reinforced in the
words of one veteran activist who noted that the lack of protests
against the executions of their colleagues stemmed from the workers'
belief that "the executions were a regime stand against the commu-
nists and not the workers."[13] This weak class-consciousness on the
part of the workers eventually assisted in facilitating their co-optation by the new regime.

The 1953 strike of textile workers in the Imbaba section of Cairo
confirmed the seriousness of the regime's attitude toward strikes and
those who broke the unspoken bargain. The Imbaba strike, which
involved approximately 2,000 workers demonstrating over pay and
work conditions, was met with full military force that included the
arrival of tanks and the arrest of approximately 300 workers. The
regime's overtly tough stance toward the strike was a turning point
for Egyptian workers. This incident made them realize that it was
neither worthwhile nor realistically possible to confront the new
regime in such a manner.[14]

While the regime applied heavy-handed tactics toward labor unrest, Nasser was politically astute enough not to lose the potential power of labor. This was most evident in 1954 during his power struggle with Nagib. This power struggle, which culminated in the "March 1954 Crisis," was won in part by Nasser as a result of the support he received from the labor force and the Cairo Transport Union. The general transport workers strike in Cairo on 27–28 March, in support of Nasser's "continuation of the revolution" as opposed to Nagib's preference for a return to civilian rule, paralyzed the city for two days and illustrated Nasser's popularity on the mass level. More important for the labor force, the strike not only helped to encourage "the continuation of military rule" but also "had important consequences for the Egyptian workers movement."[15] While such consequences primarily entailed the containment and control of organized labor, the strategies pursued were reflective of the multidimensional skills of authoritarian rule in modern Egypt.

Indicative of this is that while union leaders were eager to establish a trade union confederation following Nasser's official consolidation of power in 1956, the new president initially was not "fully committed to the idea of singularity."[16] The underlying reason behind Nasser's reluctance was the fear that a confederation would not simply unify the local unions but would also result in a "sudden concentration of union power."[17] In other words, although Nasser wanted to maintain support from the labor force, his main concern "was how to forge a support coalition without getting organizationally entangled with the popular sectors."[18] One aspect that made it difficult to overlook the reorganization of trade unions was the ever-expanding number of local unions and the subsequent expansion of overall union membership. As Robert Bianchi noted, the labor laws of 1952 meant among other things that "the establishment of new unions required only registration with, but not approval from, the Ministry of Social Affairs, and the power to close down existing unions was transferred to the judiciary."[19] While this move was intended to entice workers to support the regime, it also saw the number of unions more than double and the size of worker membership almost triple during the first six years following the coup. Therefore the number of unions in Egypt reached 1,350 and worker membership expanded to 430,000 by 1958.[20]

In this regard, the establishment of the General Federation of Egyptian Trade Unions (GFETU) in 1957 can be viewed as one of the first steps to contain and control the sprawling unions.

Furthermore, the fear of creating a unified labor movement was swiftly addressed with a series of moves aimed at counteracting potential threats to the system, the first of which was the issue of the new federation's leadership. As Joel Beinin points out: "The government did not take any chances on the political composition of the leadership of the federation. The government submitted the names of the seventeen members of the executive board of the GFETU to the founding conference. There were no nominations from those attending the conference, and no election was held."[21] In addition to placing government co-opted men at the top of the confederation hierarchy, the establishment of the GFETU also streamlined the organization of unions by placing them all under the umbrella of one of 121 newly established federations. The adoption of the unified labor law in 1959 acted to further consolidate centralized control over labor with the reduction of these federations to 65. The law also "reduced the [employment] probation period to three months, cut working hours to 8 per day, and doubled the differential for shift work."[22] Later in the same year, additional benefits were bestowed upon the workers, including the extension of health insurance regulations to all industries, an increase in the number of paid holidays, as well as an increase in both sickness days and severance pay.[23] The regime's strategy was to tighten the reins on the organizational structure of labor while endowing the workers with the necessary benefits to keep them subdued. This pattern of enticing labor support while strengthening the policies of containment and control continued throughout the 1960s and was particularly evident in 1961, 1964, and 1968.

The socialist decrees of July and October 1961 resulted in the nationalization of a large segment of the commercial and manufacturing enterprises as well as the implementation of additional land reforms. Nasser justified these policies on the basis that "they represented the first application of true socialism, and that they became necessary because an exploitative private sector seemed bent on milking the public sector."[24] Yet as John Waterbury observes:

> That the decrees were improvised is undeniable; equally so is the fact that they were not primarily motivated by economic factors. . . . Nasser was a leader acutely conscious of potential threats to his regime and his control. Whenever possible he anticipated these threats (real or imaginary) and tried to preempt them. . . .

> Dismantling the upper reaches of the private sector therefore contributed directly and commensurately to regime strength by placing the levers of economic control in its hands.[25]

The consolidation of economic control also entailed a consolidation of labor control. The 1961 socialist decrees expanded the public sector and transformed the state into the biggest employer of labor. As such, an additional series of laws beneficial to labor were issued at the same time as these decrees. These laws constituted a huge commitment on the part of the state to further enhance the living standards and welfare of labor. The laws "reduced the work week in industrial establishments to 42 hours, doubled the minimum wage, introduced a social insurance scheme and committed the government to provide administrative jobs to all university graduates and manual employment to all graduates of secondary schools."[26] Furthermore, provisions for worker representation on the management boards of all the public-sector companies were created.[27] Regardless of the economic consequences that resulted from such a move, the political motives behind this governmental patronage was the co-optation of a large segment of the Egyptian labor force. In doing so, the regime was mobilizing labor support against the bourgeoisie it was crushing. Moreover, through such generous patronage, it was in a better position to tailor the role of trade unions as it saw fit. The establishment of the Ministry of Labor in 1962 indicated this to be the case.[28]

The Ministry of Labor was assigned two primary roles: the placement of graduates into the newly guaranteed public-sector jobs, and the reorganization of unions. Union affiliation was transferred from the Ministry of Social Affairs to the newly established Ministry of Labor. The fact that Nasser intended to further reorganize the structure of unions is apparent in his choice of the first minister of labor, Anwar Salama. As the first (and presidentially appointed) head of the GFETU, Salama was a co-opted unionist. Moreover, not only was he "appointed Minister of Labor to preside over the corporatist reorganization of the unions,"[29] but it was also assumed that he would maintain his GFETU position. That Salama personally insisted on resigning from his GFETU position[30] did not contradict the fact that as minister of labor he streamlined the GFETU from 121 federations to a more governmentally controllable 59 within the same year. However, within one year, the number of workers represented on the board of directors (a maximum of nine members on any board) was formally increased from two to four.[31] Even more radical were the provisions provided by the electoral decrees of November 1963, which stipulated that half the legislature must be composed of workers and peasants. These co-optation strategies were followed by the reinforcement of stringent state control. For example, the same decrees required electoral candidates, including those running in legislative and union elections, to be members of the Arab Socialist Union (ASU). As in the case of the legislature, this meant that unruly labor activists could be denied ASU membership and hence the opportunity to run for union positions. Another significant policy aimed at controlling organized labor was the implementation of the 1964 trade union law. One of the prominent outcomes of this law was that it reduced the number of union federations to just twenty-seven,[32] thereby permitting an even further centralized tightening of unions. In terms of financing, the 1964 trade union law stipulated that membership fees for the local unions be distributed as follows: 10 percent for the confederation, 25 percent for the federation, 25 percent for administrative expenses for both local and federation levels, and 5 percent to be held in reserve. Consequently, local unions were left with only 35 percent of their membership fees. Such limited funds weakened local unions to the degree that they were unable to sufficiently fund the daycare centers, housing projects, and social events that they were formally obliged to provide to their members.[33]

One of the most significant consequences of this overall reorganization of unions in the 1960s was that it created overtly weak organizational links between the local union, federation, and confederation structures. The leadership bodies, as the local unions pointed out, were "failing to keep the rank and file informed of their activities, neglecting the lower bodies' concerns, and not organizing summations of union work in order to foster improvement."[34] As one worker remarked:

> In some workplaces we feel the existence of a new kind of feudalism called "union feudalism." . . . [T]he links between the different organizational levels [are] no longer reliable and an indication of this is that in some workplaces the management tries to block the unionists and paralyze their activity and the federation does not intervene. And this causes the workers to lose their trust in the local [unions].[35]

This in fact was the aim. Nasser understood the potential power of organized labor and, as with any group or organization, the strategy was to keep its organizational structure weak in order to preserve his own monopoly on power. The generous patronage that was bestowed upon the workers meant that ultimately Nasser could achieve his desire with minimal obstructions from the Egyptian labor force. In assessing the union predicament under Nasser, one senior unionist explained:

> In terms of prestige and job security, labor never had it so good as under Nasser. He changed the social status of workers and gave them positions in parliament and on company boards. Of course all this was at a price, there were political boundaries we could not cross. He gave us a lot, so he did not expect us to make demands. Even the basic right of workers to strike was forbidden. But in general, this did not matter much to the average workers because they knew they were much better off than before 1952.[36]

The degree to which Nasser's strategy of co-optation and control paid off was most evident in the wake of Egypt's June 1967 defeat by Israel. The humiliation of the defeat along with the country's increasing economic crisis, which resulted in a deterioration of overall living standards, produced an ideological disillusionment across the country. In the case of labor, such disillusionment translated into mass marches that were largely organized by university student activists. By February 1968 Nasser was compelled to visit the industrial Cairo suburb of Helwan to personally appeal to the workers to disengage from these marches. Furthermore, in a series of meetings that followed, Nasser listened to union concerns as "each federation president rose in turn to present a list of long-ignored demands for greater union authority and autonomy."[37] Nasser's subsequent promise of reforms was a strategy to subdue labor. In turn, the success of this tactic "allowed the regime to isolate and suppress the more persistent and violent student movement in the months ahead."[38] In doing so, labor was again an isolated entity that remained organizationally weak as Nasser went on to encourage "still greater organizational rivalry" within the labor movement until his death in 1970.[39] There is little doubt that the primary objective of preventing the emergence of autonomous and cohesive organizations within civil society was realized in the case of Nasser's trade unions. As the following section illustrates, similar patterns of containment and control were extended to the professional syndicates.

Professional Syndicates

While professional syndicates existed from as early as 1912 with the establishment of the Bar Syndicate, their expansion was most evident during the post-1952 period. When the Free Officers took power, nine syndicates existed, later increasing to fourteen during the Nasser era. The total membership base almost doubled from 179,838 in 1963 to 307,817 by 1971.[40] However, in contrast to trade unions, professional syndicates were never organized into a general federation or higher organization. Rather, each syndicate was "governed by the law under which it was established."[41] Consequently, as Eberhard Kienle points out:

> There was no apparent common denominator among the professions organized into syndicates. . . . In the absence of a common denominator, the creation and continued existence of syndicates rather seems to have reflected the nature of relations between these professions and the state. . . . Sometimes the "syndicalization" of a profession . . . was decided by the rulers in an attempt to manipulate and control the professions more easily. . . . In other cases, syndicalization, was, at least in part, a response to the demands of the "professionals" themselves, who tried not only to advance their own interests through official state recognition but also to establish formal structures that would enable them more easily to capture resources controlled and distributed by the state.[42]

Attempts to control syndicates were undertaken largely due to the fact that professional associations in Egypt have possessed an additional characteristic that extends beyond that of a profession-based interest group—namely that of a political entity. This is largely linked to the fact that their emergence at the turn of the twentieth century coincided with the country's independence struggle. Reflective of this emerging political role were the early activities of the Bar Syndicate. As one author points out:

> In the period that extended from 1919 to 1921, lawyers through their professional syndicate played a leading role in the Egyptian national struggle. They declared their strike in support of the Egyptian national demands and participated in the national demon-

strations. Last, but not least, they issued resolutions that called for the condemnation of the British colonial plans.[43]

Neither the pre-1952 nor the post-1952 regimes desired such overt political participation by professional syndicates. Attempts to depoliticize and control professional syndicates in the post-1952 political system can be detected on various levels. For example, when the Bar Syndicate announced in its 1954 General Assembly meeting that it supported the restoration of parliamentary politics, the new military government passed a law in December of that year dissolving the Bar Syndicate council in retaliation. The suspension of the syndicate's activities and the prevalence of a government-appointed "guardian" syndicate council thus remained in place until 1958. Indeed, the resumption of its activities did not take place until a number of concessions were formalized through the passing of a new syndicate law in 1957.[44] In the case of the Press Syndicate, the implementation of Law 185 of 1955 restricted membership so as to exclude newspaper owners.[45] In view of the fact the Press Syndicate was established (by Law 10) in 1941 and half of its founding mem bers were newspaper owners,[46] the implementation of Law 185 implied a radical restructuring of the syndicate's internal structure. This, in turn, excluded the bourgeoisie from participation and culti-vating a potential power base.

Indeed, none of the professional syndicates were exempt from governmental efforts of control. For example, a presidential decree issued in March 1958 stipulated that all syndicate members wishing to enter syndicate council elections must first be members of the National Union.[47] This move, as in the case of trade unions, was a tactic aimed less at politicizing syndicate leaders and more at exclud-ing nonconforming individuals by denying them party membership. The Arab Social Union, which came to replace the National Union, also became utilized as a tool to further contain the activities of pro-fessional syndicates. Not only were all syndicate council members expected to be active members of the party, but also "every profes-sional syndicate was asked to form an ASU committee that worked closely with the ASU's federation."[48]

With Nasser's firm consolidation of power, professional syndi-cates became increasingly viewed as unnecessary entities in the new socialist order. As Nasser declared in 1962, professional syndicates have "mainly pursued their own selfish class interest. . . . In our attempt to dissolve the differences between classes, professionals must be considered as members of the working class. They must join the workers in newly organized General Labor Unions."[49] The rallying of the disparate syndicates, including lawyers, doctors, and engineers, assisted in the prevention of their permanent dissolution. However, the ultimate saviors of syndicates were the ASU's leftist leaders, who believed that "the syndicates could be refashioned into useful channels of controlled participation."[50] As such, professional syndicates "were forced to adopt the functions dictated by the regime."[51] In some instances, the dictates of the regime entailed a struggle in which a compromise would eventually be reached. The Engineers Syndicate is an apt example.

While under government pressure in 1965 to allow syndicate membership to industrial school graduates, the Engineers Syndicate refused. In turn, relations between the government and the syndicate remained hostile until a compromise was reached in 1967 that allowed for industrial school graduates to be provisionally accepted on the condition that they abandon the right to vote or participate in syndicate elections. While this may appear a limited victory, the fact that Nasser did not impose his will in an absolute sense is primarily linked to his judgment of the skills held by the members of that particular syndicate. As one author points out: "The government could not force the Engineers Syndicate to accept membership of the graduates of the industrial schools . . . [because it] depended on engineers more than they depended on [government]. Their professional skills were crucial to its agricultural, industrial and housing policies."[52] However, in most instances the syndicates were compelled to bend to the will of the regime. For example, in the case of the Bar Syndicate this meant accepting a new 1968 law that authorized the admission of public-sector lawyers. This move is significant since it "allowed the government to use this professional group (which outnumbered the private practitioners) to push in its own candidates to the post of *naquib* [syndicate head]."[53] Moreover, the role of the Press Syndicate in supporting the university demonstrations of 1968 and mirroring the general discontents of the post-1967 period led to the implementation of Law 76 in 1970, shortly before Nasser's death. The new law not only dictated that one of the main objectives of the syndicate was to "enhance the socialist ideology among newspaper readers," but also stipulated that journalists could not be granted syndicate membership in the absence of a university degree.[54] That journalists could not practice their profession without syndicate membership was an indirect effort by the government to control the number of individuals entering the profession. More important, this exclusionary measure was intended to ban the type of individuals most likely to sympathize and relate to the political and economic concerns of the masses in the post-1967 atmosphere.

The diverse and relatively small membership base of professional syndicates in comparison to trade unions meant that the patterns of manipulation and control over labor could be extended to syndicates with relative ease. After all, due to the socialist policies of this era, by the time of Nasser's death in 1970 the state was also the largest employer of professionals. Hence, dependence on state employment and patronage, along with the application of constrictive laws to block potential challenges, not only allowed Nasser to divide the political bases of syndicates but also to incorporate them under the regime's control.

Civil Society Under Sadat

The containment and blatant weakening of civil society by Nasser proved beneficial to Sadat for several reasons. On one level, it allowed Sadat to move away from the populist policies of his predecessor with the relative ease that arises in the absence of strongly represented constituencies. Also, the dynamics of containment and control that were implemented prior to his ascent to the presidency meant that even with a change in policy orientations, it remained possible to maintain the tactics of his predecessor over civil society. This aspect is well documented by the continuities and changes experienced by trade unions and professional associations under Sadat.

Trade Unions

The strategies of containment and control of trade unions under Nasser were further developed and enhanced under Sadat. In contrast to Nasser, Sadat lacked the charismatic appeal of his predecessor, whose socialist policies gave him additional popularity among the masses. Yet it was due to such policies that Sadat inherited an economy that was underdeveloped and in debt. Because of the frustrating economic situation and his power struggle with Nasser's old guard, Sadat's early years were marked by labor unrest and strikes.

The first of these strikes involved 10,000 workers at the Helwan Iron and Steel Company in August 1971. The striking workers went as far as taking hostage "their managers, the delegates of the Ministry of Industry, the representatives of the governing party, as well as the secretary general of the trade unions, who was sent personally by Sadat to persuade the workers to end their strike."[55] As with the numerous other strikes and sit-ins that followed,[56] the Helwan case was a matter of the workers taking action themselves in the absence of formal union support. The fact that workers held official union representatives captive indicates the degree of anger felt by the workers toward their union representatives, whom they felt represented the government. Sadat's reaction to the strikes was similar to that of Nasser: repression and concession. For example, during the Helwan strike 3,000 people were arrested and detained, yet "Sadat quickly promised to investigate and ameliorate worker's grievances."[57]

The 1973 war with Israel and the newly gained legitimacy that Sadat acquired from it encouraged him to address Egypt's economic problems more directly. In spring 1974 Sadat moved away from his predecessor's socialist policies and formally adopted the economic "open-door" policy—the *infitah*. The fear of opening the economy to international competition produced anxiety among workers, who felt Sadat was moving away from the "social contract" of his predecessor. This anxiety was reinforced by Sadat's demoralizing comments that "the public sector was a parasite draining the Egyptian economy."[58] The additional strain of increasing inflation, which was amplified by the 1973 war debts and the emergence of foreign goods in the Egyptian market, did little to soothe workers' anxieties. As a consequence, a new wave of labor unrest emerged between 1975 and 1976.

The most violent of these protests took place in the predominantly textile-manufacturing area of Mahala al-Kobra in March 1975. The government attempted to put an end to the Mahala strike by sending in the army. This move resulted in the arrest of 2,000 people and the death of approximately 35.[59] The waves of labor unrest in the mid-1970s were addressed with a mixture of coercive tactics and concessions to workers such as increases in wages and benefits. However, none of these waves of unrest were formally organized and coordinated by the trade unions on behalf of their members. Strikes were still illegal and the senior union leaders were not prepared to risk their own co-opted positions for the sake of the workers. Consequently, the workers took matters into their own hands when sufficiently aggravated, as was the case in Mahala. In some cases young union activists on the local level participated in the coordination of strikes. However, such moves tended to arise out of a personal conviction to the cause rather than a desire to act as formal union representatives. Abd al-Rahman Khir, currently the deputy chairman of the military production federation, was one example.

As a young local union representative within the military production federation in 1975, Khir played a key role in organizing one of the first major protests against Sadat's economic reforms. The protest, which started in the Bab al-Loq train station in January 1975, resulted in the mobilization of 100,000 workers. According to Khir, the Bab al-Loq train station was chosen as a protest site because thousands of Cairo-based industrial workers congregated there each morning en route to their jobs in Helwan. When these thousands of workers failed to turn up to work and news of the strike reached Helwan, the workers who were already there also took up the protest, walking off their jobs and out onto the street.[60] The fact that Khir was instrumental in organizing such a major protest against Sadat's *infitah* policy was linked to his leftist ideological conviction, a conviction that later translated into membership in the Tagammu' Party after its establishment in 1977. As a trade union official, his role in the protest was not something that the formal union structure was even aware of at the time. In fact, the minister of labor and head of the GFETU, Salah Gharib (1971–1976), was notorious for his role as an informant to state security in regard to labor activists. As such, not only did Gharib disapprove of the Bab al-Loq protest, but he also sent trusted associates to the scene in an effort to discover who the organizers were.[61]

On one level, the absence of formal representation and coordination of strikes by unions meant that while such protests were spontaneous in nature, they were easy for the security forces to swiftly quell. However, the informal role of some local unionists in the coordination and organization of these wildcat strikes was not overlooked. The implementation of Law 35 of 1976 (later modified in 1981), in regard to trade unions, included attempts to rectify this predicament and reinforce governmental control over the entire union structure. For example, the law introduced a new indirect electoral system that further alienated union officials from their constituents and reinforced their dependence on the government. As Robert Bianchi explains, "Elected positions at all levels of the union hierarchy [became] filled nearly simultaneously, with higher-echelon leaders being chosen by lower-echelon leaders after a screening of all candidates by the Socialist Prosecutor's Office. Furthermore, the term of elected leaders . . . lengthened gradually from two years to three years in 1976, and to four years in 1981."[62] Put simply, the new electoral system tightened governmental control over the selection of union activists on all levels. Furthermore, the penalty for striking was increased to imprisonment with hard labor as a consequence of Law 3 of 1977.

The mechanisms of control also extended to electoral malpractice and indirect government interference in the union elections, the results of which were illustrated in the last union elections (1979) under Sadat. These elections were marked by an absence of competition not just on the local level, but also "at the federation and confederation levels, where there was virtually no turnover in leadership."[63] This was not surprising considering that a more coercive campaign against opponents, particularly among the leftists, during the 1979 elections led hundreds to resign from the Tagammu' Party in order to escape increasing state harassment. The end result was that the leftists barely won 120 local union seats from a total of 4,000. The increase in repression during Sadat's last two years silenced dissent from union activists, and by 1981 most of the 120 leftist union representatives found themselves languishing in prison along with the thousands of Sadat's other real and perceived opponents.

While tightening government control of trade unions and repressing voices of dissent, Sadat attempted to appease the workers. For example, between 1977 and 1978 Sadat's concessions included increases in pensions, salaries, and minimum wage. These concessions were not insignificant, since they actually resulted in keeping the "workers' wages ahead of inflation."[64] The point, nevertheless, is that such concessions were presented directly from the president to the workers. This subsequently allowed the president to appear to be voluntarily bestowing his patronage and goodwill on the workers unconstrained by any organizational body. Sadat's tactics illustrate that although he was moving away from the populist policies of his predecessor, the aspect of containment and control over civil society remained intact. The extension of such authoritarian policies was also evident within the sphere of professional associations.

Professional Syndicates

Professional syndicates under Sadat witnessed certain transformations that indicated a change of direction from the Nasserite era. First, the 1970s saw the establishment of five new syndicates (raising the total to eighteen) and an expansion in total syndicate membership to over 700,000 by the time of Sadat's assassination. Furthermore, syndicates, unlike trade unions, began to be affected by Sadat's changing economic and political policies in a positive way. On the economic side, the *infitah* encouraged the syndicates to convert part of their revenues—such as their government subsidies, membership fees, and stamp taxes—into private commercial investments. These investments and profit-making ventures changed the traditional perceptions of leadership within the ranks of syndicates. For example, as was the case for trade unions, "when professional syndicates were weaker and poorer, the patronage of well-connected leaders was often viewed as a valuable asset to the group as a whole."[65] However, with their new commercialization these same types of potential leaders (who continued to dominate trade unions) became increasingly viewed within syndicate circles as "opportunists trying to enrich their cronies and advance their own political careers."[66] The move from a single party to a multiparty system only reinforced the syndicate transformations as opposition factions began to compete with members of the president's newly created party, the National Democratic Party (NDP), in syndicate council elections.[67] Furthermore, rather than pull each other down, the opposition forces maintained a unified front in the face of government domination and Sadat's unpopular policies. One such example was the battle between Sadat and the Press Syndicate following the 1979 Camp David Accords. As one author documented:

> Many journalists rejected the idea of making peace with Israel and criticized Sadat. The regime forced some journalists to write in favor of the accords, and whoever criticized them was prevented from publishing. This decision led many journalists to leave the country and criticize Sadat's regime from abroad. . . . However, it was difficult for Sadat to reach a compromise [with the criticizing journalists], so he offered another alternative. He asked the press syndicate to revoke their membership, but they refused and insisted on its sovereignty. As a consequence, Sadat decided to change the press syndicate into a social club where journalists could meet and relax. . . . [However], the lawyers syndicate, together with the journalists . . . forced the government to change its decision.[68]

While the economic and political changes in the Sadat era were transforming the nature of syndicates, it is important to view such transformations in the context of the personal authoritarian system that prevailed. Hence, although the president backed down from his threat to turn the Press Syndicate into a social club, he still managed to curtail the already limited press freedom with his infamous "Law of Shame" in 1979 and the establishment of a predominantly government-appointed Higher Council for the Press (HCP) in 1980. The "Law of Shame" curtailed press and opposition views on Sadat's policies by turning antigovernment views and opinions into a defamation crime against Egypt. The HCP supervised the three categories of newspaper ownership (state, party, and syndicate). Half of the HCP's fifty board members were appointed by the Shura (Consultative) Council, while the other half consisted mainly of state broadcasting and newspaper editors and managers. The syndicate was allowed only one seat on the council. The result was that "these arrangements placed control of the press more firmly than ever in the hands of non-journalists and diminished the syndicate's already marginal authority to vanishing point."[69]

In the case of the Bar Syndicate, its controversial anti-Israeli position and its members' attacks on Sadat, who they dubbed the "treasonous president" for his signing of the peace treaty, simply led to the dissolution of the syndicate council in 1981 on charges of "illegal political activities." In addition, five of the dissolved council members found themselves arrested in the mass roundups of September 1981.[70] In this regard, Sadat demonstrated to the syndicates that the political and economic transformations that he pursued, and that they benefited from, should not be mistaken for genuine liberalization and autonomy from state domination. This, it would seem, is the same message Mubarak has been reinforcing since assuming the presidency.

Civil Society Under Mubarak

Civil society under Mubarak has witnessed considerable expansion. In addition to the current twenty-three trade union federations and twenty-four professional associations, the number of legal political parties has reached seventeen and there are currently 17,000 officially registered nongovernmental organizations (NGOs). However, civil society remains as weak an entity under Mubarak as under his predecessors. In the case of professional associations the constraints have been overtly evident and on the increase since the 1990s, while the autonomy of trade unions has been marginalized to such a degree that it is difficult to distinguish them from the state. In addition, the emergence of independent human rights groups in the 1980s has resulted in a new battle for the government in trying to preserve its domination of power within civil society. Therefore, in addition to assessing the development of trade unions and professional associations since Nasser and Sadat, the relatively new phenomenon of human rights NGOs is analyzed below.

Trade Unions

The co-optation of the trade union structure over the previous two decades has resulted in a pattern whereby workers have little choice but to resort to wildcat strikes and spontaneous demonstrations in efforts to communicate their grievances to the government. While this trend began to emerge rather prominently under Sadat, it peaked under Mubarak. The decline in benefits and pay for workers, the gradual easing of state subsidies, and the cessation of guaranteed state employment for high school and college graduates were all part of the economic restructuring that Mubarak was compelled to continue upon taking power. Therefore, following a period of relative calm on the labor front following Sadat's assassination, discontent began to reemerge in 1984 as workers began to feel the effects of such policies. For example, the implementation of a 1984 insurance law that doubled the contribution of pension and health insurance plans for workers coincided with Mubarak's decision to raise the prices on certain subsidized foods, resulting in an outbreak of isolated strikes and demonstrations around the country.

The worst of these protests was a three-day strike-turned-riot in Kafr al-Dawar. Initially the demonstrations were relatively peaceful, but the intervention of the Central Security Forces (CSF) escalated the strike into a violent confrontation through their use of tear gas and automatic rifles. As one author noted, when the CSF confronted the workers, the workers and their families responded by attacking the police forces with stones. This subsequently resulted in the death of three demonstrators and 220 arrests.[71] More important, the brutal response of the government heightened mass anger, resulting in "all

symbols of the state [in Kafr al-Dawar] being violently attacked."[72]
It was only after the government promised not to raise the food subsidies in the town (as opposed to raising them nationally) and post-
pone the implementation of the new insurance law that order was
restored.[73] Again, the same pattern of worker uprisings, followed by
repression and eventually some form of concession (when necessary
to restore order), can be detected. What was remarkable was the
overtly progovernment position taken by trade unions during such
protests. The 1986 Esco strike is another apt example.

The Esco textile plant in Shobra al-Khayma (Cairo) witnessed a
17,000-strong worker sit-in over their demand for their one-day-per-
week holiday payment in January 1986. While the workers were
legally entitled to one day of paid leave per week, the management at
Esco, along with the management of all the other national textile
mills, decided to omit this payment—presumably in an effort to save
money. In turn, all the textile workers found themselves being paid a
twenty-six-day monthly salary instead of their thirty-day entitlement.
The Esco workers decided to challenge this matter in court. When
the court ruled in the workers' favor, the management challenged the
decision in the appeals court and subsequently lost again. However,
the management refused to recognize the verdict, thus leaving no
choice for the workers but to strike. The January strike, which took
the form of a sit-in on the Esco premises, was put on hold after three
days when "a ministerial 'committee of five' including representatives of the Union Committee and the General Union of Textile
Workers was established to examine the workers' demands."[74] The
union's progovernment stance was highly evident when its representatives on the "committee of five" agreed with the government representatives on a compromise to pay the workers for two instead of
their four days of holiday leave.

Again, the workers were left to fend for themselves. They threatened another sit-in strike and refused their February paychecks, after
which the government conceded to pay the additional two days of
holiday leave, but not until one year later, in February 1987. The
offer was refused and 5,000 Esco workers initiated another sit-in on
27 April. In contrast to the workers, the union committee had agreed
to the government's offer of withholding two days' holiday pay for a
year on the basis that it was putting "the country's huge budget
deficit" into consideration.[75] Consequently, it condemned the April
strike

as a "conspiracy" against "the gains of the workers," and agreed during a meeting with the minister of interior that security forces storm the premises and arrest the strikers. The next day, on April 28, the police stormed the Esco plant and ended up arresting and detaining 500 workers until their release by the State Prosecutor one month later. During that period, the "Union Committee refused to provide any assistance to the detainees."[76]

This type of union opposition in regard to labor protests and strikes came to be a prominent trait of the Mubarak era. The deterioration of relations between workers and trade unions reached a level whereby it was no longer uncommon for workers to challenge their own union representatives. Illustrative of this predicament were the workers from the Helwan Iron and Steel Company. In summer 1989, with help from their two elected workers on the management board, they were able to secure a long-awaited raise in pay. However, their union committee attempted to claim the credit for it. The degree of animosity the workers felt toward their union committee prominently and spontaneously surfaced in their decision to start a campaign to have the committee replaced. Instead, the minister of industry fired the two board member workers, Mohamad Mustapha and Abd al-Rahim Haridi, who had helped negotiate the pay raise. This led to a spontaneous sit-in during which workers took hostage the vice president of the company and demanded the reinstatement of Mustapha and Haridi. In addition, they also demanded an increase in the incentive pay that the two men were in the process of negotiating on their behalf prior to being fired. While the president of the company agreed to the incentives increase, the two men were not reinstated. The result was another sit-in, with 16,000 workers participating. The workers increased their demands, which entailed not only the reinstatement of Mustapha and Haridi but also the dissolution of the union committee. The reactions of the union committee, the trade union leaders, and the government were indistinguishable from each other. In the words of one author:

> When the workers occupied the plant and raised their independent demands, members of the union committee fled the plant. The trade union leaders not only condemned the sit-ins as the work of a "subversive minority" but also urged the management and the security forces to end the occupation by storming the plant. At dawn [the next day] the steel plant was stormed in an extremely harsh manner. The Minister of Interior Zaki Badr said that if one

percent of the workers died during the ending of the sit-in, he
would consider the operation successful.[77]

Although concessions were made, including the reinstatement of
Mustapha and Haridi, they came at a price. The storming of the sit-
in resulted in the death of one worker, the arrest and detainment of
hundreds, and the torture of two workers suspected of leading the
sit-ins.[78]

There are no official records available on the number of strikes
and protests that took place from 1984 to 1990, but a conservative
estimate would point at over 300.[79] However, the economic restructuring that took place during the 1980s was not sufficient to assisting
Egypt's development. As one Egyptian official pointed out, the government came to terms with the fact that, "after the debt crisis in
1987 . . . it became inevitable to undergo a comprehensive reform of
the economy, especially after realizing the inefficiency of the partial
reforms undertaken during the 1980s, and that the rescheduling of
foreign debt in 1987 was useless."[80] The result was the introduction
in 1991 of a comprehensive economic reform and structural adjustment program (ERSAP) via the implementation of Law 203. The
cornerstone of this program was the transfer of a large section of
public enterprise into the private sector. Since the private sector cannot function unless it is profitable, the government was required to
remove excess labor from the industries allocated for privatization in
order to enhance sale prospects. Part of the retrenchment process was
to take the form of voluntary early retirement packages for male
workers between the ages of fifty and fifty-eight and female workers
between the ages of forty-five and fifty-eight—all of whom were
required to have worked a minimum of twenty years within the public sector. However, while the privatization program started in 1991,
the early retirement program did not gain momentum until the post-
1995 period. As one union official admitted, "The government's policy on privatization since 1990 is very slow."[81]

The slow implementation of the ERSAP can be linked to two
main factors regarding the workers. The labor unrest of the 1980s
illustrated to the government that even with the co-optation of trade
unions, the workers were still capable of initiating strikes and
protests independently and with significant clout. Second, the workers had reached a level of confrontation whereby their demands were
beginning to extend beyond material issues. That workers such as

those from the Helwan Iron and Steel Company had begun to challenge their representatives in the unions reflected the increasing political awareness and confidence emerging within the rank and file. In this regard, the passing of Law 12 of 1995 was intended to overcome these aspects by weakening the link between workers and unions even further. This aspect was evident from two main perspectives. First, although workers on fixed-term contracts (i.e., most public-sector workers employed since 1978, when the government began to stringently rationalize permanent contracts) had the right to vote in union elections, they were not permitted to seek candidacy in such elections.[82] It is the workers in this sector who, during any privatization process, are the easiest to displace. Thus the aim of barring them from union elections has been to prevent their emergence as union representatives. After all, the workers in this sector have the most to lose and would be the most likely to oppose the government's privatization plans.

Second, outgoing union leaders, according to Law 12, were permitted "to stand for reelection on the sole basis of having been elected to their positions previously." In other words, it was no longer necessary "to be reelected at their own firm before being reelected to the board of the Federation or to one of its twenty-three branches."[83] What this move suggests is that for those individuals sitting on the board of the federation, genuine representation of workers as obtained through electoral support at the grassroots level continued to be an asset that was not particularly desired by the government. Rather, the clause indicated that the position of co-opted union leaders was further secured and ensured minimal challenges to government in the process. Furthermore, the benefits endowed upon union representatives and workers elected to the boards of companies increased substantially and is estimated to have reached approximately 30,000 Egyptian pounds (U.S.$8,571) a month.[84] In addition to these factors, the continued co-optation of union leaders into the political system means that under the Mubarak presidency, it remains common to find individuals who simultaneously represent workers and government. For example, the current president of the GFETU, Sayid Rashid, is also a veteran member of the president's ruling party (the NDP) and a member and deputy speaker of the People's Assembly. In addition, twenty-one of the twenty-three federation heads are NDP members,[85] and at least ten GFETU leaders entered the legislature as NDP deputies in 2000.[86]

In this context, the intertwined and conventional clientelist relationship between government and trade union leadership is increasingly maintained and reinforced in the postpopulist era. The degree to which this strategy has preserved government domination is reflected in the unions' overtly passive attitude toward economic restructuring since 1995. One example has been the nature of union input for the unified labor law of 2003 (Law 12).

Within a framework constructed by the International Labour Organization (ILO), negotiations on the new law included three groups: government (formally represented by the Ministry of Manpower and Immigration), capital (formally represented by the Egyptian Federation of Industries), and workers (formally represented by the GFETU). While the presence of prominent lawyers indicated that capital entered into the collective negotiations well prepared, the workers "were mostly represented by a small number of leaders of [GFETU] (essentially one person) without additional support."[87] Not surprisingly, certain elements within the law during its proposal were not favorable to the Egyptian worker. For example, the proposed law intended to: (1) make it easier for an employer to hire and fire employees, (2) shorten the length of paid annual holidays, (3) shorten the length of paid and unpaid maternity leave, and (4) link pay increases to market profits as opposed to what currently is an annual right.[88]

However, while plans for the unified labor law began as early as 1992 and a final draft of the law was "legally revised by the Legislation Department of the State Council in 1996,"[89] the government did not present the law to the legislature for debate until the summer session of 2002. It was finally passed in the parliamentary session of April 2003. It is clear that the reason for the delay had little to do with resistance from union leaders. As Aisha Abd al-Hadi, from the GFETU's executive council, previously claimed, "Our position remains in favor of the law and we continue to call on the government to send it through parliament."[90] In this context, it was not the GFETU that was blocking the implementation of the new law, but governmental fears of worker unrest. As one opposition party leader noted, "The law has been ready since 1996 but the government has not had the courage to put it through the Assembly. . . . [T]he government is trying to appease the workers first before implementing it."[91]

Such appeasement has meant a 25 percent increase in workers' overall benefits since January 1999.[92] Furthermore, it has given the

GFETU the opportunity to hold conferences and meetings with workers in order to communicate the government's message. While a record of the number of conferences held by the GFETU after 1995 is unavailable, it is estimated that the GFETU held approximately twelve conferences related to privatization during 1998 alone.[93] Such conferences have covered a range of issues relating to privatization, including its effect on workers' social services, insurance, and overall welfare. The fact that these union-organized conferences have been utilized by the government as a propaganda opportunity is reflected in the comments of the deputy chairman of the GFETU in regard to the early retirement scheme. In his view, the policy of early retirement initially caused apprehension and feelings of insecurity among the workers. Moreover, certain "leftist" workers attempted to aggravate the situation to their advantage. As a consequence, the GFETU arranged several conferences in which both government officials and union leaders "explained" to attending workers the system of early retirement and its potential benefits.[94] The absence of a two-way dialogue, as the mechanisms of containment and control are intended to ensure, would be expected in such a situation. As Ali Hilmi, chairman of the Helwan Iron and Steel Company, admitted, "It is very difficult to influence government decisions."[95] This is especially the case for trade unions. Consequently, the economic reforms have resulted in the early retirement of 250,000 workers, the selling or liquidating of 114 public-sector companies, and submission to the legislature of the long-awaited labor law in summer 2002. There is still a long way to go, however. The debt crisis internally remains at approximately U.S.$30 billion, while external debts have reached U.S.$27 billion.[96] The weakening and co-optation of trade unions means that in the midst of such economic turmoil, workers will continue to depend on strikes and protests as their main avenue of communication with the state. The fact that 150 documented strikes and work stoppages took place in 2001 is one indication of this predicament.[97] Yet the government, intent on maintaining its power monopoly, does not see any reason to change the established patterns of domination and control over trade unions. Indeed, passage of the unified labor law in early April 2003, in a form more or less unchanged from that of the original 1996 proposal, further reinforces this assumption. The most prominent feature of the law consists in the few "concessions" that have been made, the most significant being the right to strike, but only on the condition that a strike be approved by the weak and regime-controlled GFETU.[98]

Professional Syndicates

In contrast to trade unions, efforts to maintain domination and control over professional associations under Mubarak have been complicated by two interrelated factors. First, the repoliticizing of syndicates that began under Sadat expanded even further as opposition parties continued to cooperate within the syndicate sphere in their efforts to acquire some autonomy from state domination. Second, a new phenomenon emerged in syndicates that did not exist under Nasser or Sadat. This phenomenon entailed the participation and infiltration of the Muslim Brotherhood into the syndicates on a level that overshadowed all other opposition gains within this sphere.

The Muslim Brotherhood first gained a foothold in the Doctors Syndicate council when it participated in the 1984 syndicate elections and won seven of twenty-five council seats. In 1987 it achieved an absolute majority in the Engineers Syndicate when it won fifty-four of sixty-three council seats. By 1992 it had gained a landslide victory in the syndicate council elections of five of the country's most prestigious and wealthiest professional syndicates, namely those representing the engineers, doctors, lawyers, pharmacists, and scientists.[99] The Brotherhood's increasing interest in syndicate activities in the late 1980s and early 1990s went hand-in-hand with the increasingly exclusionary measures imposed by the government on legislative elections (see Chapter 3). Just as the Brotherhood's efficient organizational capabilities served it well in the 1980s legislative elections, the same organizational capabilities also served it well in syndicates in the late 1980s and early 1990s. This is reflected in the words of one former independent syndicate council candidate who claimed that the Brotherhood's success in syndicate elections was not because its candidates were "more influential than other candidates over syndicate members, it was because the Brotherhood were more organized."[100] This view is indirectly acknowledged by Ibrahim al-Za'farani, a prominent Muslim Brotherhood member. In his view, the Brotherhood achieved victories in professional syndicate elections because "we offered a model for a good agenda, organized work and fair, free elections. People did not elect us because we pray more than others or have beards but because we manage to get things done efficiently."[101] The Brotherhood proved such efficiency when in September 1992 it won fourteen of twenty-four seats on the Bar Syndicate council and Sayf al-Islam al-Banna acquired the position of secretary-general. This particular electoral outcome was significant on several levels. As the first professional association to be established in Egypt, the Bar Syndicate has traditionally been a highly vocal defender of liberalism and secular thought. Consequently, the success of the Brotherhood in winning more seats in this traditionally liberal entity than did the NDP and the secular opposition parties combined, appeared overtly challenging to the regime. Furthermore, the electoral outcome reflected an indirect challenge in that "on a symbolic level, [the group] was able to introduce the son of the Brotherhood's founder, Hassan al-Banna, into a leadership position."[102]

One month later, the Brotherhood demonstrated its efficiency and superior organizational skills on a popular level when a major earthquake hit Cairo and left 500 people dead and thousands homeless. The earthquake, which hit on a Thursday afternoon after most government offices had closed for the weekend, also illustrated the inefficiencies of the government in comparison. While the Muslim Brotherhood reached the disaster areas almost immediately and used the Humanitarian Relief Committee (HRC) of the Doctors Syndicate to organize and provide medical relief, food, clothing, and other necessities to the victims throughout the weekend, government-backed assistance did not arrive until Saturday morning. During that time both the Doctors Syndicate and the Brotherhood-dominated Engineers Syndicate also set up emergency relief centers and donated money from their respective syndicates to help the families most affected by the earthquake. In addition, the Engineers Syndicate used its members' skills to inspect the safety of approximately 10,000 residences before allowing the families to return home. As Joshua Stacher noted, "While the Islamists worked round-the-clock little to no response came from the government for at least thirty-six hours."[103]

The government's reaction to this show of initiative and efficiency on the part of the syndicates was to ensure that such acts of autonomy would not be repeated in the future. As one legal observer pointed out, "The state saw this as a direct challenge to its legitimacy since the ruling National Democratic Party did not do as much."[104] Consequently, "both syndicates . . . were accused by the state of using humanitarian assistance to gain popularity and undermine the role of the state."[105] In retaliation, the government

> promptly issued military decrees under the emergency laws "pro-hibiting the raising of funds or the distribution of goods except through the Ministry of Social Affairs or through the Red Crescent." Furthermore, Egyptian troops were sent into the popular neighborhood of Sayyida Zainab to dismantle the make-shift tents the Brotherhood had erected to help the injured and displaced per-sons leaving "the innocent victims . . . to wallow in the mess."[106]

In addition to militarily decreed Law 4 of 1992,[107] the government implemented Law 100, regarding professional syndicates, in 1993. According to Law 100, syndicate elections would only be valid if at least 50 percent of registered members voted in the first round of elections and 30 percent in the second round. If the stipulated per-centage was not reached, Law 100 authorized the state to appoint board members. Moreover, according to the same law, syndicate offi-cials were no longer authorized to organize and supervise their own elections as was the case previously. Rather, this task was transferred to the judiciary. In this regard, the syndicates were tied to the judici-ary and were no longer free to set elections without first taking the judiciary's schedule into consideration.

However, the main obstacle of Law 100 was the impracticality of gaining such a high voter turnout, which was intended to leave the government room to maneuver and reinforce its control over syndi-cates. Indicative of this impracticality, syndicate elections have tend-ed to produce an average voter turnout of 8–12 percent of registered members.[108] Thus, while a professional association such as the Bar Syndicate has approximately 250,000 registered members, it would become a difficult if not impossible task to ensure a 125,000-voter turnout as stipulated under the new law. As one syndicate member points out:

> A 50 percent membership turn-out in elections is impossible for many reasons. Some syndicate members may have work commit-ments on election day, some may be sick or traveling, some might have not paid their annual membership fees on time [to be eligible to vote], some people don't even care about the elections and just never turn up. In fact, some members could be dead but their membership status is unchanged and are therefore still counted as members.[109]

Law 100 was enforced on the Bar Syndicate three years later. When in April 1996 the syndicate held demonstrations against government policies, the government retaliated by accusing it of financial irregularities, dissolving its council, and placing it under judicial sequestration. Ironically, it was this Brotherhood-dominated council that raised benefits for syndicate members and introduced new measures of financial accountability. Since taking power in 1992, the syndicate council had provided benefits that included a raise in the pension of retired syndicate members from 170 Egyptian pounds (U.S.$50) per month to a more respectable 700 Egyptian pounds (U.S.$205) per month. In addition, a subsidized medical policy giving all syndicate members a 30 percent discount on their medical fees was implemented. Previously, medical assistance was informally accessible only to a limited number of prominent syndicate members who had personal connections on the council. That the Brotherhood was able to reform and upgrade lawyers' benefits and pensions was largely linked to the implementation of an accountable system of expenditure that had not existed before. Prior to this new accounting system, council members were able to spend as much syndicate money as they pleased, since there were no legal limits on council payments for the purchase of goods and services. This undoubtedly left much room for financial irregularities on the part of certain individuals, but as one lawyer explained: "If a council member had previously contracted his brother to do some work for the syndicate at an overinflated rate, of course it is wrong and it can be considered stealing from the syndicate, but until the accounting system was implemented, this activity would not have been considered illegal."[110]

In this regard, if financial irregularities within the syndicate genuinely gave the government cause for concern, it is difficult to justify why such concerns did not arise prior to the financial reforms of the post-1992 period. Furthermore, it is interesting to note that after three years of being under sequestration, the Cairo Court of Appeals ruled in October 1999 that the government's decision to dissolve the Bar Syndicate council was illegal and that the court-appointed custodians had illegally extended their tenure. Nevertheless, regardless of the various lawyer protests, sit-ins, and legal challenges, the predicament remained unchanged. Instead, a new committee was appointed and a date for new council elections was subsequently set for April 2000 and later extended to September

2000. The promised elections did not materialize on either date and the Bar Syndicate remained under sequestration.[111] The Bar Syndicate's state-appointed custodians repeatedly justified the absence of new elections on the basis that they were "drawing up a list of all registered lawyers"[112] and therefore elections could not be held until this list was completed and presented "to the judicial committee in charge of syndicate elections."[113]

The reluctance on the part of the government to set an election date was invariably intended to break the Bar Syndicate's emerging autonomy and the Muslim Brotherhood's role within it. Indicative of this was the arrest of twenty professionals from the Muslim Brotherhood during the same month of the court ruling. Charged with "membership of an illegal group and incitement against the government,"[114] fifteen of those arrested were sentenced by a military court to three to five years in prison.[115] Obviously, such a move did not go unnoticed. As one report pointed out, "The arrests and trial before the military courts coincided with preparations for elections to the boards of professional syndicates and to the People's Assembly."[116] In addition, the government allegedly attempted to compile a "national list" prior to committing itself to an election date. According to one source, "government agents allegedly approached opposition parties and suggested that the parties come up with the names of individuals they wished to nominate for office [so that] opposition candidates and regime lawyers . . . would together represent a formidable challenge to the Brotherhood campaign."[117] However, not all opposition parties wanted to participate in this alleged alliance,[118] and this apparent lack of cooperation with the government further stalled the elections. It was not until February 2001, almost five years after the Bar Syndicate had been sequestered, that elections were held, but they failed to achieve the minimum 50 percent voter turnout as stipulated in Law 100. While a new election date was set for two weeks later, the government achieved its objectives and managed to marginalize the gains of the Muslim Brotherhood to only two seats.

In the face of government-imposed obstacles, the Muslim Brotherhood has continued its efforts to participate in disparate syndicate elections, albeit on a more limited scale. It went as far as supporting government-nominated syndicate chairmen, as reflected in the 1997 and 1999 Press Syndicate elections. The reason for this, as one syndicate observer explains, is that "the Brothers . . . are not only trying to make a comeback to syndicate politics, but they want to do so with the support of government."[119] This strategy is highly unlikely to succeed.

The 1999 Press Syndicate elections saw Brotherhood allies win only two of twelve council seats.[120] The legalized opposition parties did not fare much better, with their combined total of four seats.[121] The objective here was to marginalize not just the Muslim Brotherhood, but all elements independent of government control as well. The success of the Muslim Brotherhood in the syndicate elections during the late 1980s and early 1990s was reflected upon by a senior Brotherhood member:

> Admittedly we enjoyed a monopoly, but this was through the ballot box, and the trend was being toned down as other forces in the syndicates organized themselves, and put forth persuasive agendas just like the Islamists. . . . This experience should have nurtured democracy in Egypt. These spaces should have been left to function without any state intervention because the development of democracy ultimately hinges on a collaborative relationship between state and civil society institutions.[122]

These comments overlook a fundamental aspect in regard to the prevailing system of rule, namely that regime interference was precisely intended to hinder democratic development in order to maintain the government's monopoly on power. The government did not pursue professional syndicates because of their Islamist affiliation, but rather because these entities were showing signs of independence and character. It would not have pursued the syndicates with any less vigor had there been a secular liberal group instead of an Islamist group at the forefront of these events. Indeed, the emergence of modern and overtly secular human rights groups under Mubarak illustrates this to be the case.

Human Rights Groups

Human rights organizations have been the most contentious groups to emerge in the Mubarak era. A large part of this controversy stems from the regime's perception of what constitutes human rights and its inability to comprehend attempts by civil society groups to defend them. Put simply, it is an issue in which definitions and viewpoints invariably differ. The Western democratic perspective regards the

Universal Declaration of Human Rights (UDHR), in particular the first twenty-six articles of the declaration, as its basic guideline for human rights. Incorporated in these articles are the basic rights of people to life, liberty, security, and equality. Moreover, freedom of expression, peaceful assembly, association, and religion as well as freedom from discrimination, torture, and "inhuman or degrading treatment or punishment" (Article 5) constitute core tenets of the declaration.[123] In this context, human rights "are grounded in notions of equality and non-discrimination [and consequently] all human beings deserve to be treated with equal concern and respect."[124] Therefore, because human rights are grounded on notions of equality and nondiscrimination, it is "no accident that civil and political freedoms are better realized in democracies than other political systems."[125] In contrast, the less democratic a system is, the more likely its rulers are to place significance on issues that emphasize the socioeconomic and cultural rights of an individual. In general, such rights are perceived within the sphere of "the right to work and to just and favorable conditions; the right . . . to social security, and to an adequate standard of living; and the right to physical and mental health, education, and participation in cultural life, and to benefit from scientific, literary, or artistic production."[126]

While such rights are also subject to varying interpretation depending upon individual regimes, the authoritarian perception takes the stance that political participation should function not within "autonomously defined public spaces" but within "a state-controlled arena in which any discussion of issues must be made in codes and terms established by the rulers."[127] As the cases of trade unions and professional associations highlight, the Mubarak regime has been diligent in the maintenance of such a view.

The perpetual renewal of emergency law in Egypt is most indicative of the government's perceptions of human rights. The ban of most forms of political participation, such as the gathering of individuals and the distribution of political material without prior state security authorization, indicates that emergency rule is used not simply to contain suspected extremist activities, but also to control legitimate political activities. Consequently, while Amnesty International's 2001 report on Egypt noted that "hundreds" of political detainees held under emergency legislation had been released, it also pointed out that "thousands" of others, "including possible prisoners of conscience," remained in detention under such legislation.[128] As a highly respected and powerful international organization, Amnesty International is in an advantageous position to publicize its concerns and to defend disparate human rights in the international arena. However, this is not the case for Egyptian organizations working within this field. As one senior Egyptian government official explains, "Human rights means having the right to pray, the right to your religion, the freedom of work, the freedom of movement. . . . How can [human rights] organizations get involved with the politics of the state and say there is freedom or no freedom? This is none of their business."[129] In view of such perceptions, efforts to control the development of Egyptian human rights organizations can be detected on several levels, most blatantly within the legal sphere.

The legal sphere and the case of the Egyptian Organization for Human Rights. The first Egyptian human rights organization, the Partisans Association of Human Rights in Cairo (PAHRC), was formally established in 1977, shortly and separately followed by the Partisans Association of Human Rights in Alexandria (PAHRA), which was established in 1979. These organizations had little problem acquiring a legal status because they functioned as mouthpieces for the government rather than as independent defenders of human rights. Although the PAHRA is now defunct, the PAHRC continues to act as a government mouthpiece. Hence, when the Egyptian government is accused of human rights violations in the international arena, the PAHRC's main role is to deny such accusations through its formal press releases.[130] It was not until 1987 that Egypt witnessed its first independent human rights organization, the Egyptian Organization for Human Rights (EOHR). The EOHR's independent views are reflected in the fact that it remains to date a legally unrecognized entity. Law 32 of 1964, governing civil associations, has proved indispensable to the regime in this regard.

As mentioned previously, one of the stipulations of Law 32 has been the right given to the authorities to reject the founding of an organization "if the environment has no need for the services of another association."[131] This particular stipulation continues to be used under Mubarak as a mechanism by which the Ministry of Social Affairs can exclude certain organizations from civil participation. In this respect, while there are 17,000 nongovernmental organizations currently registered with the Ministry of Social Affairs, the use of Law 32 for exclusionary purposes has been most evident in the field of human rights, and the Egyptian Organization for Human Rights reflects this predicament. In 1985 the EOHR was initially a branch of the then newly founded Arab Organization for Human Rights (AOHR). However, by 1987 it had managed to establish itself as an independent entity and by 1990 it had begun its formal application for legal status. In 1991 the Ministry of Social Affairs, as a consequence of Law 32, decided to reject the EOHR's application on the grounds that another organization working in the same field already existed and hence the EOHR's existence was "not needed."[132] In other words, the government used the existence of the PAHRC to render the existence of the EOHR redundant.

In fact, it was not until 1999 that two more human rights organizations (out of approximately eighteen in existence)[133] managed to acquire legal standing. Furthermore, this appears to have been due to an unintentional loophole on the part of the authorities. These two organizations, the Center for Human Rights Legal Aid (CHRLA) and the AOHR, acquired legal status largely as a consequence of Law 153 of 1999, a short-lived and controversial piece of legislation that was intended to replace Law 32 and that provided the CHRLA and the AOHR the opportunity to register. One of the stipulations of the new law governing NGOs was that the Ministry of Social Affairs had to respond to any given application within a period of sixty days of receiving it or else the application would be considered accepted. It is argued that the applications of both organizations were accepted primarily as a preemptive measure a few days before a visit by Mary Robinson (the UN High Commissioner for Human Rights) to Cairo.[134] Such an argument has some foundation, since the haste in which the organizations were accepted under the new law appeared to be a rather erratic move on the government's part, which had previously failed to recognize both the AOHR and the CHRLA since their establishment in 1985 and 1993 respectively.

However, while Law 153 allowed the AOHR and the CHRLA to finally attain legal status, its stipulations made it no less constraining than Law 32. In fact, Law 153 was rejected at both the national and the international level. The main points of contention focused on conditions in the new law that empowered the minister of social affairs to reject an NGO board of trustees, dismiss it, and appoint other candidates of the minister's choice. Moreover, the scope of activities remained curtailed under the pretext that NGOs were prohibited from participating in activities "recognized only for political parties . . . professional syndicates or trade unions."[135] In addition, the inclusion of penalties for NGOs that participated in activities that could be interpreted as threatening to "public morality" or "national unity" led one international group to conclude that "these provisions have the effect of enabling the authorities to label the activities of human rights advocates as political and therefore illegitimate. Additionally, activities such as the provision of legal aid or commenting on legislation arguably overlap with the activities of the bar association for example, and so could be prohibited to NGOs. . . . [S]uch terms are vague and are open to abuse by [the] government."[136] Finally, as a consequence of Law 153, NGOs were also expected to file applications to the government and await approval prior to any foreign funding even though "the draft recommended by the consultative committee had explicitly authorized the receipt of funds from foreign institutions with an institutional presence in Egypt."[137]

The disparity between governmental views on the role of NGOs in comparison to the views of human rights organizations and Western governments was most poignantly reflected in their differing stands with regard to this law. While a statement cosigned by Amnesty International, Human Rights Watch, and the International Federation of Human Rights maintained that the law "restricts the right of freedom of association as guaranteed under the International Covenant on Civil and Political Rights," the United States was even more to the point. As then–State Department spokesman James Rubin pointed out, "This is the wrong direction to go if Egypt wants to energize civil society and promote development."[138] However, the Egyptian government justified the law on the basis of security concerns. Claiming that such measures "were necessary to prevent the establishment of organizations with hidden agendas using funding from abroad"[139] and that the law was not intended "for the creation of 14,000 political parties" illustrates this point.[140] Hence it was the foreign reporters covering the new law who were being "undemocratic,"[141] not the government of Egypt, according to the minister of social affairs.

In view of the imposition of such constraints, some organizations, such as the Group for Democratic Development (GDD), felt the necessity to disband in protest.[142] The EOHR, like the majority of human rights organizations, took the view that legal recognition even under overt governmental constraints is realistically more advantageous than the perils of functioning illegally. On the surface, this decision appeared to be a positive move. After submitting its application, the EOHR received a response from the Ministry of Social Affairs on 26 July 2000 informing its leaders that the organization had been registered as an NGO. However, rather than sending the EOHR its NGO license a few days later as expected, the government had a change of heart. Instead, it gave the EOHR a letter informing members that "the administration" was postponing "its decision of registering [the EOHR] at the request of the security authorities."[143] When in 2000 Law 153 was subsequently invalidated by the Supreme Constitutional Court on the grounds of its unconstitutionality,[144] the government reverted back to Law 32 and the EOHR as well as other organizations denied legal recognition returned to the Supreme Administrative Court in efforts to continue their long battle for legal recognition.[145] An end to this battle is still a long way ahead. In June 2002 the government passed Law 84, a carbon copy of Law 153, albeit this time via the formal procedural channels that had proclaimed Law 153 unconstitutional. While Law 84 has yet to enter into force, the Egyptian government has bided its time and again shown its relentlessness in securing a dominant position over the associations of civil society and the ability of human rights organizations to function legally.

Other constraints on human rights organizations. The constraints imposed on illegal human rights organizations are well illustrated through the example of the EOHR, whose inability to gain a license means that the organization must confront severe economic hardship. As a consequence, arrears in employee wages, office rent, and even bills for basic services such as electricity and telephones constitute but a few of its financial problems. Equally important is its inability to finance research and hold events conducive to its role in civil society. Thus, while the EOHR does admit to having some money, which it raised a few years earlier, its illegal status prohibits it from accessing its bank account for fear of government reprisal.[146]

This fear stems largely from the circumstances surrounding the EOHR's role in investigating police conduct following two murders that took place in the predominantly Coptic village of Al-Kosh in the Upper Egyptian governate of Sohag in 1998. In an effort to solve these murders, the police rounded up hundreds of villagers, who subsequently endured brutal treatment while in detention. The EOHR's role in monitoring the situation and sending its official report to the Egyptian media and foreign human rights organizations can be considered a routine approach, one it had adopted on numerous occasions since its establishment a decade earlier. The difference was the international attention this particular case received, and the fact that certain international newspapers, such as Britain's *Daily Telegraph,* grossly exaggerated the events of that incident.[147] In reaction to the foreign criticism, the Egyptian government promised the police officers involved in the Al-Kosh investigation "bonuses" of 1,000 Egyptian pounds (U.S.$285) for their "good work."[148]

The EOHR, in contrast, found itself in the midst of a slanderous media campaign spearheaded by *Al-Osbo'a,* an independent progovernment newspaper. Under the caption "The Price of Treason" and arguing that the EOHR was a servant for "foreign and hostile paymasters," *Al-Osbo'a* printed a copy of a U.S.$25,000 check that had been paid to the EOHR by the British Parliament's Human Rights Commission.[149] What it failed to point out was that the check was the second installment of a U.S.$42,000 funding project started in 1996 to provide women and disabled people in deprived areas with legal assistance and rights awareness.[150] In other words, the check was neither paid nor indeed used to fund the EOHR's report on Al-Kosh. Rather, the report had cost the EOHR less than U.S.$100 to produce. Emphasizing the absurdities of the accusations, Hafiz Abu Saada, head of the EOHR, was compelled to point out that "not even Mohammed Hasanin Haikal or Thomas Friedman would get paid twenty-five thousand dollars for a report."[151]

The media campaign that *Al-Osbo'a* leveled against the EOHR provided the government with sufficient justification to arrest Abu Saada on three potentially serious charges: "receiving money from a foreign country in order to damage the national interest, spreading rumors which affect the country's interest and violating the decree against collecting donations without obtaining permission from the appropriate authorities."[152] As these charges indicate, the monitoring of human rights abuses is interpreted by the government as a crime bordering on treason. As such, it is understandable that since Abu Saada's release after six days in detention, the EOHR is keeping its activities to a minimum. The fact that the government was subjected to intense international pressure as a consequence of the arrests, combined with the fact that the EOHR provided the necessary documentation in court proving that the British funding stemmed from a

separate project started 1996, resulted in the government's decision
to close the files on this particular incident.[153]

The incident nevertheless served as a covert warning to the
EOHR and similar organizations that such activities are neither welcomed nor tolerated by the government. As a direct consequence, the
EOHR itself ceased solicitation of foreign funding. Abu Saada
explains:

> In 1993 we started taking foreign funds because we found that the
> punishment for taking them without formal approval is six months
> in prison. So we decided to take the risk. After 1998, we discov-
> ered that if we continued, under martial decree for Law 4, we
> risked being tried in a military courts and being sentenced to
> between seven and fifteen years in prison. Since the Ministry of
> Social Affairs refused to give us formal authorization, we decided
> it was no longer worth the risk.[154]

On an interrelated level, negative public portrayal of human rights
activities is another tactic aimed at alienating these organizations
from the grassroots. As the EOHR's encounter with *Al-Osbo'a* illustrated, it is not very difficult for the Egyptian media to portray such
organizations as dangerous, foreign-funded enemies of the country.
Such negative publicity is enforced not only if certain NGO activities appear to be politically sensitive—as in the case of Al-Kosh—
but also if they appear to be gaining popularity among the people.
Illustrative of such a predicament is the "Teachers for Democracy"
project, started by the Group for Democratic Development[155] in
summer 1999.

Additional pressures—the "Teachers for Democracy" case. The
"Teachers for Democracy" project started with sponsorship from the
Danish International Development Agency (DANIDA). It was the
first in what had been intended to be a series of training sessions for
primary school teachers. The aim of the pilot project was to provide
teachers "with the necessary communication skills and training to
disseminate democratic values among their pupils."[156] Consequently,
topics in the program included rather basic aspects such as "the use
of participatory and creative learning processes, the role of the
teacher in a democratic classroom, and communication skills."[157]
The pilot project was popularly received, with more than 200 teachers applying for 100 available positions. In the course of the pilot

session, experienced teachers were brought in to evaluate the program and their findings were subsequently sent to the Ministry of Education along with an offer from the GDD to assist in future teacher training programs organized by the ministry. However, the governmental response illustrated a less than enthusiastic reception of such initiatives.

The minister of education, Hussein Kamel Baha'eddin, ordered that each of the teachers who had participated in the program be deducted two week's salary. Moreover, in an interview with the newspaper *Akher Sa'a* of 5 April 2000, Kamel Baha'eddin justified his ministry's opposition to the program on the basis that the GDD had used it as a platform to teach participants "freedom of sexuality and atheism."[158] Perhaps more alarming was the fact that approximately thirty of the participants were arrested and interrogated by state security forces. By adopting what had amounted to a smear campaign and punishing the teachers who had participated, the government sent an overt warning to the public about the allegedly dangerous nature of the GDD and the consequences to be faced if they did not maintain their distance from such organizations. As the director of GDD's project pointed out following the incident, "If you are a poor teacher and I come and invite you to attend this type of course again, will you accept? Of course not."[159] Indeed, efforts to alienate the GDD were also apparent in November 1999 when, following a conference held by the GDD for national universities, the minister of higher education, Mofid Shihab, sent a letter to all the faculties of the national universities informing them that the GDD was an organization that produced materials harmful to the state. Consequently, he ordered them to cease all cooperation with it.[160] In view of the "Teachers for Democracy" debacle earlier that year, it was hardly unexpected that the orders of the minister were swiftly implemented.

Given the hostile stance the state takes toward human rights groups, combined with its overt reluctance to legally recognize these activist organizations, even when they are willing to play by the ill-defined rules of the game, it is clear that governmental perceptions of civil society in contemporary Egypt remain at odds with those of its Western counterparts. Thus, while some human rights organizations do take the risk of illegal participation, while continuing their struggle for legal recognition, they do so with the knowledge that the authorities can "come at any time and close your shop."[161] As the case of the GDD illustrates, the disparate and "very hard pressure"[162] imposed from above sometimes leaves human rights groups with only one option, to preemptively close shop—the only form of protest that the Egyptian government approves and supports.

Conclusion

The case examples of trade unions, professional associations, and human rights groups illustrate the consistency of the containment and control strategies in Egypt over the past fifty years. While presidents and policies have changed since the 1952 coup took place, the exclusionary and repressive tactics over civil society established by Nasser under the populist-socialist umbrella have been well preserved by both his successors. The fact remains that the "socialist gains" of the 1950s and early 1960s could not be maintained. Political and economic policies have changed and society has diversified as disparate groups, opinions, and demands have emerged. The repressive tactics of the present government reflect its unwillingness to accept this very real situation. It is intent on preserving society's side of a bygone "social contract" even though it is economically impossible to keep its own side of the bargain.

So far, the established patterns of containment and control have allowed the present government to preserve the political status quo as it continues to apply and extend such tactics to both traditional and new sociopolitical forces. However, these authoritarian policies have not only hindered the emergence of autonomous groupings and organizations, but have also created abnormal and erratic patterns of behavior within civil society. The increase in labor strikes and riots over the past decade reflects the despair of the Egyptian labor force with its own trade unions and formal channels of communication. The desperation of opposition parties and groupings within the political arena has led to their adoption of professional associations as alternative avenues of political participation. The refusal of the government to recognize human rights groups has rendered them criminal in the eyes of the law and isolated them from the same society they work to defend. While this is a small price to pay for a system intent on maintaining its political domination and monopoly on power, the consequences of such repressive tactics do not end there. The emergence of extremist reactionary activities, as reflected by the clandestine Islamist forces, is also largely a product of the system's repressive policies. This phenomenon is examined in the next chapter.

Notes

1. Norton, *Civil Society in the Middle East,* p. 7.
2. Ibrahim, "Democratization in the Arab World," p. 28.
3. Ibid.
4. Norton, *Civil Society in the Middle East,* p. 7.
5. Ibid.
6. al-Sayyid, "A Civil Society in Egypt?" p. 282.
7. Ibid.
8. Salem, *The Despotism of the Bureaucratic State.*
9. Ibrahim, "Democratization in the Arab World," p. 39.
10. Said, "The Roots of Turmoil," p. 66.
11. Vatikiotis, *The History of Modern Egypt,* p. 401.
12. Beinin, "Labour, Capital, and the State in Nasserite Egypt," p. 74.
13. Abd al-Rahman Khir, deputy chairman of the Military Production Union, Egyptian Federation of Trade Unions, interview by author, 19 June 2002, Cairo.
14. Ibid.
15. el-Shafei, "Trade Unions and the State in Egypt," p. 15.
16. Posusney, *Labor and the State in Egypt,* p. 60.
17. Bianchi, *Unruly Corporatism,* p. 136. This fear was further encouraged by both the minister of social affairs and labor, Husayn al-Shaf'i, and the minister of interior, Zakariya Muhi al-Din. See ibid.
18. Sunar, "The Politics of Interventionism." Cited in Ayubi, *Overstating the Arab State,* p. 208.
19. Bianchi, *Unruly Corporatism,* p. 128.
20. Vatikiotis, *The History of Modern Egypt,* p. 401.
21. Beinin, "Labour, Capital, and the State in Nasserist Egypt," p. 75.
22. Posusney, *Labor and the State in Egypt,* p. 59.
23. Ibid.
24. Waterbury, *The Egypt of Nasser and Sadat,* p. 77.
25. Ibid., p. 78.
26. el-Shafei, "Trade Unions and the State in Egypt," p. 16.
27. Ibid. Also, these laws are analyzed in Posusney, *Labor and the State in Egypt,* pp. 69–73.
28. The Ministry of Labor is formally known as the Ministry of Manpower and Immigration.
29. Bianchi, *Unruly Corporatism,* p. 139.
30. Ibid.
31. el-Shafei, "Trade Unions and the State in Egypt," p. 16.
32. Bianchi, *Unruly Corporatism,* p. 131.
33. Posusney, *Labor and the State in Egypt,* p. 87.

34. Ibid., p. 89.

35. Ibid.

36. Khir interview, 19 June 2002.

37. Bianchi, *Unruly Corporatism,* p. 137.

38. Ibid.

39. Hatem, "Professional Associations in a Developing Country," pp. 137–138.

40. Bianchi, *Unruly Corporatism,* p. 95.

41. Kienle, *A Grand Delusion,* p. 37.

42. Ibid.

43. Hatem, "Professional Associations in a Developing Country," pp. 27–28.

44. For details on the main concessions, see ibid., p. 44.

45. Ezz el-Din, "Press Law 93/95," p. 27.

46. Ibid., p. 26.

47. Hatem, "Professional Associations in a Developing Country," pp. 44–46.

48. Ibid., p. 80.

49. Minutes of the Preparatory Committee, 1962, pp. 70–71, cited in ibid., p. 74.

50. Bianchi, *Unruly Corporatism,* p. 92.

51. Hatem, "Professional Associations in a Developing Country," p. 77.

52. Ibid., p. 8.

53. Ibid., p. 80.

54. Ezz el-Din, "Press Law 93/95," p. 28.

55. Lafif Lakhdar, "The Development of Class Struggle in Egypt" (1978), p. 67, cited in el-Shafei, "Trade Unions and the State in Egypt," p. 17.

56. See Posusney, *Labor and the State in Egypt,* chap. 3, for an in-depth analysis of various labor protests.

57. Posusney, *Labor and the State in Egypt,* p. 160.

58. Khir interview, 19 June 2002.

59. Ibid. The only other time that the military intervened in labor unrest under Sadat was during the 1977 "bread riots," which left thousands injured and resulted in seventy-nine deaths. The bread riots emerged as a consequence of Sadat's announcement of the lifting of state subsidies on some basic foods and goods as part of an International Monetary Fund stabilization program. While the whole country erupted in rioting upon hearing the news, it was the workers across Egypt who first walked out and led the protest.

60. Khir interview, 19 June 2002.

61. During the 1971 Helwan Iron and Steel Company sit-ins mentioned earlier, it was actually Salah Gharib whom Sadat had sent personally to mediate as the head of the GFETU and whom the workers kept hostage overnight.

62. Bianchi, *Unruly Corporatism,* p. 129.

63. Posusney, *Labor and the State in Egypt,* p. 112.

64. Ibid., p. 138.

65. Bianchi, *Unruly Corporatism,* p. 98.

66. Ibid.

67. Although a new constitution was promulgated in 1971, Sadat's "corrective revolution" did not include changes to syndicate laws. Consequently, Law 8 of 1958 remained intact until 1977, when it was updated to allow independents and opposition members to run in syndicate elections. However, a new stipulation was added that required potential candidates to first obtain clearance from the office of the state attorney general.

68. Ezz el-Din, "Press Law 93/95," p. 35.

69. Bianchi, *Unruly Corporatism,* pp. 110–111.

70. Ibid., pp. 111–112.

71. el-Shafei, "Trade Unions and the State in Egypt," pp. 23–24.

72. Ibid., p. 24.

73. Ibid.

74. Ibid., p. 26.

75. Ibid.

76. Ibid., pp. 26–27.

77. el-Shafei, "Trade Unions and the State in Egypt," p. 34.

78. This incident and other major strikes in the 1980s are well documented in ibid.

79. el-Shafei, "Trade Unions and the State in Egypt," p. 19. It is estimated that 1986 witnessed 50 labor protests and 1988–1989 witnessed 153 incidents of labor unrest.

80. Khattab, "Constraints of Privatization in the Egyptian Experience," p. 5.

81. Mustapha Mongy, deputy chairman of the GFETU, interview by author, 5 December 1998, Cairo.

82. Kienle, "More Than a Response to Islamism," p. 227.

83. Ibid.

84. Author interview with union activist, 19 June 2002, Cairo.

85. Khir interview, 19 June 2002.

86. These are: Sayed Rashid, Hussein Magawir, Fathi Nematallah, Fathi Abdel Latif, Abdel Aziz Mustapha, Mohammed Salama, Mohammed Wahbalahi, Adrey al-Mishnib, and Sayed Rostum. Ibrahim Lutfi, deputy chairman of the Federation of Military Production, GFETU, and member of parliament (NDP), interview by author, 19 June 2002, Cairo.

87. al-Fergany, *Impact of the Proposed Labor Law,* p. 6.

88. Hoda al-Mirghani, economist for the Federation of Egyptian Industries, interview by author, 27 May 1999, Cairo.

89. al-Fergany, *Impact of the Proposed Labor Law,* p. 5.

90. *Al-Ahram Weekly* (11–17 February 1999).

91. Abd al-Ghafar Shokr, senior member Tagammu' Party, interview by author, 27 January 1999, Cairo.

92. Ibid.

93. Ibid.

94. Mongy interview, 5 December 1998.

95. Ali Hilmi, chairman of the Metal and Steel Industries Company, interview by author, 14 November 1998, Helwan.

96. "Business in Brief."

97. Hassan, "Work Rules."

98. Lussier, "Striking a Balance?"

99. Assam al-'Ariyan, assistant secretary-general of the Egyptian Medical Syndicate and senior Muslim Brotherhood activist, interview by author, 25 January 2001, Cairo.

100. al-Sheikh, "Liberal Lawyers Syndicate Council Candidate Interview."

101. Abdel-Latif, "No Partners in Power."

102. Stacher, "Moderate Political Islamism," p. 65.

103. Ibid., p. 72.

104. Kamal Khalid, lawyer, interview in Apiku, "Rushed Syndicate Law Under Constitutional Fire."

105. Ibid.

106. Stacher, "Moderate Political Islamism," p. 72.

107. Law 4 "forbids collecting, receiving, declaring or even asking for donations for facing effects of disasters or accidents or risks or for any other purpose without permission from the ministry of social affairs." Although it was initiated as a consequence of the 1992 earthquake and the Muslim Brotherhood's role in providing relief, this decree has been abused against other activists, namely Hafiz Abu Saada of the EOHR in 1998 and Saad Eddin Ibrahim in 2000.

108. Sullivan and Abed-Kotob, *Islam in Contemporary Egypt,* p. 133.

109. Khalid Fouad, lawyer and former independent Bar Syndicate council candidate, interview by author, 18 January 2001, Cairo.

110. Ibid.

111. Apiku, "Syndicate Sit-In Pays Off."

112. Apiku, "Lawyers Call for Self-Rule."

113. Ibid.

114. U.S. Department of State, "1999 Country Reports on Human Rights Practices: Egypt."

115. See *Cairo Times* (23–29 November 2000).

116. U.S. Department of State, "1999 Country Reports on Human Rights Practices: Egypt."

117. Apiku, "Government Keeps Islamists Out of Syndicate Elections."

118. The Nasserite Party apparently refused to participate in such an alliance. See ibid.

119. Apiku, "Government Keeps Islamists Out of Syndicate Elections."

120. Apiku, "Nafie Wins Syndicate Elections with Some Opposition."

121. Ibid.

122. Abdel-Latif, "No Partners in Power."

123. Monshipouri, *Democratization, Liberalization, and Human Rights in the Third World,* p. 17.

124. Gillies, *Between Principle and Practice,* p. 16.

125. Ibid., p. 17.

126. Monshipouri, *Democratization, Liberalization, and Human Rights in the Third World*, p. 17.

127. O'Donnell and Schmitter, *Transitions from Authoritarian Rule*, p. 48.

128. Amnesty International 2001 report, Arab Republic of Egypt.

129. Schemm, "NGOs New Big Brother Ready to Help."

130. I would like to thank Dr. Mustapha al-Sayyid for sharing this information with me.

131. Salem, *The Despotism of the Bureaucratic State*.

132. Hafez Abu Saada, secretary-general of the EOHR, interview by author, 3 August 2000, Cairo.

133. Approximate figures derived from Abu Saada interview, 3 August 2000.

134. Jasir Abd al-Razik, then director of Hisham Mubarak Legal Center, interview by author, 6 August 2000, Cairo.

135. See Advocacy Alert, "President Mubarak Should Not Ratify Restrictive New Law."

136. Ibid.

137. Ibid.

138. "NGO Law Passed in Full."

139. Apiku, "Notorious NGO Law Thrown Out."

140. Social affairs minister Mervat Tellawi as reported in "Egypt: Human Rights Development," Human Rights Watch 1999 report.

141. Schemm, "NGOs Divided over Resistance to New Law."

142. Negad al-Borai, lawyer and head of the now defunct GDD, interview by author, 30 July 2000, Cairo.

143. Howeidy, "Destitute but Determined." Also Abu Saada interview, 3 August 2000.

144. Interestingly, the Supreme Constitutional Court's invalidation of Law 153 was based more on technicality rather than content. According to Article 175 of the constitution, since the law fell into the category of being "complementary to the constitution," it should have been reviewed by the Shura Council, which did not happen, before being passed by the People's Assembly. Thus the law was invalidated. Apiku, "Notorious NGO Law Thrown Out."

145. The EOHR did in fact present its case to the Higher Administrative Court after its initial application was rejected in 1990. The court, however, sided with the ministry and rejected the EOHR's case in 1991. Since then, the EOHR has been in the process of appealing to the Supreme Administrative Court. Abu Saada interview, 3 August 2000.

146. Abu Saada interview, 3 August 2000.

147. For example, while the EOHR's report claimed that the police threatened the detainees with rape and crucifixions, the *Daily Telegraph*'s report indicated that these acts were actually carried out. See Aikman, "Egypt's Human Wrongs."

148. Digges, "Rights Groups Recoil at Egypt Law."

149. Aikman, "Egypt's Human Wrongs."

150. Abu Saada interview, 3 August 2000.
151. Ibid.
152. Aikman, "Egypt's Human Wrongs."
153. Abu Saada interview, 3 August 2000.
154. Ibid.
155. The GDD was a nongovernmental organization established in 1995 with the aim of promoting democratic development in Egypt. The pressures it faced from the government led it to voluntarily close down in 2000.
156. GDD newsletter, winter 1999.
157. Ibid.
158. al-Borai interview, 30 July 2000.
159. Ibid.
160. Ibid.
161. Abu Saada interview, 3 August 2000.
162. al-Borai interview, 30 July 2000.

5

Egypt's Islamists: From Fundamentalists to "Terrorists"

Political opponents are invariably influenced by the type of political system in which they function. As Lisa Anderson aptly observes:

> The particular platforms and programs of both governments and their opposition . . . reflect a great variety of sources: ideological beliefs, cultural heritages, historical norms, and economic interests. Opposition, however, has the unusual characteristic of being defined partly by what it opposes; it develops within and in opposition to an ideological and institutional framework and, as such, reveals a great deal not only about its own adherents, but also about the individuals, policies, regimes, and states in authority.[1]

Furthermore, according to the same author, "The absence of a reliable, transparent institutional framework for political opposition to work within not only hampers the routinization of opposition of all kinds but magnifies the profile and broadens the constituency of 'rejectionist' or 'disloyal' parties."[2] In the case of Egypt, these "rejectionist" or "disloyal" parties have predominantly taken the form of Islamist groupings. On this basis, the argument presented in this chapter is that, in contrast to popular perceptions, it is because these groupings are "extremist" that the state has little choice but to suppress them. It is the "rejectionist" approach by the political system and the tactics used to suppress disparate Islamist groupings such as the Muslim Brotherhood, Al-Jama' al-Islamiya, that are largely responsible for the prevailing Islamist challenge that contemporary Egypt faces. This chapter will not only raise questions as to why the Islamists have emerged as the most popular opponents within the contemporary Egyptian political system, but also exam-

ine the role of the state in shaping the nature and perceptions of
such opponents.

The Emergence of Islamists

Political Islam in its contemporary, participatory, and popular form
emerged in 1928 with the establishment of the Society of the Muslim
Brothers (Muslim Brotherhood). The original aim of its founder,
Hassan al-Banna, was the "reform of hearts and minds, to guide
Muslims back to the true religion, and away from the corrupt aspira-
tions and conduct created by European dominance."[3] This view
stemmed from the ideas of earlier Islamic thinkers and reformers
such as Jamal al-Din al-Afghani, his disciple Mohammed Abdu and,
Abdu's disciple Rashid Rida. These Islamic thinkers questioned the
increasing domination of Western colonial powers and attributed it to
the ignorant, corrupt, and fragmented nature of Islamic polities. The
failings of the Islamic polities, they argued, were not intrinsic to
Islam but were due to the fact that Islam "had been subverted by the
dynastic empires, and forgotten in the degeneration and corruption of
religion in the later centuries."[4] Connected to this perception is an
underlying difference between the Muslim Brotherhood and these
earlier Islamic thinkers in regard to attitudes toward the oppressor.
For example, "whereas for Abdu Europe, the oppressor, was at the
same time the model for progress and strength, for the later [Islamic
activists] the West was both oppressive and culturally threatening."[5]
In addition, while the intellectual influence of Islamic thinkers such
as al-Afghani, Abdu, and Rida was considerable socially, their success was limited since they failed in transferring such ideas "into the
field of political struggle or of incorporating them into the modern
state."[6] The establishment of the Muslim Brotherhood is a significant
milestone in this regard and for the disparate Islamist groupings that
subsequently followed both in Egypt and in the region. It spearheaded the shift of Muslim political thought in the contemporary era into
the arena of active political participation.

Active political participation by the Muslim Brotherhood
emerged on several levels and in conjunction with a broad range of
social and educational activities. On one level, the Muslim
Brotherhood initially did not reject the established political order
when it emerged. Rather, it perceived the monarchy and society to be

"in need of reform to make it fully Islamic, in both the moral and social sense."[7] Since the Muslim Brotherhood was formally established under the umbrella of a charitable society, its attempts to encourage such reforms included a strategy by al-Banna to teach "children in the daytime and their parents at night."[8] In a society where education was limited to a small section of the population, the Brotherhood's charitable Islamic education undoubtedly contributed to its popularity and expansion across the country. However, this expansion and popularity was not spontaneous; it emerged from hard work and a focused vision. As Richard Mitchell points out:

> In the first three years of the life of the Society, its primary goal was the enlargement of its membership in and around Isma'iliyya. Banna and selected deputies pursued this goal by direct contact, touring the countryside on the weekends and during vacations, preaching most usually in mosques but also in the homes, clubs, and other meeting-places of the people. The use of the mosques gave the speakers the legitimacy and respectability they needed. Direct communication with the people in their homes, at their work, and in their places of leisure added to that legitimacy the quality of sincerity and the personal touch.[9]

The popularity of the Brothers was further enhanced because, as one author observes, "Their consistent defense of the national cause (Palestine, Suez, British evacuation) gained them respect and legitimacy on purely secular terms and beyond their own circle of sympathizers."[10] It is on the basis of such popularity that some of the Brotherhood's prominent members, including al-Banna, competed as independent candidates in legislative elections for the first time in 1942. The result could not have been more disappointing, since "they were all defeated—be it because of government manipulation or British intervention."[11] This intervention is not surprising because of the group's increasingly popular base of support. The tense and antagonistic relationship between the state and the Brotherhood increased in proportion to the latter's popularity and growth. In this context, it was not unexpected that the Brotherhood's dissolution in 1948 coincided with its most notable achievement in its then two-decade history. This is well observed by Mitchell, who notes that

> the Brothers most notable achievement was the assistance they rendered to the besieged Egyptians caught in the 'Faluja pocket' created by the Israeli advance after the second truce had broken down in

October 1948. In the field the Brothers helped to run supplies
through the encircled forces; in Cairo the Society joined with others to press the Egyptian government for more volunteers to relieve
the trapped garrison. Naqrashi [the prime minister] refused and it
was only in the following February, after the armistice agreements,
that the pocket was relieved. The Faluja excitement reached its
highest pitch in November 1948. Early in the next month the
Society of Muslim Brothers no longer legally existed.[12]

The decree ordering the dissolution of the Brotherhood was based on
accusations by the state's prosecution that "the organization, after it
grew strong, assumed 'political goals'; the secret apparatus was created and the rover group was trained to assist it in the ultimate political goal of taking power."[13]

It should be noted that national and regional issues such as the
British presence in Egypt and the Jewish question in Palestine creat-
ed a highly charged political atmosphere in the 1930s and 1940s.
Along with the Brotherhood, disparate movements representing
nationalistic tendencies, such as Misr al-Fatat (Young Egypt), and
leftist tendencies, such as the Communist Party, were also active participants within Egypt's political arena. While the Muslim
Brotherhood sometimes resorted to violent tactics—most notably in
December 1948, when members assassinated Prime Minister
Mahmoud Naqrashi in retaliation for ordering their dissolution—this
was not a particularly uncommon phenomenon during that period. In
addition to the Muslim Brotherhood, "other extremist organizations
of the national-social variety also appeared in the 1930s, which sanc-
tified further violent politics—and political violence."[14] The emergence of political violence under the monarchy was not an exclusive
Islamist pursuit, but rather was connected to an attitude of desperation born out of wider socioeconomic and political discontent. As P.
J. Vatikiotis points out, "Apart from the further dilution of direct
British influence over political affairs in the country in the 1930s,
there were serious domestic political, social and economic factors
which contributed to, and facilitated the emergence of new organized
groups subscribing to violent ideologies. These were not only
opposed to the established order, but also ready to challenge its
authority by violent means."[15]

The Egyptian government also retaliated in kind. Indicative of
this was the manner in which it disposed of al-Banna in 1949.
Although not an Islamist sympathizer, Mohammed Heikal acknowl-

edges that following the assassination of Naqrashi, the new prime minister, Ibrahim Abdel Hadi, ordered the vindication of his predecessor. In Heikal's words: "The attack on [al-Banna] was planned and carried out by the head of the special police department responsible for the safety of ministers (*haras el-wizarat*). With two policemen from his department in civilian clothes he ambushed and killed [al]-Banna in Cairo's Queen Nazli Street at 9 o'clock in the evening of 12 February 1949."[16] It is clear from al-Banna's assassination that "the Abdel Hadi government was uncompromising in its suppression . . . of the Brotherhood," as was the Naqrashi government.[17] Due to the Brotherhood's ideological opposition to "secular, liberal constitutional parties, especially the Wafd (the main . . . party in Egypt before the Free Officers' revolution in 1952),"[18] King Farouk cultivated its support to counteract the popularity of the newly elected Wafd government in 1950. The matter was encouraged following a court battle over the Brotherhood's dissolution in September 1951. The court retreated from the state's argument, which gave "legal sanction . . . to the existence of the Society "[19] This legality lasted until 1954, after which the Brotherhood, like the Islamist groups that were to follow, was confined to the realms of illegal political participation. The significance is that, following its creation, a pattern emerged with regard to the group and its relationship with the state. Namely, the state used the groups as a tool to counteract opponents (as in the case of the Wafd) and external threats (as in the Arab-Israeli conflict). In this vein, the Brotherhood proved useful.

On the other hand, the ability of the Brotherhood to mobilize mass support and organization meant that first and foremost, it was regarded with overt suspicion and hostility by the state. This pattern by the state of adopting "cooperative" and "coercive" tactics constituted a cycle that was not simply maintained and enhanced in the post-1952 republic, but significantly contributed toward determining the disposition of Islamist opponents in the contemporary era.

Islamists Under Nasser

The post-1952 republic under Nasser directly influenced two important aspects of the development of Islamist groups in contemporary Egypt. On one level, it crushed the Muslim Brotherhood movement in a manner unprecedented to date. On another level, the brutality involved in the regime's approach to the Brotherhood produced a reactionary Islamic ideology that not only was extremist in its inter- pretation, but also was the foundation of the more radical Islamist groups that emerged in the late 1960s.

The relationship between the newly established Revolutionary Command Council (RCC) and the Brotherhood began, during the first few years, with some form of mutual toleration. Indeed, the new regime went as far as attempting to co-opt the organization by offer- ing three ministerial posts to Brotherhood members. However, when the Brotherhood's guidance council was presented with this option, its members refused. Indicative of this move, Shaikh Hassan al- Baquri, the only one of the RCC's three proposed Brothers who accepted a ministerial position, was dismissed from the group. The reasons behind the decision to reject the RCC's offer were based on the following considerations:

> (1) The fear that the Society would lose its "popular" quality, i.e. sully itself with power; (2) the fear . . . of bringing down the wrath of foreigners and minorities on the regime and thus complicating its problems. Other more mundane considerations seemed to be operative: (1) behind each ministry stood an army officer who had the real power; (2) with only three ministries, the Brothers would invariably be outvoted and would be compelled to lend their names to decisions that . . . they could not support.[20]

The RCC's move to co-opt the Brotherhood was not surprising given that on 16 January 1953 all existing political parties and groups except the Muslim Brotherhood were abolished by decree. The regime had alienated all opposition political forces in the country. In the case of the Brotherhood, this was not a confrontation the RCC was willing to risk after just six months in power. The Muslim Brotherhood, after all, "represented the largest organized popular force in the country."[21] The Brotherhood's rejection to formally ally with the government was hard- ly problematic for the new regime, which after consolidating power subsequently dissolved the group in January 1954. The confrontations between the regime and the Brotherhood peaked on 26 October 1954, when an assassination attempt against Nasser, then prime minister, dur- ing an Alexandria rally resulted in the shots being heard on the radio in Egypt and across the Arab world. It did not help the Brotherhood's position that Nasser, who was unhurt, regained his composure and delivered a speech that was essentially a public rela tions coup.

While the formal role of the Brotherhood in this attack still remains unclear, Nasser used this opportunity of overwhelming public support in its aftermath to remove Mohamad Nagib from the presidency and occupy the position himself. Just as important, the assassination attempt "provided [Nasser] with the opportunity of being done with the Society of the Muslim Brothers. On the following 9 December, six men were hanged; thousands of other Brothers were already imprisoned, and the organization had been efficiently crushed."[22] Put simply, the relationship between the Brotherhood and the new regime was understood on the following terms:

> At the outset of the July Revolution there was a good deal of cooperation, and even some ideological affinity, between the Ikhwan [Brotherhood] and the Free Officers. . . . The falling out between the Ikhwan and Nasser was not a mere misunderstanding. It was the result of an open struggle for power; and when Nasser won, he had to decide how to deal with the Ikhwan organization, with Islamic fundamentalism and voluntary Islamic organizations, and with those classes and groups that had been most responsive to the appeal of the Ikhwan.[23]

The coercive and brutal manner in which the Nasserite regime pursued the Brotherhood in the post-1954 era resulted in the birth of Islamist radical thought as reflected by the works of its chief ideologue, Sayyid Qutb, a Brotherhood member. Following the assassination attempt on Nasser, Qutb was accused of being affiliated with the movement's secret apparatus and in 1955 was sentenced to fifteen years' imprisonment.[24] The torture that he and other Brotherhood members faced at the hands of the regime at that time, and the subsequent massacre of twenty-one of his prison-mates in 1957, transformed him. Indeed, Qutb went "from a very liberal writer in Egypt into the most radical fundamentalist thinker in the Arab world, converting his imprisonment and ferocious torture into a radical political theology of violence and isolation."[25] Reflective of this, Qutb's "most important books or gospels of radicalism—*Fi Zilal al-Qur'an, Ma'alim fi al-Tariq, Hadha al-Din, Al-Mustaqbal li Hadha al-Din,* and others—were written because of and in spite of, the torture that he and others tolerated year after year."[26] In other words, Qutb "was horrified by the barbarism of the camp guards, by the inhumanity with which they had let the wounded die."[27] Hence his radical writings were undoubtedly shaped by "the concentration camp in which the author spent ten years of his life" and the fact that he had become very "well acquainted with the underside of 'Arab socialism.'"[28] From such a vantage point, Qutb interpreted the Nasserite regime as representative of "the model of *jahiliya*."[29] This meant that society was "ruled by an iniquitous prince who made himself an object of worship in God's place and who governed an empire according to his own caprice" rather than according to Islamic teachings.[30] As a result, in his writings Qutb called upon Muslims "to undertake *jihad* [armed rebellion] against their leaders because they had replaced God's *Shari'a* with their own man-made laws."[31] Qutb was released from prison only to be rearrested in 1965 and charged with plotting to overthrow the government. He was subsequently hanged in 1966, but his writings survived and, more important, "marked the starting point of the road along which the militants of the Islamic movement would travel."[32]

The brutal tactics of the Nasser regime not only paved the way for the emergence of a more radical Islamic ideology, but also crippled the Brotherhood's relatively moderate movement, creating a void that contemporary Islamic groups were more than willing to fill. As one author notes, "While in political and organizational limbo, the Ikhwan could neither hold the allegiance nor nourish the religious commitment of a new generation of fundamentalists."[33] This aspect became overtly evident when, upon assuming power, President Sadat turned to the Islamists in an effort to cultivate support for his own political motivations.

Islamists Under Sadat

While in his early years in power Nasser viewed the Brotherhood as his main political threat, Sadat perceived the leftists and Nasserists as the main obstacle to both his consolidation of power and efforts to move away from Nasser's ailing socialist experiment. Overcoming such a threat entailed the removal of Nasser's old guard on the elite level as well as the dismantling of the Arab Socialist Union (ASU) and its replacement with a multiparty system created from above. While Sadat did not allow for the legal recognition of religiously based political parties, the president did allow Islamist groups to participate on several levels in the socioeconomic and political arena. In some instances such groups "were supported organizationally and financially by the authorities."[34] It should be noted that Sadat's attempt to revive the Islamist movement was not a particularly difficult undertaking. The void left by the Brotherhood, along with the spread of Qutb's radical Islamic thought, meant that before Sadat came to power new religiously based groups had emerged as underground movements by the late 1960s. As Leonard Binder notes: "Many new local, and often small and secret organizations were founded after 1965, some of which challenged the vestige of the Ikhwan, and others of which simply did their own religious thing. Some were highly politicized and militant while others sought the comfort of fraternal association and the consultation of mutual cooperation."[35]

The growth of such groups can be linked to Egypt's military defeat in 1967 and, to some degree, Nasser's inadvertent encouragement when he released hundreds of Brotherhood prisoners. Also, Nasser's rhetoric shifted toward an Islamist orientation and, "as if to rationalize the defeat by Israel . . . [he] resorted to Islamic slogans in his addresses to the masses."[36] These emerging religious groups found the 1967 defeat conducive to the recruitment of supporters because "Egypt's military weakness had created fertile ground for the growth of religious ideals because the defeat was perceived as a punishment for Egypt's pursuit of socialist, rather than Islamic, ideals. Only when Egypt returned to Islam would God support the nation's war against Israel."[37] The post-1965 Islamist movement was thus already gaining ground and would prove to be a formidable challenge to the Nasserist and leftist movement, as Sadat had intended. It also helped that, as a former Islamist student in the 1970s points out, "The majority of our generation were Islamists because of our disillusionment with Nasserism, but if things had worked out differently, most of us would have been Nasserists."[38]

Sadat's courtship of the Islamists during the early 1970s focused initially on reconciliation with the Muslim Brotherhood. This included the release of Brotherhood prisoners and the encouragement of its exiled members to return home, primarily from Saudi Arabia and the Gulf states. Indeed, it was upon "Sadat's instruction" that presidential adviser Mahmud Mo'awwad Jami' came to an agreement with exiled senior Brotherhood members, such as Yusif al-Qaradawi and Ahmed al-'Asal, to release Brotherhood prisoners in return for letting "bygones be bygones."[39] Such reconciliation also meant that,

although the organization was legally unrecognized, "the government did not interfere when the Muslim Brotherhood rebuilt its
organization."[40] However, because the Brotherhood was largely a
shadow of its former self and throughout the 1970s remained in the
process of reconstruction, the Brotherhood was less appealing to
potential recruits during this period than other emerging Islamist
groupings. As one former Al-Jama'at member explains, "The Muslim
Brotherhood had just come out of Nasser's prisons, they were worn
out and just wanted to make peace with the government—al-Jihad
and al-Jama'at were young groups that had different ideas—they
were more appealing to the youth."[41] Sadat's encouragement of this
Islamist youth movement facilitated the birth of student associations
(Al-Jama'at al-Islamiya) in universities because, as the president
explained to his adviser, "I want us to raise Muslim boys, and to
spend money on them, so they can become *rakizitna* [our anchor]."[42]
The atmosphere at the time is well documented by prominent
Egyptian writer and political observer Mohammed Heikal:

> Much money was . . . going to the universities, where lavish exhi-
> bitions of religious literature were frequently staged. Societies
> were promoted to provide students with what was described as
> "Islamic costume," veils for the girls and *galabiyehs* for the boys.
> . . . But most energy was devoted to ensuring that the students
> were correctly represented in their unions. To give just one exam-
> ple: in the elections for student unions in Alexandria University [in
> 1978] . . . candidates from the Islamic association won all sixty
> places in the Faculties of Medicine and Engineering, forty-six out
> of forty-eight in the Faculty of Law, forty-three out of sixty in the
> Faculty of Pharmacy. . . . Knowing that they had the support of
> higher authority, the Islamic students began to behave as if it was
> they who were running the universities. . . . Any students who
> openly disagreed with the Islamic groups were subject to discipli-
> nary action. Boys and girls seen walking together were beaten up. .
> . . It was clear that the religious students were not simply tolerated
> by the authorities but actively encouraged by them.[43]

The development of Al-Jama'at appeared a to be natural progression in such a nurturing and supportive political environment. Such a
conducive environment and Al-Jama'at's rapid growth in popularity
and appeal can also be viewed as a consequence of its harmless ideological outlook, as Al-Jama'at's main concern until the late 1970s
was the spread of *al-Dawa* (Islamic calling) among the student bod-

ies and on some levels of society. While Al-Jama'at managed to monopolize the Islamist movement during the 1970s, the smaller, more radical militant groups remained marginalized until the late 1970s, when Egypt's political atmosphere changed due to Sadat's controversial policies. Sadat's 1974 economic open-door policy (*infitah*) had produced a huge socioeconomic gap between the rich elite and the poor majority by the late 1970s. The Camp David Accords, which Sadat signed with Israel in 1979, added fuel to the opposition's fire because they resulted in Egypt's isolation from the Arab world and formal expulsion from the League of Arab Nations. In addition, Sadat's decision to give refuge to the Shah of Iran in defiance of the new Islamic Republic (1979) was also a move that was regarded, particularly by the Islamists, with much contempt. It should be pointed out that Sadat's political liberalization in the mid-1970s meant that along with the Islamists, a wide spectrum of groups, including the legalized opposition parties, the intellectuals, and what remained of the socialists and Nasserists, were also airing their disfavor. However, the Islamists were perceived as the prime threat by the president. His reaction to this threat is aptly described by Mohammed Heikal:

> Realizing that the groups posed an increasing threat, he unleashed a series of responses that signaled the end of the regime's positive involvement with the groups. He withheld subsides from the student unions that were dominated by the Islamists; in 1979 his regime outlawed the activities of the religious *jama'at;* and the Central Security Forces shut down Islamic summer youth camps in Alexandria, Cairo and Zagazig. This . . . deprived the *jama'at* of their legal cover, their organization, and their funds.[44]

Rather than contain Al-Jama'at, the regime's policies enhanced its position so that it not only began to enjoy "an aura of martyrdom" but also began to preach "among the people, making new recruits in the poor neighborhoods."[45] The result was the expansion and amalgamation of its power base outside the realm of the university campus. It united with smaller Islamist groups, particularly in Asyuit and other Upper Egyptian cities, to create a broad organization under the banner of Al-Jama' al-Islamiya (The Islamic Group). Such a politically charged anti-Sadat atmosphere proved to be a unifying force for the radical militants and in particular for the establishment of Tanzim al-Jihad in 1977. The founders of Jihad, Salim al-Rahal and

Hasan Halawi, were previously members of the Islamic Liberation Party (ILP), a minor militant group whose main claim to fame had been a futile attack on the Military Technical Academy in Cairo in 1974. By 1979 the Alexandria-based organization had expanded to Upper Egypt and, more significant, to populated working-class areas in Cairo. During the same period, Mohammed Farag, Jihad's Cairo leader, managed to unite Jihad's urban branches under his authority. In addition, the increasing political tensions proved such a strong unifying force that Farag, along with Al-Jama's Karam Zouhdy, came to an agreement whereby Jihad and Al-Jama' formed an alliance (Al-Jihad al-Jama') under the spiritual guidance of Shaikh Omar Abdel Rahman in 1980.

The conflict between the state and the Islamists reached its peak in September 1981, when Sadat silenced his critics through the wholesale arrest of approximately 1,500 intellectual, religious, and political individuals—of whom the majority were Islamists. Within a month, Islamist militants assassinated Sadat during the annual 6 October military parade. According to the official investigation files, the president's assassin, Khalid al-Islamboli, justified his actions by arguing during interrogation, "I did what I did because the *Shari'a* was not applied, because of the peace treaty with the Jews and because of the arrest of Muslim *'Ulama* [clergy] without justification."[46] In an interview following the assassination, another Jihad member described the political system as "a corrupt one whereby we hear of a member of parliament having been involved in the drug traffic business, of a minister who is presently being tried for having taken advantage of his position, and of individuals becoming millionaires overnight."[47] While these views were a major source of discontent, the September arrests and their personal implications for al-Islamboli were the catalyst behind his actions.

Al-Islamboli's younger brother, Mohammed, the leader of Al-Jama' at the Asyuit faculty of commerce, was among those arrested. As Gilles Kepel notes, when al-Islamboli discovered that his brother "had been dragged out of bed in his pajamas and 'taken away' . . . he was seized with a burning feeling of revolt [and] told his mother that he would seek vengeance, and that 'every tyrant has his end.'"[48] Al-Islamboli's personal motivation is reinforced by his decision and determination to carry out the assassination even though other group members had reservations about the haste with which it was planned. 'Abbud al-Zumur's insistence "on establishing a link between the assassination . . . and the preparations for a 'popular' revolution inclined him to oppose Khalid al-Islamboli's plan at first. . . . But 'Abbud was ignored and on the night of 26 September the . . . group decided to set plans for the assassination in motion."[49] The point is that while Sadat may have thought that he had little option but to contain the increasingly challenging Islamists through mass arrests and torture, such coercive actions resulted in an equally brutal reaction. As one author noted, the president's "crackdown on al-Jama's activists in the late 1970s and early 1980s culminated in his assassination by Jihad, and the further militarization of Islamic politics."[50] Indeed, while Nasser's ruthless crackdown on the Brotherhood gave birth to radical militant Islamism, Sadat's crackdown enhanced radical militant tendencies. The reinforcement of such tactics by the state under Mubarak not only reinforced this predicament, but consequently elevated it to the international level as well.

Islamists Under Mubarak

The rise of politically motivated violence involving Islamists is striking. As one report points out:

> During the first four years (1982–1985) of Mubarak's term, there was hardly any violence—a total of thirty-three casualties, averaging eight casualties annually. The third four years (1990–1993) were by far the bloodiest, not only of the Mubarak presidency but also of this century. There were 1,164 casualties—averaging 291 casualties annually. To put it differently, of the first twelve years of Mubarak's presidency, the last four appropriated nearly 92 percent of all casualties due to politically-motivated violence involving Islamic activists.[51]

These data indicate the manner in which state-Islamist relations have developed under Mubarak. Indeed, the Mubarak era has produced an unprecedented expansion of politically motivated violence involving Islamists and an upsurge in the number of Islamist prisoners. Mass military trials have been established for these civilian opponents,[52] and equally important, the Islamist sociopolitical movement has proceeded from the realm of religious fundamentalism into the realm of political terrorism. These developments emerged largely as a consequence of, and a reaction to, the various state policies toward the

Islamists during the 1980s and 1990s.

In the aftermath of Sadat's assassination, the adoption of stringent state policies toward the Islamists emerged in light of the mass
arrests. Of the approximately 500 Islamists arrested, twenty-four
individuals were charged with direct involvement in Sadat's assassination. This group comprised individuals who directly carried out the
assassination, who knew about it before it happened, and who directly assisted in setting up the operation. Five were executed, seventeen
were sentenced to life imprisonment with hard labor, and two were
found not guilty of the charges. The second group of suspects comprised 302 Islamists who were arrested in what came to be known as
the case of Al-Jihad al-Kobra, or Greater Jihad. These individuals
were charged with being leaders of an illegal organization "that
implemented the assassination, entering head of security offices in
Asyuit on the 8th of October 1981 and stealing gold from jewelry
shops."53 Of this group, 132 were found guilty and all received sentences of between ten years and life in prison. The third group of
arrests comprised 178 suspects who were charged with being members of an illegal organization. All suspects were arrested in October
1981 following Sadat's assassination and all had to serve their term
in addition to the two years awaiting trial.

An in-depth ideological platform stating Al-Jama's goals,
beliefs, and strategies did not exist until 1984, when a group of Al-
Jama' leaders serving life sentences in the aftermath of Sadat's assassination wrote *Mithaq al-'Amal al-Islami* (Conventions of Islamic
Action),54 a 231-page document in which Al-Jama's radical and violent tendencies were formally acknowledged. In addition to explaining the group's goals, creed, and its understanding of Islam, the document detailed its aim to establish "Islam as a totality in each soul . . .
and in each society,"55 to be accomplished on the conditions that people be "made to worship their Lord" and that "a *khalifa* [caliphate,
religious-political leadership] on the model of prophethood (*nabi-
wa*)" be established.56 The group's move toward violence was
reflected most prominently in the document's section on *tariq,* or
approach to achieving its goal. It consisted of two levels, a reaffirmed commitment to *al-Dawa,* which was the group's main strategy until the late 1970s, and an adoption of jihad (holy struggle).
Jihad was interpreted as a two-stage process that entailed "gentle
preaching, meeting 'bad deeds' with 'good deeds' to influence
reform in the path of Islam. If this does not succeed, *Jihad* then

requires the use of physical force."[57] The point is that Al-Jama's official ideological platform came to resemble that of its smaller, more militant partner, Al-Jihad. Hence, the concept of jihad and Qutb's writings became major influences on Al-Jama's ideological orientation. More important, Al-Jama' leaders produced the *Mithaq* after being sentenced to life imprisonment for being "leaders of an illegal organization" following the 1981 roundup, indicating that the harsh prison sentences reinforced their belief in the accurateness of Qutb's ideology and contributed to their public declaration of militant radicalism. Furthermore, the increasingly coercive nature of state polices toward the Islamists throughout the 1980s simply served to encourage these activists to put their imprisoned leaders' militant ideology into practice.

The Nature of State Policies

The early 1980s under Mubarak, despite the postassassination crackdowns, can be viewed as a tolerant period not only for secular political opponents, but also for the Islamist groups. As mentioned in the previous chapters, attempts to control wholesale opposition gains in legislative and syndicate elections were not overtly brutal. Instead, they focused on semicovert methods of containment such as the application of constraining participatory laws and disparate co-optation tactics. The use of blatantly coercive tactics by the state in that period was limited. The fact that "during the first four years of Mubarak's term there was hardly any [political] violence" can be interpreted as an outcome of such a policy.[58]

The virtual absence of state coercion against Islamist opponents during the first part of the 1980s can be attributed to the fact that Mubarak was in the process of consolidating his power base within the military, National Democratic Party (NDP), legislative, and executive realms. As a consequence, Mubarak presumably felt that the mass Islamist arrests following Sadat's assassination had removed the main threat to his new leadership, thus leaving him free to concentrate on the more important task of consolidating his personal power within the formal state apparatus. That state support for the Islamists had been withdrawn and a large number of their leaders had been imprisoned suggests that these illegal entities were no longer in the position to challenge the state. The regime's "looser political style and efficient and discreet use of repression" led Kepel to argue, in 1985, that this tactic had enabled the regime to rob "the Islamist movement of its role as a surrogate for all challenges to the political order."[59]

However, the Islamist challenge to the system reemerged. The Muslim Brotherhood had used the 1970s as a reconstruction period and by the 1980s had emerged as the main opposition force within parliament. The Brotherhood was represented with eight seats and thirty-eight seats in the 1984 and 1987 legislative elections respectively. While the Brotherhood overcame the legal restrictions imposed by the exclusionary party-list system through electoral alliances with legal parties in both elections, its unprecedented electoral gains in the 1980s reflected its superior promotional and organizational capabilities. This was reinforced because the Brotherhood also gained a foothold within the professional syndicate elections by the late 1980s. In regard to the group's rise within legislative and professional elections, emphasis of its participation and gains within the formal political arena during the 1980s worked for the communal favor of the Islamists in general. This is because all the Islamist groups had an informal alliance, since regardless of their disparate methods they pursued the same ultimate objective—the implementation of *sharia*. Consequently, the various groups "at either end of the Islamist spectrum chose not to vilify one another,"[60] leading the government to conclude by 1987 that it was "unable to exploit internal divisions within the Islamist movement."[61] This view is reinforced by a former Al-Jama' leader who notes, "The 1980s started as a great period for us. Islamists were popular, people respected us, the slogan *al-Islam howa al-hal* [Islam is the solution] was used by all of us, any gain by one group was a gain for all of us. Even in prison, we were treated as political prisoners—not as terrorists."[62] The same view is reinforced by other Islamists, such as Montasir al-Zayat:

> Many of us who were arrested after Sadat's assassination were released by October 1984. Mubarak gave some political space so we were participating visibly and legitimately in professional associations, student bodies and legislative elections. *Al-Islam Howa al-Hal* was a slogan used by all of us, not just the Muslim Brotherhood. We were very popular with the people and because the state was tolerant, we did not initiate any violence against the state between 1984 to 1987.[63]

The participation of the Brotherhood within the electoral arena was beneficial to the Islamist movement because it remained within the formal framework of Egyptian politics. As a consequence, this allowed the Brotherhood access to mainstream politicians and media outlets. It reinforced the organization's mainstream appeal on the grassroots level, while allowing it to continue its own established sociopolitical activities. Therefore, it is not surprising that the Brotherhood's confidence remained high as its call for *sharia* persisted.

Following the Brotherhood's 1984 electoral performance, the Islamists' demand for the implementation of *sharia* opened a cycle of debate and activism that peaked in June 1985, when the radically oriented shaikh Hafez Salama organized a march in Cairo. In a move indicating that the period of political tolerance was beginning to decline, the government not only refused to issue a permit for this demonstration but also took the precaution of sealing Al-Nor mosque, from which the demonstration was intended to commence. The security forces also detained more than 500 activists prior to the day of the march. A few weeks later the government replaced radical shaikhs such as Salama and Omar Abdel Rahman with "others appointed by the Ministry of Endowments."[64] The intention was to curtail their influence, as these radicals attracted popular followings especially in Cairo, Alexandria, Suez, Fayoum, and Upper Egypt.

The government's containment strategies gained further momentum between 1986 and 1987 partly as a reaction to the short-lived Central Security Force (CSF) riots in February 1986. While the riots were initiated by a group of CSF troops following a rumor that their period of conscription was to be extended, the Islamists aggravated the situation by using the disturbance to air their own grievances against the state. As Robert Springborg notes, the riots

> provided an opportunity for radical Islamists in the Giza area to vent their rage. . . . These activists torched numerous establishments that had been left unscathed by the soldiers and that had attracted the wrath of Islamists because they sold alcoholic beverages and/or catered to Western or Westernized clienteles. The riots also had a profound effect on Upper Egypt, not only because they seemed to inspire radical Islamists there, but because deserters from the CSF sold or gave their weapons away, most of which were acquired by gun-loving *Saidis* (Upper Egyptians), a significant percentage of whom were radical Islamists.[65]

The removal of Ahmed Rashdi as minister of interior as a consequence of the CSF incident, and his replacement by the former governor of Asyuit, Zaki Badr, in May 1986, indicated that a direct coercive stance toward the Islamists had been decided.

Rashdi was known to be an advocate of dialogue between the
state and the Islamists. In contrast, Badr rose to prominence because
of his intolerance of the Islamists in his Upper Egyptian governate
and the manner in which he cooperated with drug barons in the
region in his quest to fight them. This aspect remains an incomprehensible move to the Islamists. The fact that a senior state official
cooperated with drug barons against "religious" people like themselves only reinforced their views of the corrupt and religiously ignorant (*jahiliya*) nature of the political system. The promotion of such a
person to the position of minister of interior reaffirmed this belief,
especially in view of the swift changes in security tactics he implemented once in office.

The first indication of a change in national security policies was
detected five days after Badr assumed office in May 1986. In an
approach that was used again during the 2000 legislative election to
prevent voters from entering the polling stations, the security apparatus began sealing off popular mosques in Upper Egypt. This prevented people from congregating around the popular shaikhs who were
attempting to circumvent their earlier removals by appearing as guest
speakers outside their hometown bases.

The first such incident occurred at Al-Rahman mosque in
Aswan, were Shaikh Omar Abdel Rahman had been invited from his
Fayoum base to give a sermon. Because Abdel Rahman was the spiritual head of Al-Jama' and Jihad and a popular religious speaker in
his own right, the turnout was expected to reach several thousand.
However, when the inhabitants of Aswan and the surrounding villages arrived, they found themselves confronted with security forces
who had surrounded the mosque premises. The security forces were
equipped with rubber bullets and tear gas canisters, which were lib-
erally used to disperse the angry crowd. Apart from nonfatal casualties caused during the ensuing clashes, more than sixty people were
arrested, the first major Islamist group arrest since 1981. The arrests
would expand within a few days when the security forces began
applying the same tactics to other popular mosques in the region.

Al-Rahman mosque in Minya and Al-Jama' al-Sharqiya'
mosque[66] in Asyuit witnessed the same predicament, with approxi-

mately ninety and two hundred arrests respectively, and the number
of citizen arrests increased with every popular mosque and shaikh
the government attempted to isolate. These arrests induced serious
and politically oriented charges of "attacking the government"
(meaning the security forces). In reality, the majority of those arrested were not members of any Islamist organization, but were villagers
(albeit sympathetic to the Islamist cause) excited at the prospect of
hearing the sermon of popular guest shaikhs in their local mosques.

Their fury and subsequent clashes with the security forces cannot be regarded as politically planned or motivated, but rather as an
impulsive reaction to being denied entry into their respective
mosques. The fact that they were all eventually released without
charge after spending two months in detention strongly indicates that
they were not Islamist activists. The point, nevertheless, is that a
large number of civilians in Upper Egypt found themselves incorporated into the realm of "Islamist" activists by the state.

The escalation of security tactics against the Islamists was evident in July 1986, when the radical shaikhs were placed under house
arrest. The first was Shaikh Omar Abdel Rahman in Fayoum, followed by Shaikh Hafez Salama in Suez and Shaikh Ahmed Mihlawi
in Alexandria, among others. Ironically, while Shaikh Mihlawi maintained a popular following among the Islamists, he was known to
maintain a public and vocal anti-jihad stance. Nevertheless, as a radical shaikh with a mass following, his house arrest, like those of
Abdel Rahman and Salama, was based on the rational view that iso-
lating him was the most effective option for avoiding clashes with
the public.

The state did not consider these concerns when it entered its
most brutal and irrational confrontation with the Islamists in summer
1987. During this period, particularly between the months of May
and June, a massive operation of wholesale Islamist arrests was carried out, resulting in approximately 3,000 people detained.[67] This
move was justified by the security forces as a response to several
assassination attempts by Islamists in early May. Apart from the
sheer number of those arrested, this move was significant for several
other reasons, among them the fact that the mass arrests were preceded in April by the Brotherhood's impressive gain of thirty-eight seats
in the parliamentary elections. This is significant because it meant
that the group had received 9 percent of the vote or, as one author
points out, "more than half a million votes, despite the heavy-handed

methods of the Ministry of Interior, which supervised the election."[68] The Brotherhood's 1987 electoral gains were also significant because on the eve of election day approximately 2,000 Brotherhood members and supporters were arrested in what was clearly an effort aimed at curtailing their gains.[69] What this suggests is that, characteristic of authoritarian rule, the government had entered a stage of panic as it began to feel the Islamist threat on several levels. The Islamists had won the largest proportion of opposition seats in parliament, the radical shaikhs were more popular and harder to contain than expected, and to add further insecurity, the Islamists were also gaining ground on other levels of electoral competition. As Joshua Stacher notes, the Islamists during the 1980s were "increasing their ranks among national professional associations such as the Councils of Administration in Clubs of University Professors in Cairo, Alexandria, and Asyuit. Additionally, student unions in the national universities were being re-controlled by young Islamists."[70] To add to governmental anxiety, the Brotherhood acquired its first professional syndicate gains in 1984, when it won seven of twenty-five Doctors Syndicate council seats, and gained nearly absolute control of the Engineers Syndicate by acquiring fifty-four of sixty-three council seats by 1987.

While the government responded to such threats with the implementation of laws that constricted Islamist gains within the formal electoral arena, it is not erroneous to argue that the mass arrests witnessed in summer 1987 were a reactive impulse based on the government's growing anxiety. Through the arrests of thousands of people, the government assumed that wholesale repression would solve the matter once and for all. Such a coercive and ultimately unsuccessful strategy highlights the insecurity and fragility of an authoritarian system of rule. Furthermore, this careless approach only served to expand the framework of confrontation from the political context to also include personally motivated violent retaliations against the state.

One reason for the emergence of violence is that a large number of those arrested were not necessarily Islamist activists but were assumed to be guilty by the state because they had "Islamist" tendencies, such as donning a beard and attending sermons and prayers at mosques considered by the state to be Islamist-controlled. In addition, the mass arrests included the indiscriminate roundup of family members, friends, and neighbors of Islamist activists. In an unprecedented move beginning in late 1986, roundups of female family members became common, a particularly significant event for understanding the emergence of personally motivated violence against the state. As one Islamist lawyer explains:

> The shock of being arrested was nothing for most men in comparison to the humiliation they felt when their women were arrested by the police and humiliated in public view. When police officer Ahmed Ala' was murdered in the late eighties in Fayoum, his killers were caught and brought to trial. They did not deny the fact that they killed him even though they knew they would be executed for this crime. They were protecting their honor and one of them admitted it in court and said "I killed him because he came and arrested my wife and dragged her into the street in her night-clothes in front of all the men to see. I did it to defend my honor [*sharaf*]."[71]

The death of police officer Mohammed Mahran in late 1986 in Asyuit was one of the first murders to have been motivated on such revenge for the mistreatment and humiliation of women family members at the hands of the security personnel. According to several Islamist sources, many subsequent acts of violence against the security forces in the post-1987 period emerged from personal rather than political motivations.[72] This issue is also touched upon in the wider context of a vendetta. In the words of one author:

> The violent campaign of the Islamists against the government, particularly in Upper Egypt, is intertwined with the common practice of vendetta [*tar*]. For example, if an Islamist from Asyuit is killed by the security forces, the whole family or village seeks vengeance from the family of the individual who killed him or ordered his killing, irrespective of the political context of the incident.[73]

In this context, the mass arrests by security forces in 1987 instigated an increase in violent confrontations between the state and Islamists. More important though, in its wholesale and careless approach the state also alienated and infuriated many others caught in the middle of this sphere.

The post-1987 confrontations soon gained another dimension. Not content with the arrest, imprisonment, and torture of the Islamist activists and their supporters and family members, the security apparatus adopted the use of forced exile and extrajudicial killings. For example, whereas Shaikh Omar Abdel Rahman was initially placed under house arrest, in 1989 he was then forced into exile. According to one eyewitness:

> While Shaikh Omar was under house arrest in 1989, he asked if he
> could be allowed to go to do Umra' (a lesser form of pilgrimage
> than Hajj). On the last day of Ramadan, he was given permission
> and we took him to Cairo airport to catch his plane to Saudi
> Arabia. When we arrived at the airport, we discovered he was
> among the list of banned travelers to Saudi. We did not really know
> what to do . . . the state security people who had accompanied us to
> the airport made it clear that we could not take him back home.
> They told him that he must leave the "country one way or another."
> We therefore spent the entire day running around the airport trying
> to inquire where he can go. . . . Sudan was the only country that did
> not require a visa prior to the purchase of a ticket, so we bought
> him a ticket at the airport. . . . [T]hat was his last day in Egypt.[74]

The decision to force Shaikh Omar into exile may have seemed a discreet option for the security forces at that point. After all, his blind-
ness and the fact that he was an Al-Azhar-educated cleric gave him
vulnerability and a legitimate religious authority that distorted his
radical orientation. Thus, forcing him into exile was a tactic intended
to permanently remove him from the scene without turning him into
a "martyr" in the process. Such considerations were not taken into
account when a "secular" Islamist leader was targeted for assassination less than a year later.

Ala' Mohiydin, a medical doctor from Asyuit and spokesman for
Al-Jama', was assassinated on 2 August 1990 when four security
personnel dressed in civilian clothes approached him on a Cairo
street, shot him, and then escaped in a waiting car. Mohiydin's assassination became still another turning point in the escalation of politically motivated violence by Islamists against the state, as the state's
adoption of extrajudicial killings in turn became an alternative means
of escalating its conflict with the Islamists. Al-Jama' tried to justify
the assassination of the former speaker of parliament, Rifa't al-
Mahgob, in October 1990 as a direct retaliation for Mohiydin's
assassination—even though al-Mahgob was not originally the intended target.[75]

The fact that the Islamists were retaliating in kind not only took
the government by surprise, but increased its insecurity and paranoia.
As a consequence, the more it perceived the Islamists as a threat to
stability, the harsher it applied its coercive apparatus to society in its
pursuit of Islamist targets. Indicative of this were the government's

attacks on villages and working-class areas including Imbaba in Cairo and Dayrot and Sanabo in Asyuit governate between 1991 and 1995, targets considered to be Islamist breeding grounds. In what can be regarded as combined police and military operations, one observer notes, "Homes, mosques, and entire villages were raided and there was a massive wave of arrests; at least forty-five people died during the raids. It was almost as if anyone who had a beard and lived in the alleys of the 'popular' neighborhoods were being rounded up."[76]

In an effort to legally justify the coercive tactics of the security apparatus, the state implemented amendments to the penal code and the law on state security courts via Law 97 in July 1992. Not only did such amendments expand application of the death penalty, but equally important they expanded the definition of terrorism so as to incorporate "spreading panic" and "obstructing the work of authorities."[77] Having expanded the nature of "terrorist" crimes punishable under the penal code, the government was now in the dual position of being able to brand virtually anyone it deemed fit as a "terrorist" and hence "legally" bring such individuals to trial before military tribunals. This strategy was made possible due to a 1966 military judiciary law regarding states of emergency, according to which "the President of the Republic has the right to refer to the military judiciary any crime punishable under the Penal Code or under any other law."[78] In a 1993 ruling the Supreme Constitutional Court (SCC) reaffirmed the president's right to refer any crime to a military tribunal. This, in turn, sealed the fate of hundreds of civilian defendants, who under military trial were deprived not only of independent civilian judges, but also of any right to appeal the verdicts handed down by career-trained officers appointed by the minister of defense.

The more repressive the measures implemented by the state, the more the spiral of violence escalated, as Islamists continued to direct (and retaliate with) numerous acts of violence against the regime and anything they perceived to be associated with it. Such acts have included the assassination of state officials and public figures, the bombing of the Egyptian embassy in Pakistan, violent attacks on tourists and Egyptian civilians, as well as numerous assassination attempts against President Mubarak.[79] The politically (and personally) motivated violence that ensued between Islamists and the state during this period not only culminated in the 1997 Luxor massacre but also resulted in 1,300 fatal casualties between 1990 and 1997.[80]

In 2001 the number of Islamist political prisoners was estimated at 15,000–20,000.[81]

On one level, the Islamists viewed their increasingly violent outbursts as their "defense against state violence."[82] Yet as Dan Tschirgi notes, by 1997 Al-Jama' leadership came to terms with the fact that in regard to violence "a change of strategy [was] in order."[83] Tschirgi explains that this shift took place not because of its fear of state repression but because "available evidence—particularly the *Gama'a's* apparent soul searching after the Luxor massacre—indicates the group's methods, if not its objectives, became progressively more repugnant to the Egyptian public."[84] This view is reinforced by a former Al-Jama' member:

> The Al-Jama' leaders have been revising the organization's ideology even before the 1997 Luxor massacre. . . . [T]hey had revised their previous interpretation of Islam in order to prevent damage to society and the killing of innocent people. Initially, the fight was between the Islamists and the state, but the society who we were meant to be protecting and defending got hurt instead. . . . Islam says that if the rulers are not ruling according to *sharia* then they are illegitimate and it is the duty of Muslims to remove them. However, in reality if it is impossible to remove them or fight them because they are too strong and in the process your family and your community will be harmed, then Allah forgives you for it is not in your power to remove them.[85]

As the comments indicate, the underlying conflict between the Islamists and the Egyptian state has not been resolved and the political system continues to be perceived as an illegitimate entity.

The Islamists, in the form of Al-Jama', came to realize that the state's blatant use of aggression in its efforts to control and contain them had inadvertently baited them into retaliation, and that they had started an armed struggle that they could not win. Equally important, in the process they saw themselves being marginalized from the sphere of political activity and being pushed into the category of terrorists.

It has since emerged that the renouncing of violence by Al-Jama' was analyzed and explained in a four-volume book that was apparently written in July 1997 prior to the Luxor massacre, but did not reach the bookshelves until January 2002. The book, *Taslit al-Dawa,* was written by eight imprisoned Al-Jama' leaders, only one of whom, Hamdi Abdel Rahman, has been released. Apart from declar-

ing an end to armed confrontation, the book explains why Al-Jama'
leaders were wrong in their original interpretation of what constitutes
jihad and why they conceded that violence directed at Copts, tourists,
and even the security forces was neither justifiable nor indeed religiously legitimate (*halal*). Abdel Rahman has questioned publicly
why it took five years for the book to be published. In his view, "If
these publications were made public in time, it would have prevented
the Luxor massacre."[86]

One plausible reason for the delay in publication is that the government misinterpreted the Al-Jama' leaders' call for a retreat from
violence as a sign of its defeat. Hence the government's announcement that there would be no concessions on its part since it would
"not talk to terrorists."[87] Rather than return the gesture by showing
leniency toward many of the Islamist prisoners languishing in prison,
the government discredited the Al-Jama' leaders in the eyes of their
followers and the "other members of leadership living abroad who
were either noncommittal or downright hostile to the steps taken by
their imprisoned colleagues."[88] More important, the government's
contempt toward the Al-Jama' leaders provided a group of junior Al-
Jama' members with an irrational sense of justification to retaliate
with further bloodshed. As one Islamist argues, "The 1997 Luxor
massacre was not authorized by Al-Jama' leadership. It was planned
and carried out by an independent group of its young members. They
wanted to prove that the call for a truce was not because the organization was broken as the government claimed and that it still had the
capabilities to resume violent confrontations."[89]

The most positive aspect to emerge out of the Luxor debacle was
that the Al-Jama' leadership abroad united with their imprisoned
counterparts to formally declare a cease-fire in March 1999. But on
some levels the cease-fire declaration was interpreted as a progovernment concession:

> Al-Jama' leaders at home and abroad in effect conceded defeat by
> declaring a unilateral suspension of armed action. . . . This unilat-
> eral declaration of a cease-fire represented . . . an acknowledge-
> ment of the dismal failure of its armed insurrection. . . . Al-Jama'
> appeared to have dug its own grave, and its belated attempt to proj-
> ect a human face by declaring a unilateral cease-fire was a sign of
> weakness, not strength.[90]

This narrow interpretation overlooks the fact that, for certain groups in society, Al-Jama' did have a human face, otherwise it would not have emerged as a popular force—a force that produced sufficient anxiety for the government to unleash its coercive apparatus with full might. By retaliating in kind with the state, Al-Jama' lost its human face, because as one former Al-Jama' member notes, "It became difficult to function as a normal and civil organization when you are at the mercy of *amn al-dawla* [state security]."[91] A former Jihad member is more direct in his interpretation of the cycle of violence: "The state dug a hole of violence for the Islamist youth and then threw them in it. Don't forget these [Islamists] were all young people who thought nothing of returning the fire. Also, the pressure on us was so intense from the state that retaliation overrode common sense."[92]

While politically motivated violence is difficult to justify, it is not an uncommon phenomenon. One of Samuel Huntington's early observations was that the emergence of a new group in society also entails new demands, such as finding "avenues of access to the political leaders and the means of participation in the political system."[93] The absence or blockage of such avenues, as he argued, leads a group to feel frustrated and alienated.[94] Moreover, if these patterns continue for an indefinite period of time, it is not incomprehensible that the group in question may attempt "to enforce its demands on the system through violence, force, or other means illegitimate to the system."[95] In this context, the Islamists in Egypt have not been an exceptional case, especially when the state's attempts to block the avenues of participation shifted toward repressive and coercive means. What is problematic is that while the heavy-handed tactics of the state may have eventually led it to gain the upper hand in its confrontation with the Islamists on the national level, they contributed toward shifting the conflict into the international arena.

The International Arena

In 1981, *Al-Dawa,* the Muslim Brotherhood's mouthpiece, printed the following editorial:

> The United States is the leader of the international crusade and neo-colonialism. The Muslim world in general and the Arab region in particular are considered prime targets for American designs because of their energy resources, strategic location, and tremendous markets. The United States would not permit competition

from any rival in its quest to monopolize the pillage of Islamic wealth. . . . The United States implements its schemes through both its own CIA and the client Muslim rulers who sold out their religion, country, nation and honor. The price for selling out is for these client rulers to stay in the seat of power.[96]

Twenty years later, on 11 September 2001, the United States witnessed four connected terrorist attacks that resulted in the destruction of the World Trade Center and part of the Pentagon. While the economic toll has been enormous, it is the human toll of nearly 3,200 deaths that has made these the deadliest terrorist attacks ever witnessed by the world. U.S. intelligence networks, in cooperation with their international counterparts, identified Saudi dissident Osama bin Laden and his Al-Qaida network as being responsible for these attacks. It was not the first time Washington had accused bin Laden of attacking the United States and its interests. The August 1998 bombings of the U.S. embassies in Kenya and Tanzania are also believed to have been masterminded by bin Laden, who incidentally had declared an "Islamic international front to fight Jews and crusaders" in February that year.[97] This apparent "front" was founded on the militant ideology that "to kill Americans and their allies, both civil and military, is an individual duty of every Muslim."[98] Of particular significance here is that such a call generated support from disparate Islamists including, most notably, exiled members of the Egyptian Islamist groups Al-Jihad and Al-Jama'. Indeed, reports shows that "Egyptian activists . . . perished when US long range missiles destroyed bin Laden's headquarters in Afghanistan"[99] in the 1998 retaliation strikes for the embassy bombings. This indicates that links with bin Laden and Egyptian militants existed long before the 11 September 2001 attacks.

The assumption that bin Laden's Al-Qaida network was formally allied with Egypt's Al-Jihad, at the least, was publicly confirmed in early October 2001 in a videotaped statement aired before the commencement of U.S. air strikes against Afghanistan. This videotape gave some insight into the extent of Egyptian Islamist involvement with bin Laden. As one report noted, rather than being bin Laden's deputy, Ayman al-Zawahiri appeared to be "bin Laden's equal" on the video.[100] This speculation was reinforced when "al-Zawahiri . . . spoke before bin Laden and at some length. . . . [T]he protocol and body language confirmed what [terrorist experts] had long suspected:

that the two men shared command of their merged organizations."[101]
The FBI's subsequently released a list of the twenty-two most wanted terrorists showing six to be of Egyptian origin, making Egyptians
the largest nationality represented therein.

The emergence of a strong militant Egyptian connection on the
international front is not wholly surprising. As the editorial in *Al-
Dawa* indicated, the United States has long been perceived by the
Islamists not only to be a neocolonial power exerting domination
over the Muslim *ummah* (nation), but also the patron of the repressive and corrupt regimes that exist.

It is interesting to note that the 1993 bomb explosion at the
World Trade Center was found to have been linked to Egyptian militants, including Al-Jama's Shaikh Omar Abdel Rahman. Abdel
Rahman's arrest and conviction in the United States for being the
"spiritual" leader of the four men who carried out the attack has sub-
sequently led President Mubarak to claim that he had warned the
United States not to grant the blind shaikh a visa. As the president
commented in an interview, "When [the U.S. government] asked me,
I told them, 'No, you're going to pay a heavy price. You [Americans]
kept him and he bombed the World Trade Center in '93.'"[102] Indeed,
Abdel Rahman did manage to obtain a U.S. visa from his base in
Sudan in 1990, but it was Egypt's security apparatus that had thrust
Abdel Rahman into the international arena through his forced exile.
Regardless of the president's warning, the fact that Abdel Rahman
was expelled from Egypt in the first place meant it was only a matter
of time before the international arena was exposed to the consequences of the radical shaikh's extremist ideology.

Ayman al-Zawahiri's rise to the international stage of terrorism
can also be interpreted as a direct consequence of the Egyptian state's
policies toward the Islamists. Al-Zawahiri, like many imprisoned
Islamists, fled Egypt in 1984 following his release from prison to
escape the increasingly repressive tactics of the state. He experienced
such tactics following Sadat's assassination when he was arrested
along with other radical activists in the "Greater Jihad" case. As with
Abdel Rahman, al-Zawahiri's case was dismissed, but he was convicted of carrying a weapon and remained in prison until 1984. According
to a former friend, during his time in prison al-Zawahiri was severely
tortured—an aspect that in itself is not unique. However, the severity
of the torture was particularly significant in that it was intended to
force him to testify against his comrades—especially his officer

friend Essam al-Kamari, who was subsequently executed after al-Zawahiri's testimony and a military tribunal.[103]

The point is that this experience caused great guilt and distress to al-Zawahiri and undoubtedly amplified his hatred toward the system and his determination to destroy it. Indicative of this, al-Zawahiri's main focus during his time in Saudi Arabia, Sudan, and Afghanistan remained the fall of the Egyptian political system. When in April 1996 Shaikh Khalid Ibrahim, the head of Al-Jama' in Aswan, called for a one-year cease-fire, al-Zawahiri was one of the most vocal opponents to this idea. Al-Zawahiri labeled Ibrahim's call a manufactured "media bang" and presented a declaration on 20 May 1996 in which he stated that Ibrahim and his supporters should "fear God" and not "give the Egyptian system the opportunity to win time [by holding] back the Egyptian youth."[104] It is also worth noting that al-Zawahiri's decision to support bin Laden's call for an "Islamic international front to fight Jews and crusaders" in February 1998 and his group's role in the August 1998 U.S. embassy bombings occurred less than a year after the 1997 Luxor massacre, during a period when the Al-Jama' leaders in Egypt were publicly reassessing their violent strategies. Thus, while the majority of radicalized Islamists in Egypt were reassessing their interpretation of jihad and use of violence, al-Zawahiri and his fellow Islamists in exile chose to distance themselves and joined forces with bin Laden and his Al-Qaida network. Having fled from Egypt with bitter experiences and emotions toward a system that increased their diaspora throughout the world, they found bin Laden's radically violent outlook appealing in comparison to the adjustments of their Egyptian-based counterparts. In this regard, by joining forces with bin Laden, al-Zawahiri and his fellow Egyptian Islamists abroad may have shifted their focus toward attacking the United States, but in principle the Egyptian state remained the underlying enemy. As one Islamist points out:

> Their participation in attacks on the United States is no more than an ideological revision. Shifting the confrontation to the United States is a strategy which they see as refocusing to the roots of the problems back home because not only is America helping Israel and hurting the Palestinian and Iraqi people, more importantly it is the force that is responsible for protecting our brutal dictators.[105]

According to Montasir al-Zayat, a former friend of al-Zawahiri, the failure of the armed operations that were carried out against the

Egyptian state and the organizational problems that emerged as a consequence of the mass arrests weakened the Islamist capabilities inside Egypt. Such factors were thus taken into consideration when forming the alliance with bin Laden. In other words, this shift in strategy and the alliance were born out of practical considerations as opposed to a change in perception toward the Egyptian political system.[106]

The arrest of Islamists abroad and their extradition to Egypt, including one of al-Zawahiri's aides, Ahmed Salama Mabrok, combined with Al-Jama's declaration of a unilateral cease-fire, meant that in order for al-Zawahiri and his followers to continue their anti-regime activities, the alliance with bin Laden became a viable option. The main difference was that in this alliance, bin Laden had managed to convince al-Zawahiri to cease the armed attacks against Egypt in order to focus on the bigger picture, namely the United States and Israel. As al-Zayat notes, this shift in strategy was not "in harmony with [al-Zawahiri's] style and . . . his original belief of finalizing the conflict with the Egyptian authorities."[107] However, he agreed to this change in focus not only out of practical considerations, but also because by attacking the United States he could show that "he was standing up against American aggression and by this win the sympathy of the Arabs and Muslims which he had lost with the failure of earlier operations."[108] For al-Zawahiri and his Egyptian collaborators abroad, the United States is to a large degree perceived as an alternate avenue to the same end—the fall of the Egyptian government.

It would of course be erroneous to hold the Egyptian state solely responsible for the emergence of Islamic militancy in Egypt and its expansion into the international arena. Nevertheless, the repressive tactics of the Egyptian state over the decades are a significant contributing factor to the manifestation of terrorism against the regime and, ultimately, the U.S. patron state. The inability of the Egyptian system to regulate political dissent in a civil and orderly manner means that when faced with a threat that is potentially capable of challenging the political status quo, it resorts to repression as the primary solution to the problem. As a consequence, what initially emerged as a series of spontaneous retaliations against the Egyptian system developed into a national and international conflict.

Conclusion

Political Islamist activism in contemporary Egypt illustrates the dynamics and consequences that arise when certain social forces emerge and are legally and coercively excluded from the formally defined political order. Equally important, political Islamism was encouraged to flourish by the ruling elite for their own political purposes—whether to counteract an external power, or an internal threat such as the leftists and Nasserists. While the existence of ideological and political disillusionment, poverty, unemployment, alienation, and other socioeconomic factors have heightened the appeal and popularity of political Islamism at the grassroots level, the role of the state in allowing it to breed to suit its own particular objectives cannot be overlooked. Furthermore, in its militant form, political Islamism did not emerge and expand in a vacuum; rather, the state's coercive and ineffective strategies of containment bear much responsibility.

While such strategies allow for the preservation of personal authoritarianism, their effects both domestically and internationally are evident. The concluding chapter examines the long-term prospects of political development in such an environment and their consequences for Western systems.

Notes

1. Anderson, "State Policy and Islamist Radicalism," pp. 18–19.
2. Ibid., p. 19.
3. Zubaida, *Islam, the People, and the State*, p. 48.
4. Ibid., p. 45.
5. Ibid., p. 46.
6. Ibid., p. 47.
7. Kramer, "The Integration of the Integrists," p. 211.
8. Zubaida, *Islam, the People, and the State*, p. 47.
9. Mitchell, *The Society of the Muslim Brothers*, p. 9.
10. Kramer, "The Integration of the Integrists," p. 211.
11. Ibid.
12. Mitchell, *The Society of the Muslim Brothers*, p. 58. It is worth noting here that Muslim Brotherhood forces fighting in Palestine, upon being informed of the decree, decided to continue fighting under the banner of the Egyptian army rather than accept the offer by the authorities of laying down their arms and returning to Cairo.
13. Mitchell, *The Society of the Muslim Brothers*, p. 75.
14. Vatikiotis, *The History of Modern Egypt*, pp. 319–320.
15. Ibid., p. 320.
16. Heikal, *Autumn of Fury*, p. 124.
17. Ibid., p. 124.
18. Zubaida, *Islam, the People, and the State*, p. 47.
19. Mitchell, *The Society of the Muslim Brothers*, p. 84.

20. Ibid., p. 108.

21. Kepel, *Muslim Extremism in Egypt,* p. 26.

22. Mitchell, *The Society of the Muslim Brothers,* p. 151.

23. Binder, *Islamic Liberalism,* p. 340.

24. Of the fifteen years, Qutb served ten.

25. Moussalli, *Moderate and Radical Islamic Fundamentalism,* p. 96.

26. Ibid., p. 98.

27. Kepel, *Muslim Extremism in Egypt,* p. 28.

28. Ibid., p. 46.

29. Ibid.

30. Ibid., pp. 46–47.

31. Sullivan and Abed-Kotob, *Islam in Contemporary Egypt,* p. 43.

32. Ibid., p. 57.

33. Binder, *Islamic Liberalism,* p. 341.

34. Ayubi, *Political Islam,* p. 75.

35. Binder, *Islamic Liberalism,* p. 341.

36. Sullivan and Abed-Kotob, *Islam in Contemporary Egypt,* p. 44.

37. Ibid.

38. Kamal al-Said Habib, former Al-Jama' al-Islamiya activist, interview by author, 19 February 2002, Cairo.

39. Sullivan and Abed-Kotob, *Islam in Contemporary Egypt,* p. 44.

40. Ibid.

41. Gamal Sultan, editor-in-chief of *Al-Manar al-Jadid* and former Al-Jama' al-Islamiya member, interview by author, 16 February 2002, Cairo.

42. Cited from Sullivan and Abed-Kotob, *Islam in Contemporary Egypt,* p. 73.

43. Heikal, *Autumn of Fury,* pp. 133–134.

44. Ibid., p. 74.

45. Kepel, *Muslim Extremism in Egypt,* p. 149.

46. Heikal, *Autumn of Fury,* p. 44.

47. Ibid., p. 46.

48. Kepel, *Muslim Extremism in Egypt,* p. 210.

49. Ibid., p. 213.

50. Gerges, "The End of Islamist Insurgency in Egypt?" p. 593.

51. Ibrahim, *Egypt, Islam, and Democracy,* p. 72.

52. The Egyptian Organization for Human Rights (EOHR) provides figures indicating that the number of political prisoners in Egypt has been growing at an alarming rate. In 1990, for example, the number of political detainees was approximately 5,000. By early 1998, the EOHR estimated that this number had expanded to 15,000–20,000 detainees, the majority of whom have disparate Islamist orientations.

53. al-Zayat, *Ayman al-Zawahiri.*

54. The authors were Najih Ibrahim, 'Asim Abd al-Majid, and 'Isam al-Din Dirbala, under the supervision of Shaikh Omar Abdel Rahman, who was also among the group rounded up in the postassassination period and was not released until 1984.

55. Cited from Sullivan and Abed-Kotob, *Islam in Contemporary*

Egypt, p. 84.

56. Ibid.

57. Ibid., p. 85.

58. Ibrahim, *Islam, Democracy, and Egypt,* p. 72.

59. Kepel, *Muslim Extremism in Egypt,* p. 257.

60. Springborg, *Mubarak's Egypt,* p. 184.

61. Ibid.

62. Habib interview, 19 February 2002.

63. Montasir al-Zayat, Al-Jama' al-Islamiya lawyer and Islamist, interview by author, 16 February 2002, Cairo.

64. Springborg, *Mubarak's Egypt,* p. 216.

65. Ibid., p. 217.

66. Al-Jama' al-Sharqiya mosque in Asyuit witnessed the first fatality when the police shot and killed a medical school student, Shaban Rashid, while he was putting up posters around the mosque premises. He was publicizing the imminent arrival of a guest shaikh who was due to give a sermon at the mosque. Indeed, Rashid's death did not produce a wide-scale counterattack by the villagers toward the security forces, which is linked to the government swiftly authorizing a private plane to take the victim from Asyuit to the Maadi military hospital in Cairo. This conciliatory move contributed to the prevention of further bloodshed during that period. Nevertheless, the number of citizen arrests increased with every popular mosque and shaikh the government attempted to isolate.

67. Springborg, *Mubarak's Egypt,* p. 239. This estimation is also confirmed by various Islamists I interviewed in 2002 in Cairo.

68. el-Sayed, "The Islamic Movement in Egypt," p. 228.

69. Kienle, *A Grand Delusion,* p. 27.

70. Stacher, "Moderate Political Islamism," p. 33.

71. al-Zayat interview, 16 February 2002.

72. Author interviews various Islamists, 2002, Cairo.

73. Azzam, "Egypt," pp. 113–114.

74. al-Zayat interview, 16 February 2002.

75. The intended target was actually the minister of interior, Abdel Halim Mosa, but when al-Mahgob turned up at the Semiramis Hotel, where Mosa was expected to arrive, the assassins in their panic and haste mistook al-Mahgob for Badr, given the former's security and entourage, and shot him instead.

76. Weaver, *A Portrait of Egypt,* p. 155.

77. U.S. Department of State, "1999 Country Reports on Human Rights Practices: Egypt."

78. *Military Courts in Egypt.*

79. There have been thirty-three alleged assassination attempts. See Fisk, "Egypt Caught Between Islam and the West."

80. Gerges, "The End of Islamist Insurgency in Egypt?" p. 592.

81. U.S. Department of State, "Egypt Country Report on Human Rights Practices, 2001."

82. al-Zayat interview, 16 February 2002.

83. Tschirgi, "Marginalized Violent Internal Conflict in the Age of

Globalization," p. 29.

84. Ibid.

85. Habib interview, 19 February 2002.

86. *Al-Wafd* (21 February 2002).

87. Rouleau, "Egypt's Islamists Caught in a Bind."

88. Ibid.

89. al-Zayat interview, 16 February 2002.

90. Gerges, "The End of Islamist Insurgency in Egypt?" p. 595.

91. Habib interview, 19 February 2002.

92. Mamdoh Ismail, lawyer and former Jihad member, interview by author, 26 February 2002, Cairo.

93. Huntington, *Political Order in Changing Societies,* p. 276.

94. Ibid.

95. Ibid..

96. *Al-Dawa* (May 1981), p. 61, cited in Ibrahim, *Islam, Democracy, and Egypt,* p. 45.

97. Gerges, "The End of Islamist Insurgency in Egypt?" p. 597.

98. Ibid.

99. Ibid.

100. Borger, "More Than a Deputy."

101. Ibid.

102. "Q&A."

103. al-Zayat interview, 16 February 2002.

104. Ibid. Also see al-Zayat, *Ayman al-Zawahiri.*

105. Habib interview, 19 February 2002.

106. al-Zayat interview, 16 February 2002.

107. al-Zayat, *Ayman al-Zawahiri.*

108. Ibid.

6

Conclusion: Rethinking Authoritarianism

As the case of contemporary Egypt illustrates, the adoption of a formal "democratic" framework does not necessarily imply a change in the fundamental nature of authoritarian rule. In fact, personalized authoritarian rule can prove to be so overtly flexible and resilient that it can function over a long period of time, with successive rulers, and under the guise of various political structures and policies. For example, on the surface, the seemingly Western-oriented multiparty arena under Mubarak drastically differs from the socialist-oriented single-party system of governance under Nasser. Yet closer analysis reflects the existence of more similarities than differences in regard to patterns of rule and the formal structures of governance. From Nasser to Mubarak, the use of a legal-constitutional framework to curtail the influence and powers of institutions, groupings, and individuals, the distribution of state patronage to create a dependent clientelist network, the presence of electoral malpractice, and the use of state coercion to control perceived challengers all point to this trend. The position of the president as the ultimate source of power and authority remains intact. On this basis, it can be concluded that personal authoritarian rule in contemporary Egypt has become institutionalized.

Institutionalizing Personal Authoritarian Rule in Egypt

The establishment and survival of personal authoritarian rule is inherently dependent upon the absence of autonomous political institutions and groupings that can challenge a ruler's personal monopoly on power. In turn, the institutionalization of personal authoritarian rule occurs when the powers of office established by the ruler survive him and his "successors find it politically advantageous to . . . maintain [them] intact."[1] To preserve such a position means the successor must maintain the unequal balance of power. In other words, the institutionalization of personal authoritarian rule entails the maintenance of a weak political system that is never fully institutionalized in comparison to the ruler's own position. It is this aspect that places the ruler above all other political institutions and groupings and allows him to direct the policies of the state and formulate the structure of governance so that he is unhindered by formal constraints.

In the case of contemporary Egypt, the weakness of the political system in comparison to the institutionalized domination of the presidency is evident on several levels. On one level is the unequal balance of power between the formal branches of government. In regard to the executive office, the clientelist network and dependency that are derived from the president's power to appoint and dismiss ministers have rendered them little more than loyal bureaucrats subservient to their leader's personal will. In addition, presidential domination over the legislature has rendered it little more than a "rubber stamp" to formalize the policies of the president. While the judiciary appears somewhat autonomous from presidential domination, closer analysis indicates that this is not necessarily the case. The 1969 "massacre of judges" illustrated presidential power taken to the extreme as Nasser dismissed hundreds of judges who refused to abide by his decree to join the Arab Socialist Union (ASU). More common, however, are the tactics of ignoring court rulings and referring civilians to military courts via presidential decree. Such factors demonstrate the limitations imposed on the judiciary's autonomy and role by the president.

While the coercive apparatus of the state constitutes the backbone of any authoritarian system of rule, it should not be misinterpreted as an entity that is independent of presidential domination. The president's powers of appointment at the highest level within both the military and the police, combined with the extensive patronage bestowed upon officers, have resulted in a clientelist structure in which the president remains the ultimate patron. This clientelist structure makes it almost impossible for a coup to occur. For example, even though the minister of interior and the minister of defense were part of the group who attempted to purge Sadat during his first six months in power, they failed to achieve their objectives and instead were arrested. The clientelist structure and "its Byzantine complexity . . . would have made a well-timed, carefully coordinated strike difficult and security leaks inevitable."[2] The same argument can be extended to the relationship between Mubarak and Abd al-Halim Abu Ghazala, who was Mubarak's first minister of defense. Abu Ghazala, at the time, was considered to be more popular and powerful within the armed forces than the new president. In fact, because "the mechanism of balanced rivalry is seen in perhaps its most critical manifestation in the armed forces . . . [as] different military leaders and different military bodies [exist] in constant tension with one another and [serve] as watchdogs of one another,"[3] the armed forces remain as subservient to the Egyptian president as the formal branches of government.

The absence of organizational autonomy is also evident within the arena of political contest. The combination of repression and co-optation has weakened political parties, including the president's own party, to the point that they are unable to recruit mass followings. Consequently, electoral participation remains oriented toward parochial, individualistic, and patronage-based methods of cultivating voter support. Such a weak multiparty arena ensures that the president's position and authority as the ultimate source of power will not be challenged. It is this strategy of containment and control that prevents the legalized political parties from marginalizing the Muslim Brotherhood's electoral threats without the government's heavy-handed interference. The rise of the Islamists in civil society is also linked to the heavy restrictions imposed by the government on the public sphere. It is a pattern that has extended throughout the Middle East for similar reasons. In the words of one analyst:

> As the regimes of the Middle East grew more distant and oppressive and hollow in the decades following Nasser, fundamentalism's appeal grew. The Muslim Brotherhood and organizations like it tried to give people a sense of meaning and purpose in a changing world, something no leader in the Middle East tried to do. . . . On that score, Islam had little competition. The Arab world is a political desert with no real political parties, no free press, few pathways for dissent. . . . From the

> Muslim Brotherhood to Hamas to Hezbollah, they actively provide
> social services, medical assistance, counseling and temporary housing.
> For those who treasure civil society, it is disturbing to see that in the
> Middle East these illiberal groups *are* civil society.[4]

As in the case of political parties, attempts to counteract this Islamist
reemergence have not loosened the restrictions imposed on the formal public sphere, but narrowed them even further. As a consequence, restrictions on the public sphere from the late 1990s onward
have reached an unprecedented level in the Mubarak era.

Reasserting Restrictions

It is a widely accepted view that "a ruler who must assert and
reassert himself presents at least circumstantial evidence that his personal domination is flagging."[5] When this reassertion is reflected in
the form of increased attacks on groups and individuals within the
public sphere, it reinforces this assumption or at least indicates that
the regime is interpreting this assumption to be valid. This is what is
happening in contemporary Egypt. The Mubarak regime has over the
past few years expanded its focus of attacks from political parties,
nongovernmental organizations (NGOs), and the Islamists to also
include individuals whom it perceives to be obstacles to the pursuit
of its objectives.

The Case of Saad Eddin Ibrahim

Saad Eddin Ibrahim, a professor of sociology at the American
University in Cairo and founder of the Ibn Khaldon Research Center
(established in 1988, also in Cairo), was arrested during a June 2000
midnight visit by police to his home. He was subsequently detained
for forty-two days without charge. Once charged, the state's allegations that he had illegally received and misused funds from the
European Commission (which Commission auditors denied), forged
voter registration cards, attempted to bribe public officials, and tar-
nished the reputation of Egypt abroad rendered him liable to receive
a sentence of up to fifteen years' hard labor if convicted. In May
2001, Ibrahim was convicted by a state security court and sentenced
to seven years' hard labor. Twenty-seven Ibn Khaldon codefendants

were also found guilty and sentenced to prison terms of up to five years. Ten months into his sentence, Ibrahim and his colleagues were released (7 February 2002) pending a retrial.[6]

The political motivations behind the charges against Ibrahim can be detected on several levels. First, Ibrahim's research center has undertaken projects highlighting issues that the regime perceives to be highly sensitive, such as the plight of Copts, the lack of democracy, and the need for the rehabilitation of militants. More recently, two controversial factors have acted as catalysts for Ibrahim's arrest and subsequent trial. The first factor, which was indirectly used against Ibrahim during his trial, was his establishment of the League of Egyptian Women Voters (HODA) in 1998, made possible with the assistance of a European Commission grant. The organization intended to raise the political awareness of women nationwide through various means such as promotional videos and education. Furthermore, the organization intended to promote and encourage women to vote and, when necessary, assist them with practical issues such as registration and obtaining a voting card. As the 2000 legislative elections were approaching, the objective was to get the project off the ground as swiftly as possible. Not surprisingly, Ibrahim's arrest five months prior to the November elections and the forced closing of the HODA office along with the Ibn Khaldon Research Center led many to speculate that "the government arrested Ibrahim to prevent his center from monitoring . . . November's parliamentary elections."[7] The fact that the center was performing an active participatory role in regard to women voters undoubtedly touched upon a sensitive issue for the regime. While the regime may tolerate some degree of independent views and opinions, crossing the red line to actual participation is not.

Another more discreet factor that quite possibly sealed Ibrahim's fate was a magazine article he wrote on 10 June 2000 titled "The Arab World's Contribution to Political Science."[8] In this sarcastic piece, Ibrahim used the Syrian example of Bashar al-Asad assuming the presidency after his father's death to highlight the emerging trend in the Middle East of the inherited presidency, which he dubbed *gomlokiya* (republican monarchy). As a result, following the death of Syrian president Hafez al-Asad, Ibrahim was invited to a live question-and-answer program broadcast by an Arabic satellite television station. When a viewer whom Ibrahim knew personally called in to ask him his views on the possibility of Egypt becoming an inherited republic, he attempted to avoid answering the question but was eventually cornered into admitting that the possibility did exist, after which he presented a potential scenario as to how it could happen.[9] In the authoritarian world of politics, Ibrahim broke the ultimate rule: mentioning in public a sensitive topic regarding the ruling family.

The assumption that Ibrahim's arrest was politically rather than legally motivated was subsequently reinforced during his trial and sentencing. First, the fact that he was not officially charged for forty-two days indicated the lack of transparency and confusion on the part of the government in regard to his alleged "crimes." Second, during his trial the main evidence presented to the court was derived from the testimony of a state security officer, Nasir Mohi al-Din, and a number of pretrial statements made by Ibrahim's codefendants during detention. The fact that a lawyer was not present when these testimonies were given led to the suspicion that they had been coerced through police pressure. One of the defendants, Khalid Fayid, took the opportunity to distribute a flyer during his first court appearance, in February 2001, in which he urged all those present to note "the tense conditions" under which his "statements were extracted."[10] Furthermore, among other obstacles, the defense was denied access to the Ibn Khaldon Research Center, restricting it from acquiring records demanded by the state tax authority. Equally important, on the first day of Ibrahim's trial (17 February 2001), the defense, unable to properly prepare itself, had to ask the court for permission to photocopy Ibn Khaldon documents seized by state security, to which the defense had been allowed only reading access.[11] Even the sealed evidence allegedly taken from Ibn Khaldon came under suspicion, with the defense noting that some of it could have been tampered with. As one lawyer pointed out, "Boxes number four and fourteen are especially important because they contain the allegedly forged voter registration cards and voter lists, which could have been easily planted in the place of the real cards."[12]

International observers represented by the media, human rights groups, and U.S., Canadian, and European diplomats did little at the time to influence the biased outcome of the trial. Reflecting the views of many, Amnesty International and Human Rights Watch issued a statement a few hours after the verdict maintaining that Ibrahim and his codefendants had been "tried before a court that fails to meet international standards of fair trial . . . [and] we fear that the decision to convict had already been made prior to the conclusion of the trial."[13] The *Cairo Times* was equally direct when it declared in its 25 May 2001 editorial "Pharaoh's Prisoners" that the verdict "was brazen in its disregard of legal norms, brazen in its disdain for international opinion and brazen in its contempt for human rights."[14] A joint statement by six Egyptian human rights groups provided an accurate insight into the reasons behind the whole episode: "The arrest and trial of Dr. Ibrahim and his colleagues is a continuation of the state's hostile policies against civil society institutions in Egypt, aiming at the silencing of all institutions that try to participate effectively in public issues."[15]

Although Ibrahim was tried in a state security court, it was not part of the emergency division and thus Ibrahim's right of appeal could not be denied. Consequently, his defense presented an appeal to the Court of Cassation. Perhaps influenced by the highly vocal outrage of the international community, the court acknowledged on 21 March 2002 that certain procedural mistakes were made in the trial and set a retrial date of 27 April.[16] Almost one year later (18 March 2003), the Court of Cassation exonerated Ibrahim and declared him innocent of all charges. The international outrage and the public criticism leveled by the U.S. government (Ibrahim has dual Egyptian and U.S. nationality) undoubtedly played an important role in pressuring the regime into accepting an independent, civil court ruling in Ibrahim's favor.

The fact remains that the Ibrahim case is a poignant reflection on the increasing absence of governmental restraints in the state's quest for domination. To a large degree the government still achieved its intended objectives. The Ibrahim case has acted as a warning to other individuals and groups of the consequences of political activism. As the secretary-general of the Egyptian Organization for Human Rights noted, "In the last two years, lack of funding has affected our activities. . . . Prior to the NGO law and the Saad Eddin Ibrahim case we were producing 10 to 12 reports on human rights abuses a year. Now we are only producing two or three. We've also stopped producing our quarterly magazine."[17]

For the occasional activist, the message is yet to be fully absorbed. For example, Ahmad Saif, director of the Hisham Mubarak Legal Aid Center, interpreted the government's position within the following context: it does not mind the existence of human rights activists in order to enhance its international image. But domestic issues, such as those addressed by Ibrahim, are not to be publicized.

In Saif's words, "The government wants us to make an effort for the intifada . . . but it doesn't want us to work on local issues like torture [or] the misuse of power."[18] However, as the next case illustrates, even this is an optimistic interpretation.

The Case of Farid Zahran

In the regime's quest for political and social domination, no individual is considered too insignificant to be immune from the increasing crackdowns. The abduction and temporary detainment of Farid Zahran by security authorities in September 2001 is one such example. Zahran, a small publisher with leftist tendencies, was one of the founding members of the Egyptian Popular Committee for Solidarity with the Palestinian Intifada (EPCSPI), founded in 2000 in support of the Al-Aqsa intifada (uprising), which began in October of that year. The uniqueness of the group is that it comprises a small number of individuals (seven founding members) representing disparate political persuasions. In this regard, their sole point of unification is the Palestinian situation.

Prior to his abduction, Zahran and other members of the EPCSPI began to organize their efforts to assist and highlight the Palestinian cause. Their activities included sending petitions to President Mubarak urging him to break formal ties with Israel as well as a petition to the United Nations expressing concern for Palestinian political prisoners. However, most of their activities focused on the publication of literature relating to the Palestinian situation in local newspapers and magazines. Since the Palestinian-Israeli conflict is staple news in the media anyway, the publication of articles was neither particularly original nor striking. However, the EPCSPI crossed the red line by organizing conferences and political forums in regard to the Palestinian problem and holding an unauthorized anti-U.S. demonstration near the U.S. embassy in Tahrir Square on 10 September 2001. Consequently, Zahran was abducted by state security officers on 20 September 2001 while he was walking down a street in the Cairo suburb of Nasr City on his way to meet a fellow EPCSPI committee member. The meeting was actually scheduled so that Zahran's colleague could accompany him to the state security office, where he was wanted for questioning. Since state security officers abducted him beforehand, Zahran was unable to meet his colleague, who subsequently turned up a few minutes later to find a large crowd in the street who had watched the episode and believed that "state security officials had just arrested a terrorist."[19] Zahran was charged with "disseminating and possessing publications that threaten national security and injure the public good"[20] and was held in Tura prison for fifteen days before being released on bail of 5,000 Egyptian pounds (U.S.$1,000). Zahran's experience during his time in prison provides an insight into the regime's increasingly paranoid behavior.

It was clear that the charges against Zahran were a pretext for other issues of concern to the regime. While Zahran was in detention, state security officers searched his home without a warrant or formal identification to show his wife[21] and then presented him with allegedly subversive material that they claimed was found at his home. According to Zahran, "It was the first time I'd seen [the material] and I think it was the first time anybody had seen them. I think they belonged to the security people."[22]

The interrogation also focused on the demonstration of 10 September. Zahran had notified security officials about the demonstration plan and when he received no response from them, he assumed that he had permission to proceed as intended. Therefore, during interrogation, Zahran did not understand what the problem was. He told his interrogators, "You agreed to the demonstrations," to which their response was, "No, you didn't ask. You planned everything and then you told us what you were doing. If you had asked, we would have said no."[23] Most of Zahran's interrogation focused on the issue of Islamist activists, as a few Islamist-oriented activists were involved in the EPCSPI's planning meetings. Zahran denied any kind of formal alliance with the Islamists, as most of the committee members were secular intellectuals, academics, and artists. However, he admitted that "all shades of activists were welcome at committee meetings" but was clear to point out that the committee had no links or relations with "any political party or group."[24] There is little doubt that the authorities knew he was not tied to any political parties or groups, otherwise they would not have released him after two weeks in detention. It seems the objective was to preempt the possibility of a demonstration happening again. This assumption was reinforced when Zahran asked them directly during interrogation, "What are the ground rules? What are the red lines?" to which the reply was, "No street [activities] and no Muslim Brotherhood."[25]

In other words, Zahran was warned to stay out of political life—a warning that he views as senseless. In his words, "Either you have a political life and political activism or you have terrorism. There is no third way."[26] It is worth noting here that, following Zahran's release, state security has since moved on to other EPCSPI members. For example, on 13 May 2002 Gamal Abd al-Fatah, an EPCSPI member and a pharmacist by profession, was arrested. As in the case of Zahran, he was also charged with possessing printed material that was disruptive to public security. In addition, he was also charged with possessing expired medicines at his pharmacy. The next day three Islamist activists whose participation in the EPCSPI had been causing the most concern for the government were arrested. Ali Abd al-Fatah, Gamal Madi, and Ahmad Abd al-Hafiz were charged with "trying to revive the activities of a banned organization (a standard charge for Brotherhood members) and organizing an illegal rally."[27] Gamal Abd al-Fatah was subsequently released after spending one week in prison, during which time he was never questioned by security. The three Islamists remain in detention at the time of writing.[28]

The crackdown on individuals is in itself a reflection of the increasing restrictions imposed by the regime and an indication of its attempt to reassert itself on every level of the public sphere. In this regard, the government is having little problem achieving its objectives. Yet its repression of individuals as a mechanism for sending political messages in the seemingly inexhaustible quest for domination and control has extended beyond the realm of academics and activists. Indeed, the boundaries have been obscured to unprecedented levels and now reach into the private lives of apolitical individuals.

Homosexuals in Politics

The most prominent case in regard to the crackdown on alleged homosexuals for obscure political gains is the Queen Boat saga, in which fifty-two young men were arrested on 10 May 2001 and charged with "habitual practice of debauchery"—a term used to penalize activities not formally recognized by law, such as homosexuality and prostitution. The men, most of whom were rounded up from the Queen Boat, one of many nightclub vessels lining the Nile waterfront on the relatively cosmopolitan Cairo island of Zamalek, were then presented to a state security court (emergency division) for trial. The fact that an alleged vice crime was being tried in the emergency division of a military court with no prospects for appeal was in itself an overtly harsh and unjustifiable move. Furthermore, although the defense highlighted the irregularities of the evidence presented by the prosecution, such as the "conflicting testimonies, allegations of coerced confessions and inconclusive medical tests,"[29] by November 2001 the court had swiftly handed down prison sentences of up to five years to twenty-three of the defendants.[30] In December 2001 two students were arrested and sentenced to three months and one year in prison, respectively, on similar but unrelated charges.[31]

The high level of negative publicity given to these cases, the harsh sentencing of the accused, and the unprecedented use of a state security court to sentence the Queen Boat defendants (the two students were tried in a civilian court) all point to the government's politically inspired motivations. This assumption was highlighted by one human rights activist who noted, "My personal speculation is that the government is trying to portray itself as a guardian of moral values. All this is hailed in official newspapers as upholding Islamic virtues."[32] Ahmad Saif, director of the Hisham Mubarak Legal Aid Center, an independent NGO that supported the defendants of the Queen Boat case, also interpreted the government's increasing interest in the persecution of alleged homosexuals within a political context: "There was a change in government attitudes after the last [2000 legislative] elections . . . [w]hen the Ikhwan [Muslim Brotherhood] won a big membership [of parliament]. The government is trying to prevent the Ikhwan membership from mobilizing the people in the street. They say, 'Look! We too try to serve God.'"[33]

The targeting of alleged homosexuals by the government does appear to be linked to its increasing obsession with the Islamists. Yet the 17 seats acquired by the Islamists in a 454-seat parliament monopolized by the National Democratic Party (NDP) can hardly be perceived as a serious threat warranting such tactics. That the current regime is willing to publicly ruin the lives and reputations of apolitical civilians for its own political ends illustrates the emergence of yet another dimension of its repressive strategies, a trend that the post–11 September 2001 "war on terrorism" has only facilitated.

The War on Terrorism: Egypt, the United States, and the International Front

This book began with an examination of how political support on the international front, particularly from the Western democratic front, combined with economic incentives, can act as an effective instrument for curtailing or prolonging the life-span of particular authoritarian regimes. It was also pointed out that international support is ultimately linked to international interests. In this regard, whether the international arena chooses to prolong or undermine an authoritarian regime depends primarily upon its own particular interests. In the post–11 September 2001 world, the interests at stake and the basis on which choices are made have become clearer. Regimes that do not necessarily share the official U.S. worldview have been targeted for eradication, as was the case of the Taliban in Afghanistan and Saddam Hussein's regime in Iraq, or ostracized, as was the case of the authoritarian regimes in Iran and North Korea, which were labeled along with Hussein's Iraq by President George W. Bush as "the axis of evil." The authoritarian regimes of Libya, Syria, Sudan, and Cuba did not fare better. However, while such public attempts at undermining authoritarian regimes can be viewed as a potentially positive step in the long-term development of democracy, it is the selective nature of this offensive that has become more sharply evident and unsettling. For example, authoritarian regimes not dissimilar from those mentioned above have found international recognition and economic support in the post–11 September world, as in the case of General Musharaf's junta in Pakistan and the Northern Alliance in Afghanistan (as promoted in the guise of a transitional government). In addition, a more common trend has emerged in which increased repression by specific authoritarian regimes is directly and indirectly encouraged by their Western democratic patrons. A stark indication of this predicament was reflected in the contradictory position of the U.S. government with regard to two overtly authoritarian regimes in the post–11 September period, Cuba and Egypt.

In the case of Cuba, the U.S. president fervently attacked the absence of democracy. In his words, "Opposition parties should have the freedom to organize, assemble, and speak, with equal access to all airwaves. Political prisoners must be released and allowed to participate in the election process. Human rights organizations should be free to visit Cuba to ensure conditions for free elections are being created."[34] In addition, President Bush made it clear that normalization with Cuba and the prospect of economic assistance were dependent upon the establishment of a functioning democracy under a new government. In his words, "Full normalization of relations with Cuba—diplomatic recognition, open trade and a robust aid program—will only be possible when Cuba has a new government that is fully democratic, when the rule of law is respected, and when the human rights of all Cubans are fully protected."[35]

In regard to Egypt, the view differed drastically. When questioned about the need for political reform and the issue of human rights in Egypt, the U.S. ambassador to Cairo, David Welch, responded, "Egypt is our friend, and we do not put pressure on friends."[36] This position is not wholly unexpected in view of the increasingly positive U.S. interpretation of the Egyptian regime's repressive tactics in the wake of 11 September. As U.S. secretary of state Colin Powell stated two weeks after the terrorist attacks, "I . . . expressed my appreciation for the commitment that Egypt has made to working with us as we move forward to deal with the scourge of terrorism. Egypt, as you all know, is really ahead of us on this issue. . . . And we have much to learn from them and there is much we can do together."[37] On the basis of these comments, as one author noted, Colin Powell "portrayed Mubarak's heavy-handed approach to domestic security as a model for emulation."[38]

Furthermore, the United States, along with a host of international donors, extended such positive public support into practical economic assistance. While Egypt, the second biggest recipient of U.S. aid after Israel, continues to receive U.S.$2 billion worth of aid annually, the U.S. government announced in November 2001 its intentions of providing extra aid and pledged 400 million Egyptian pounds (U.S.$100 million) "to help alleviate the economic distress caused by the repercussions of the September 11 attacks."[39] The U.S. ambassador to Egypt justified this decision on the basis that "the U.S. government is pleased to be able to work with the government of Egypt to help Egypt overcome a current budget deficit resulting primarily from reduced revenues from tourism."[40]

At an international donors conference held in the Egyptian Red Sea resort of Sharm al-Shaykh in February 2002, the United States spearheaded the way for international donors to provide Egypt with another aid package totaling over U.S.$10 billion. Undoubtedly, the funds, of which U.S.$2.1 billion are to be paid initially and the remainder over the next few years, will help alleviate Egypt's increasing economic debts, which in 2002 stood at U.S.$57 billion. Nevertheless, the result is that "Egypt has secured from the US government massive aid and tacit acceptance of its human rights violations."[41] As the Egyptian government jumped onto the antiterrorism bandwagon, such human rights violations have reached rampant proportions.

The Case of Al-Waad

The group dubbed "Al-Waad" (The Promise) by the media comprises a miscellaneous assembly of ninety-four individuals with Islamist sympathies. In May 2001 its members were arrested and put on trial (seven in absentia) before a state security court on charges of unauthorized collection of U.S.$300,000 for Palestinian and Chechen assistance. On 13 October, President Mubarak issued a decree ordering the trial to be transferred to a military court. In addition, the charges were inexplicably changed to include "being part of an illegal organization, planning to assassinate government officials, destroy government buildings and arms possession."[42] The absurdity of these charges can be detected on several levels. First, the evidence presented by the prosecution was disproportionate to the charges levied at the accused. For example, the weapons presented to the court included a baseball bat, an air rifle, some knives, homemade pistols, and an antiaircraft shell (minus the antiaircraft gun). Even the military court was compelled to disqualify the baseball bat and air rifle as unsuitable evidence. The remaining evidence primarily took the form of books and documents, such as a videotape of fighting in Afghanistan and technical and engineering manuals.[43] This can hardly be regarded as serious evidence of the group's alleged intentions (and capabilities) to assassinate government officials and destroy government buildings.

Another factor relating to the evidence was the alleged tampering with police interrogation transcripts. The defense lawyers filed a complaint to the court about the deletion of certain words, such as "intifada," "Palestinians," and "Chechnya," from the interrogation transcripts. One of the defense lawyers, Hafiz Abu Saada, accused the police of deleting these words because their presence would have indicated "that this is not an armed group or illegal organization wanting to change power in Egypt, but only a group to collect funds to help and assist Muslims in Palestine."[44] Perhaps the most significant indication of the exaggerated charges faced by the group is the fact that until the mass arrests, political experts and analysts were not even aware of the group's existence. Diaa Rashwan, a prominent Islamist expert at the Al-Ahram Center for Strategic Studies, admitted that "this is the first time I have heard anything about this group—I don't really think there is a group called *al-Waad* in this country."[45] It is highly unlikely that the emergence of a militant Islamist group threatening to overthrow the government would pass unnoticed until its members were so efficiently rounded up en masse and presented for military trial.

This case is just one of several mass arrests that simultaneously occurred following the 11 September terrorist attacks. Two days after Mubarak issued the decree to transfer Al-Waad to a military trial, the president went on to issue another decree (15 October 2001) referring a separate group of 170 civilians to a military trial on charges of "terrorist activities and membership of the Islamic *Jam'at* organization."[46] On 11 November the president issued another decree referring a group of twenty-two civilians to trial in a military court on charges of "membership of the Muslim Brotherhood and inciting student demonstrations."[47] This was followed on 27 January 2002 by the arrest and referral to a military court of eight more civilians on charges of "organizing student protests and raising funds for Palestine, in addition to the usual charges of being members of a banned organization [the Muslim Brotherhood]."[48] It is worth noting here that the last two groups arrested were composed of middle-aged professionals, including university professors, engineers, and doctors. Dr. Hamdi Said, head of the Doctors Syndicate and an NDP member, spoke in support of two of the doctors who had been rounded up in the 27 January arrests. As he pointed out, "They are very well respected people, both of them are professors in the university, one is very well known in the field of liver disease and the other is a professor of anatomy. . . . I have never noticed any political activity from those two members."[49]

Whether or not these professionals are politically active is irrelevant. It remains difficult to justify their presence in front of a military court on such feeble charges. Furthermore, while it has always been very difficult to protect civilians from the prospect of military trials, the situation since 11 September has made it virtually impossible. As Mohamad Zarai, a lawyer and director of the Human Rights Center for the Assistance of Prisoners (HRCAP), noted, "Before 9/11, there were balances and pressure on the government from the international community. But post 9/11, the whole world is on one side and terrorism on the other. And by simply defending human rights by taking a stand against torture or military trials for civilians, I am placed in the position where I am accused of defending terrorism."[50]

Consequences of the Post–11 September Approach

In 1999 one expert noted that in relation to the Middle East, "We're in a very sensitive time. . . . The idea that the fundamentalist threat can only be controlled by hard military rulers prevails."[51] Since the 11 September attacks, it is clear that this perception has been reinforced. As one human rights report noted shortly after the terrorist attacks, the political arena in Egypt consists of "a narrowly circumscribed political realm and a government that does all it can to suffocate peaceful political opposition." The report goes on to note that this has subsequently produced "an environment in which the political center has been systematically silenced . . . [and] governments can credibly portray themselves as the only bulwark against extremism."[52] The fact that the international arena, particularly the United States, supports the government's portrayal of such a role only serves to protect the existence of authoritarianism and allow for continued increase in repression.

In the wake of 11 September, the rise in repression and mass arrests in the name of fighting terrorism is not the only factor indicating the continued support of authoritarianism in Egypt. Rather, that the Egyptian government continues to proclaim its pursuit of democracy while not being held accountable by its Western democratic patrons is another reflection of the West's reinvigorated support of authoritarianism in favor of genuine democratic reform. For example, in response to a question on how the process of combating terrorism has affected democratic development in Egypt, President Mubarak stated, "Not a speck. Democratic development is progressing, the freedom of the press is protected, the sovereignty of the law is upheld, the judiciary is independent and state institutions, including legislative bodies, are operational and effective."[53] Such a response is indicative of the degree to which international support has increased the regime's confidence and its ability to proclaim unsubstantiated propaganda.

The West's reinvigorated support of authoritarian allies, such as the Egyptian government, can be perceived as little more than an erroneous, shortsighted approach to addressing the increasingly threatening trend of violent extremists. In Egypt, the decline of extremist activities since 1997 has been credited to "the growing unpopularity of its criminal actions, including among Islamist sympathizers, and the extent and severity of repression" inflicted by the state.[54] While this may be the case, the fact remains that the repression did not address the fundamental issues of contention as much as it helped redirect the Islamists' strategies of confrontation and violence into the international arena. After all, the use of coercion may act to intimidate and suppress targeted opponents, but it does not help to solve the conflict. As one study notes, "Acquiescence can perhaps be achieved solely by coercion, but support and acceptance cannot . . . support and acceptance must be cultivated by the only means possible—that is, political means of persuasion, promises and inducements of whatever kind."[55] In regard to its opponents, the Egyptian government has increasingly depended on the policies of coercion and intimidation without attempting—perhaps out of insecurity and fear of undermining its own position—to examine the roots of discontent and cultivate some form of acceptance or support. In an effort to explain the reemergence of Islamic Jihad in the international arena, this aspect is acknowledged by Foad Alam, a former deputy director of state security's terrorism department. As Alam points out, while the activities of Jihad as a group "have receded in Egypt . . . the ideology remains and was not confronted properly. It's like a tree, when you cut only the branches but leave the roots. With a little water and fertilizer, the branches will grow again."[56]

In this vein, the Western and U.S. endorsement of the Egyptian government's increasing repression as part of the post–11 September "war on terrorism" will heighten the conflict. As one academic argues, the reason "why so many Arabs and Muslims hate the U.S. and look at it as a power of evil . . . [is because] through the dictators that America supports . . . America has perverted attempts to democratize the Arab world. They are hypocrites. They preach freedom and democracy, but prevent Arabs from enjoying it."[57] This view will invariably become more widespread within the Middle East if the Egyptian government, along with the other authoritarian regimes, continue to receive the increasing unconditional support of their Western allies.

It was this same Western and particularly U.S. support of the Pahlavi regime in pre-1979 Iran that discouraged the Shah from adopting either restraint or genuine political and economic reforms. The result was an authoritarian system of rule that over the years began "rotting from within . . . as repression and corruption became the two defining characteristics of the regime."[58] By the 1970s, channels of communication to the government had not only "withered and disappeared" but "the gap between the rich and poor increased, [as] the shah sought to concentrate all powers into his own hands while turning his secret police (SAVAK) loose on the people."[59] The utilization of a sophisticated coercive apparatus to strike down real and perceived opponents, along with an extremely close relationship with the United States, rendered it unimaginable that the Shah's position could be challenged. For example, U.S. ambassador to Iran William Sullivan reported to Washington in 1977 that "the Shah was in full control of the country and that the opposition was no match for the well-fortified regime."[60] Even by late 1978, when mass opposition had reached a level whereby "short of a miracle, nothing could save the Shah,"[61] Sullivan still perceived it unimaginable that the regime would fall. In fact, a few weeks before the Shah was forced into exile, the ambassador still believed that the armed forces would protect the Shah and ensure "he will not leave the country [even if it involves] a massive crackdown which will involve a lot of blood being spilled."[62]

In January 1979 the Pahlavi regime fell, but not through political opponents, who were very weak after decades of repression, but through the people themselves in "a multi-class uprising in which the lower-class masses and the burgeoning middle classes joined hands against the Pahlavi political elite."[63] Indeed, political opponents eventually unified to take advantage of the fury of the masses and transform them into an organized movement—but the underlying fact remains that it was undoubtedly a people's revolution. The fall of the Shah illustrates how a few erroneous judgments on the part of a regime and its allies can lead to its downfall. In the case of Iran, the overthrow of the Shah led to the rise of the ulama (Muslim theologians), who consolidated power and transformed what was initially a people's revolution into an Islamic one. In the process, the United States lost an ally and became the "Great Satan"—a term readily accepted by the Iranian masses given the decades of resentment they harbored as a consequence of U.S. support for their former dictator.

The case of Iran may be a prominent example, but it is not unique. Prior to the Iranian revolution, the 1950s and 1960s saw the rise of populist republics in the Middle East, all of which emerged as consequence of the decline and fall of corrupt and repressive regimes that had also claimed the support of Western colonial patrons. In turn, the birth of these populist regimes in Egypt, Syria, Tunisia, Libya, and Iraq brought little more than an alternate form of authoritarian rule in which anti-Western nationalism preceded the anti-Western Islamism of the contemporary era. In fact, the Pahlavi dynasty was born out of the first Middle Eastern military coup of the twentieth century, in 1921, in reaction to the corruption and repression of its predecessor, the Qajar dynasty. With few exceptions, the fall of authoritarian regimes in the Middle East has produced a pattern in which the old regime is replaced by another authoritarian system of rule. In most instances the new regimes turn out to be more radical and repressive than those they replaced.

Currently and in the absence of democratic reform, the political uncertainties associated with authoritarian rule continue to prevail as plotting individuals and groups resort to clandestine and occasionally violent activities. Reinforcing the uncertainty is the possibility that, "by bringing down the ruler, the plotters may very well succeed in bringing down a regime."[64] More ominous is the possibility that, while political opponents or "an active, militant, and highly mobilized popular upsurge" may become instrumental in "bringing down a dictatorship . . . [such an upsurge] makes subsequent democratic consolidation difficult, and under some circumstances may provide an important motive for regression to an even more brutal form of authoritarian rule."[65] Past experience in the Middle East indicates that the overthrow of authoritarian regimes tends to result in the latter pattern being the norm rather than the exception.

As one author noted, the rise of political Islam in its various forms has not been surprising in contemporary Egypt, "given the social ills engendered by . . . extended unemployment, especially among the qualified young; aggravated social polarization in which ill-gained wealth, insolently displayed, stood out against the growing misery of the rural and urban populations; and generalized corruption spreading right up to the highest levels of society and state."[66] The author rightly argues that in regard to such socioeconomic and political discontents, "Egypt is not an exceptional case among [developing] countries . . . without any rigorous democratic control."[67] In this regard, the fundamental issue is the progression toward genuine political liberalization and an authentic democratic framework that will assist in alleviating such problems. Political stability, peace, and development in the Middle East, like anywhere else, can best be achieved through reform rather than revolution. As mentioned earlier, foreign support may protect and prolong the life-span of an authoritarian regime, but it cannot maintain such a regime indefinitely. It is in the interest of all parties concerned, including authoritarian regimes and their international patrons, to opt for political reform rather than risk the imposed and unpredictable transformations of dissent. Consequently, the United States could start by recognizing that it is should "pressure friends" into genuine political reform. In this vein, the 11 September terrorist attacks, orchestrated to a large degree by Egyptian nationals, should be viewed as an outcome of U.S. support for a dictatorial and repressive Middle Eastern regime—not as an excuse to reinforce unconditional support for such a regime.

Conclusion

Egypt's political system illustrates the flexibility and adaptability of personal authoritarian rule. It also provides an apt example of how the adoption of a formal multiparty framework should not automatically be perceived as a move toward political liberalization and democratic transitions. Rather, to properly assess the nature of a political system, it is best to examine the formal and informal structure of government, the balance of power within it, and its relationship with society. In other words, it is erroneous to assume that a regime is liberalizing based simply on an analysis of the number of political parties and civil society groups that exist within a particular system. The balance of power and the relationship between these entities and the power-holders provide a more accurate framework of analysis.

The existence of regular elections should also be discarded as an indication of political liberalization or democratic transition. Instead, one should focus not only on the outcome of the elections but also the factors that produced such an outcome. As the case of Egypt illustrates, the adoption of a multiparty framework can act to reinforce authoritarian rule. Indicative of this is that the existence of a multiparty arena for a quarter century has achieved little in terms of allowing for the development of autonomous organized parties and groupings. Instead, it has helped to ensure that participation is contained and channeled into the regime's rigidly defined formal political arena. The creation of this arena has helped protect the exclusionary nature of the system by allowing the regime to co-opt political opponents while exercising a veto over the participation of certain groups and particular personalities perceived to be potential threats to the status quo. The negative consequences of these strategies, as examined throughout this book, are varied. They include the existence of weak political institutions and groupings, the prevalence of political individualism, and the reinforcement of the hierarchical ties of clientelism. The most recent and prominent trend has been the expansion of conflict and the rise in violent confrontations on the state-society level. While the regime's Islamist opponents remain the main focus of coercion and repression, secular political activists, human rights activists, homosexuals, workers, and voters have all been increasingly targeted over the past few years. This trend can be viewed as an indication of the increasing insecurity of an authoritarian regime determined to maintain its monopoly on power. At present, such insecurity is largely unfounded.

The survival of the Egyptian regime is secure for the foreseeable future due to several factors.[68] First, there does not appear to be any serious conflict within the ruling bloc, and particularly within the military, that would potentially cause the disintegration of the existing power structure. As discussed in Chapter 2, the dynamics of the prevailing governance structure make such a probability unlikely. Second, the support extended to the Egyptian regime by the international arena, and particularly by the United States, has not been conditional upon genuine political reform. In the absence of such pressure, the political arena in Egypt has not achieved the type of irreversible political reform that would result in regime compromises and a true democratic transition. Rather, political reform remains symbolic and therefore controllable and easily contained by the regime. Furthermore, as Adam Przeworski points out, "A regime does not collapse unless and until some alternative is organized in such a way as to present a real choice for isolated individuals."[69] In the case of Egypt, the symbolic nature of political reforms means that this choice does not currently exist. Political parties and individual activists are swiftly repressed and weakened at the slightest indication of dissent or potential leadership qualities. Militant Islamists may create violence and occasional havoc, but their potential following among the population is as marginal as for extremist groups anywhere else in the world. The Muslim Brotherhood is not a potentially viable alternative to the existing regime in that it appears to present "a real choice" only for the 1 million[70] "isolated individuals" who sympathize with it. However, the regime's persistent and ruthless pursuit of the Brotherhood indicates that the possibility of the group being left unhindered to sufficiently organize and present itself as a realistic alternative to the political status quo is currently as unfeasible as it is for the secular, legalized opposition. The post–11 September world has moved to reinforce the unfeasibility of such an option. The implications of the above factors all indicate that the adoption of repressive and authoritarian tactics may erode the regime's legitimacy, but in practical terms this is not a particularly threatening situation. As Przeworski explains:

> A regime survives when . . . the handful of people not occupied with disciplining children or gaining a livelihood is prevented from organizing by repression or cooption. . . . Only when one has the option of not disciplining children, not leaving the factory but occupying it instead, not lowering one's voice when speaking about politics but actively mobilizing others, only then is a regime threatened. If these options are not present, if one cannot engage in such behaviors without risking almost certain extinction, one may believe that a regime is totally illegitimate and yet behave in an acquiescing manner. . . . If the belief in the legitimacy of the regime collapses and no alternative is organized, individuals have no choice.[71]

This is the current situation in Egypt. The consolidation and monopolization of power by the regime renders the possibility of imminent challenges to the Egyptian system remote. This leads to the main question proposed by this book: If personal authoritarian rule in contemporary Egypt has emerged since its establishment in 1952 as institutionalized, adaptable, flexible, and continuously developing in sophistication, then why is it becoming increasingly repressive and insecure when its position is stable?

This leads us back to the fundamental essence of authoritarian rule, namely that as a dominating and oppressive political system it can never be fully institutionalized. The political uncertainty that radiates from the knowledge that a successful challenge would mark the end of a regime and perhaps the lives of the power-holders is a reality for all systems of this nature. Foreign powers can change policies and alliances, splits within the ruling elite can emerge and become sufficiently serious to fragment and weaken a regime internally, and a socioeconomic crisis can erupt into the type of mass unrest that would provide even the weakest opposition with the necessary support required to bring down a regime. These are the types of uncertainties that make even the most stable of authoritarian systems behave in an insecure and repressive manner.

The prevailing Egyptian regime is no different in terms of facing such uncertainties. While its close ties with the United States are strong and have been strengthened since 11 September, the regime is currently facing significant problems. On the economic level, the country is reaching a near crisis. In addition to its estimated U.S.$57 billion debt, the structural adjustment program is moving slowly and is producing neither the expected economic development nor the rise in employment needed to sustain the population at large. Compounding this predicament, the 2000–2002 period saw the U.S. dollar almost double in value compared to the Egyptian pound. The current state of the Egyptian economy is aptly noted in the words of Clement Henry and Robert Springborg:

> Inward looking crony capitalism, coupled to the military economy and the leviathan government with its still large public sector, generates the patronage and provides the controls required for the regime to retain its support within the state, while contemptuously ignoring or repressing what little autonomous political life remains. But this nexus of cronies, officers, bureaucrats, and public sector managers is inherently inward looking, as it feeds off rents that can only be provided by the monopolies and oligopolies of a protected economy. In 1982 Egypt exported goods worth $8.6 billion and Turkey $9.2 billion. In 1999 Turkish exports had risen to $52 billion, while in Egypt they had increased to only $14 billion. . . . The steadily more negative balances of trade and payments, and associated need for governmental borrowing, presage an economic crisis.[72]

On the political level, the Mubarak leadership is nearing its end and the seventy-four-year-old leader has yet to designate a successor. While the president refutes claims that he is preparing his son Gamal for succession, the outside observer might look upon the current state of affairs skeptically in view of the young Mubarak's appointment to senior political posts, including membership in the NDP's elite political bureau, the General Secretariat. The twenty-four-member bureau constitutes the center of the dominant party and its presidentially appointed members comprise the most senior and trusted of Mubarak's ministers. As a young and charismatic individual, should

Gamal succeed his father he might have problems with these and other members of his father's old guard should they feel threatened by any potential efforts to reform this decaying system. If Gamal is not designated as a successor, the possibility of an interelite struggle for the presidency has the potential to weaken and break the existing power bloc. After all, in the absence of the ruler, the cohesive bond that ties the ruling elite tends to rapidly falter in a personalized system of rule. Either way, the patterns that have existed since Nasser show that repression increases toward the end of a president's rule, just as it decreases at the start of his tenure. This pattern has been highly evident in the Mubarak era. If the succession process is smooth, and this is most likely to be the case, Egypt will witness a new "liberalizing" era under Mubarak's successor. Yet past and existing patterns should also temper our optimism for such a transition.

A Final Note

I would like to include here an incident that I believe is an indication of both the increasing lack of empathy on the part of the Egyptian regime over the past few years and the extent of its alienation from the people. This case does not imply that the Egyptian regime is at risk of imminent instability or collapse.

During the 2000 legislative elections, a small community in rural Egypt brought to my attention some of the problems they had encountered with the security forces. They had been denied entry to vote, which resulted in the death of a few locals as well as injury to many more. A well-publicized affair, the case was covered in the international media as well as national opposition party newspapers.

The community was angered by the lack of governmental response—whether in the form of an apology or compensation for the families of the victims. Following the scandalous publicity of the event, state security had sealed off the area to prevent further communication between locals and outsiders. After these tragedies of election day, I was compelled to sneak into the community disguised as a local, with the help of some genuine residents who took the risk out of a desperate need to communicate with the outside world. As a stream of locals sneaked in and out of the back entrance of a local notable's house, which acted as my base, state security personnel were sitting in the reception room drinking tea and observing the main entrance, oblivious to the action. During interviews and discussions, members of the community asked me to pass on their grievances, if possible, to any senior government official that might listen. They assumed that the lack of governmental response might be due to information being blocked prior to reaching a high level.

Later, I contacted a senior and highly respected public figure in government. I explained the sequence of events and highlighted the ill feelings that had developed within the community toward the government. The senior government official was very understanding and appeared to grasp how important it was to compensate the families of the victims in order to regain the community's confidence and trust. The senior government official also promised that he would contact the minister of interior and look into the situation personally. I subsequently left feeling satisfied that the problems of the community would be addressed.

The next morning at work, I was contacted on a personal mobile phone by a senior state security officer, who introduced himself and informed me that a meeting was in order. A few hours later, I arrived at the officer's state security office, which was based at the Ministry of Interior's headquarters in Cairo. The officer was sitting behind his desk drinking tea and watching an interview being conducted on the Al-Jazeera satellite news channel with a senior member of Egypt's Muslim Brotherhood. As I entered the office, he picked up the phone and asked the person on the other end to ensure that the Brotherhood interview was being videotaped. Then, after pleasantries, the officer began asking me about the election events surrounding the community in question. I relayed the same information I had narrated the previous day to the senior government official. The officer listened carefully and then proceeded to question the reasons behind my interest and concern about this particular issue. When the officer discovered that it was an impersonal matter based on humanitarian concern that had led me to seek assistance for the distraught community, and that I was not linked to the village through family or friendship ties, he was very puzzled. The officer then proceeded to justify the events to me by placing the blame on the community. He claimed that the people had not listened to the security forces and that this was what had caused the injuries and deaths. He then went on to compare the role of the state to the role of parents, and the role of citizens to the role of children. In his words, "If the parents tell the children not to go out onto the streets and the children disobey and get run over by a car, is that the parents' fault? No it is not. The same with [that local community], they misbehaved and did not follow instructions so they paid the price, is that the government's fault? No it is not, it is their own fault for being careless." After about an hour of discussions with little progress, I conceded that it was time to leave. Just before leaving, I repeated the point that my decision to bring this matter to the attention of the authorities was intended to inform them of the fragile situation so that they could hopefully do something constructive to defuse the tension and potential instability in the community. The officer smiled, thanked me for my concern, and stated that he would try to help, even though still maintaining that the locals were the ones at fault. As I was opening the door to leave, the officer looked over and said, "This is not Iran or Algeria you know. Everything is under control. . . . We will never make the same mistakes as them. There will never be instability or uprisings. . . . It will never happen here."

Notes

1. Jackson and Rosberg, *Personal Rule in Black Africa,* p. 267.
2. Springborg, "Patterns of Association in the Egyptian Political Elite," p. 95.
3. Bill and Springborg, *Politics in the Middle East,* p. 171.
4. Zakariya, "Terrorism."
5. Jackson and Rosberg, *Personal Rule in Black Africa,* p. 23.
6. "Belated Justice in Egypt." It is worth noting that on 18 March 2003 Ibrahim was eventually exonerated and declared innocent of all charges by the Court of Cassation, Egypt's highest court of appeal.
7. Radwan, "Having the Last Laugh."
8. The article was written in the London-based Arabic newspaper *Magalit al-Saudiya.*
9. Author discussion with Ibrahim family member, spring 2002, Cairo.
10. el-Ghobashy, "Public Enemy No. 1."
11. Ibid.
12. el-Ghobashy, "Business Unusual."
13. el-Ghobashy, "Echoes of Shock."
14. Ibid.
15. Ibid.
16. Elamrani, "Mistakes Were Made."
17. Lussier, "Down and Out?"
18. Ibid.
19. Hassan, "Snatched."

20. Ibid.

21. Ibid.

22. Khalil, "Home Again, with a Warning."

23. Ibid.

24. Ibid.

25. Ibid.

26. Ibid.

27. Schemm, "Rites of Passage."

28. For in-depth coverage, see ibid.

29. Khalil, "Out of Mind."

30. In May 2002 the military governor agreed to a retrial in a civil court for all but two of the fifty-two defendants thanks largely to the international outrage, which included a letter of protest from forty U.S. senators to the Egyptian authorities. The new date had not been set at the time of writing. For further details on the news of the retrial, see Elamrani, "180 Degrees."

31. "Shadow Crackdown."

32. Ibid.

33. Ibid.

34. "President Bush Announces New Initiative for Cuba."

35. Ibid.

36. David Welch, U.S. ambassador to Egypt, public lecture on U.S. foreign policy in the Middle East, American University in Cairo, 28 January 2002. For coverage, see Elamrani, "The Cost of Friendship."

37. "Remarks with Egyptian Minister of Foreign Affairs Ahmed Maher," Washington, D.C., 26 September 2001, www.state.gov/secretary/rm/2001/5066.htm. See Brownlee, "The Decline of Pluralism in Mubarak's Egypt." p. 17.

38. Brownlee, "The Decline of Pluralism in Mubarak's Egypt," p. 17.

39. USAID. See Kassem, "More Aid Now, Trade Later."

40. David Welch, U.S. ambassador to Egypt. See ibid.

41. Human Rights Watch 2001 annual world report. See Elamrani, "Hypocrisy Matters."

42. Schemm, "Terror Tactics."

43. Ibid.

44. Ibid.

45. Ibid.

46. U.S. Department of State, "Egypt Country Report on Human Rights Practices, 2001," p. 6.

47. Ibid.

48. Schemm, "The Never-Ending Crackdown."

49. Ibid.

50. Lussier, "Down and Out?"

51. Perlez, "A Middle East Choice."

52. Human Rights Watch 2001 annual world report. See Elamrani, "Hypocrisy Matters."

53. Interview with President Mubarak, *Al-Ahram Weekly* (25–31 October 2001).

54. Rouleau, "Egypt's Islamists Caught in a Bind."

55. Jackson and Rosberg, *Personal Rule in Black Africa,* p. 38.

56. MacFarquhar, "Islamic Jihad."

57. Beaumont, "The Roots of Islamic Anger."

58. Bill and Springborg, *Politics in the Middle East,* p. 381.

59. Ibid.

60. Milani, *The Making of Iran's Islamic Revolution,* pp. 111–112.

61. Ibid., p. 119.

62. Ibid., p. 125.

63. Bill and Springborg, *Politics in the Middle East,* p. 381.

64. Jackson and Rosberg, *Personal Rule in Black Africa,* pp. 58–59.

65. O'Donnell and Schmitter, *Transitions from Authoritarian Rule,* p. 65.

66. Rouleau, "Egypt's Islamists Caught in a Bind."

67. Ibid.

68. These factors are based on a theoretical argument presented in Przeworski, "Problems in the Study of Transition to Democracy," pp. 50–53.

69. Ibid., p. 52.

70. This estimation is derived from Rafiq Habib, director of the Coptic Evangelical Organization for Social Services in Egypt. Habib, who has worked with political Islamist groups in Egypt since 1989, believes that the Muslim Brotherhood has 50,000–100,000 members and approximately 1 million sympathizers. Stacher, "Moderate Political Islamism," p. 70.

71. Przeworski, "Problems in the Study of Transition to Democracy," pp. 52–53.

72. Henry and Springborg, *Globalization and the Politics of Development in the Middle East,* p. 155.

Bibliography

Abd al-Razik, Jasir. Then director of the Hisham Mubarak Legal Aid Center. Interview by author, 6 August 2000, Cairo.

Abdel-Fattah, Nabil. "A Time to Judge." *Al-Ahram Weekly* (10–16 August 2000).

Abdel-Latlf, Omayman. "No Partners in Power." *Al-Ahram Weekly* (23–29 December 1999).

Abdel-Magid, Wahid. "Assessment of the Performance of the People's Assembly, the Third Legislative Session of the Seventh Chapter, 1997/98." *Group for Democratic Development.* Cairo: Parliament Watch Group, 1998.

Abou al-Maged, Nadia. "Tempered Jubilation." *Al-Ahram Weekly* (13–19 July 2000).

Abu Saada, Hafez. Secretary-general of the Egyptian Organization of Human Rights. Interview by author, 3 August 2000, Cairo.

Advocacy Alert. "President Mubarak Should Not Ratify Restrictive New Law on Associations in Egypt." Legal Center for Human Rights, May 1999. www.lchr.org, accessed 4 January 2000.

Aikman, David. "Egypt's Human Wrongs." *American Spectator* 32, no. 3 (March 1999): 64–66.

Al-Ammar eyewitnesses. Interview by author, 5 January 2001, Al-Ammar, Qalubiya governate, Egypt.

Anderson, Lisa. "Arab Democracy: Dismal Prospects." *World Policy Journal* 18, no. 3 (fall 2001), electronic collection A8075732.

———. "State Policy and Islamist Radicalism." In *Political Islam: Revolution, Radicalism, or Reform?* ed. John L. Esposito. Boulder: Lynne Rienner, 1997, pp. 17–32.

"Annual Report 2000: Egypt." Amnesty International. www.web.amnesty.org/web/ar2000web.nsf/ar2000, accessed 13 June 2002.

Apiku, Simon. "Ahrar Crisis Gets More Intricate." *Middle East Times* (20–26 September 1998).

——. "Ahrar Evicts Renegades in Further Squabbles." *Middle East Times* (2–8 August 1998).
——. "Egypt Cracks Down on Islamist Party." *Middle East Times* (27 May–2 June 2000).
——. "Government Keeps Islamists Out of Syndicate Elections." *Middle East Times* (16 June 2000).
——. "Lawyers Call for Self-Rule." *Middle East Times* (14–20 February 1999).
——. "Nafie Wins Syndicate Elections with Some Opposition." *Middle East Times* (4–10 July 1999).
——. "Notorious NGO Law Thrown Out." *Cairo Times* (8–14 June 2000).
——. "The Plot Thickens." *Middle East Times* (15–21 March 2001).
——. "Political Parties Committee Spares Ahrar." *Middle East Times* (6–12 September 1998).
——. "Rushed Syndicate Law Under Constitutional Fire." *Middle East Times* (9–15 November 1997).
——. "Syndicate Sit-In Pays Off." *Middle East Times* (20 May 2000).
al-'Ariyan, Assam. Assistant secretary-general of the Egyptian Medical Syndicate and senior Muslim Brotherhood activist. Interview by author, 25 January 2001, Cairo.
Ayubi, Nazih. *Overstating the Arab State: Politics and Society in the Middle East.* London: I. B. Tauris, 1996.
——. *Political Islam: Religion and Politics in the Arab World.* London: Routledge, 1991.
——. *The State and Public Policies in Egypt Since Sadat.* Reading, Mass.: Ithaca Press, 1991.
Azzam, Maha. "Egypt: Islamists and the State Under Mubarak." In *Islamic Fundamentalism,* eds. Abdel Salam Sidahmed and Anoushiravan Ehteshami. Boulder: Westview, 1996, pp. 109–122.
Baaklini, Abdo, Guilain Denoeux, and Robert Springborg. *Legislative Politics in the Arab World: The Resurgence of Democratic Institutions.* Boulder: Lynne Rienner, 1999.
Baker, Raymond William. *Egypt's Uncertain Revolution Under Nasser and Sadat.* Cambridge: Harvard University Press, 1978.
Bates, Robert H. *Beyond the Miracle of the Market: The Political Economy of Agrarian Development in Kenya.* Cambridge: Cambridge University Press, 1989.
Beaumont, Paul. "The Roots of Islamic Anger." *The Observer* (14 October 2001). www.observer.co.uk/print/o,3858,4276871,00.html.
Beinin, Joel. "Labour, Capital, and the State in Nasserite Egypt, 1952–1961." *International Journal of Middle East Studies* 21 (fall 1989): 74.
"Belated Justice in Egypt." *New York Times* (8 February 2002).
Bianchi, Robert. *Unruly Corporatism: Associational Life in Twentieth Century Egypt.* Oxford: Oxford University Press, 1989.
Bill, James A., and Robert Springborg. *Politics in the Middle East.* 4th ed. New York: HarperCollins College Publishers, 1994.
Binder, Leonard. *Islamic Liberalism: A Critique of Development Ideologies.*

Chicago: University of Chicago Press, 1988.

al-Borai, Negad. Lawyer and head of the now defunct Group for Democratic Development. Interview by author, 30 July 2000, Cairo.

Borger, Julian. "More Than a Deputy: This Man Could be bin Laden's Inspiration—Zawahiri Leader with Ruthless Vision." *The Guardian* (8 October 2001).

Brooker, Paul. *Non-Democratic Regimes: Theory, Government, and Politics.* New York: St. Martin's, 2000.

Brownlee, Jason. ". . . And Yet They Persist: Explaining Survival and Transition in Neopatrimonial Regimes." *Studies in Comparative International Development* 37, no. 3 (fall 2002): 57.

———. "The Decline of Pluralism in Mubarak's Egypt." *Journal of Democracy* 13, no. 4 (October 2002): 6–14.

Bush, Ray. *Economic Crisis and the Politics of Reform in Egypt.* Boulder: Westview, 1999.

"Business in Brief." *Cairo Times* (10–16 January 2002).

Carothers, Thomas. "The End of the Transition Paradigm." *Journal of Democracy* 13, no. 1 (March 2002): 5–21.

Cassandra. "The Impending Crisis in Egypt." *Middle East Journal* 49, no. 1 (winter 1995): 10–27.

Chehabi, H. E., and Juan Linz, eds. *Sultanistic Regimes.* Baltimore: Johns Hopkins University Press, 1998.

Dawoud, Khalid. "Necessary Precautions." *Al-Ahram Weekly* (16–22 November 2000).

Dessouki, Ali al-Din Hilal. "Democracy in Egypt: Problems and Prospects." *Cairo Papers in Social Science,* 2nd ed., vol. 1, no. 2. Cairo: American University in Cairo, 1983, pp. 8–26.

Digges, Dianne. "Rights Groups Recoil at Egypt Law." *Christian Science Monitor* 91, no. 131 (3 June 1999): 6.

"Egypt." *Middle East Contemporary Survey,* vol. 11. Cairo, 1987.

"Egypt: 2001." *The World Factbook.* Washington, D.C.: U.S. Central Intelligence Agency, 2001.

Eisenstadt, S. N., and R. Lemarchand, eds. *Political Clientelism, Patronage, and Development.* London: Sage, 1981.

Elamrani, Issandr. "The Cost of Friendship." *Cairo Times* (31 January–6 February 2002).

———. "Divide and Rule." *Cairo Times* (23–29 November 2000).

———. "Hypocrisy Matters." *Cairo Times* (24–30 January 2002).

———. "Mistakes Were Made." *Cairo Times* (28 March–3 April 2002).

———. "180 Degrees." *Cairo Times* (30 May–5 June 2002).

———. "State of the Region." *Cairo Times* (13–19 July 2000).

Engel, Richard. "Government Man Set to Win Syndicate Elections." *Middle East Times* (27 July–2 August 1999).

Essam al-Din, Gamal. "Lakah Hard Times." *Al-Ahram Weekly* (23–29 August 2001).

———. "Three More Years of Emergency." *Al-Ahram Weekly* (2–8 March 2000).

Ezz el-Din, Mahitab. "Law 93/1995: A Case Study of the Role of the Egyptian Press Syndicate." M.A. thesis, American University in Cairo, fall 1996.

Farag, Sharif, and Mohamad Mursi. "Requiem for a Heavyweight." *Cairo Times* (30 August–5 September 2001).

Farahat, Nur. "Courting Constitutionality." *Al-Ahram Weekly* (31 August–6 September 2000).

Farghali, Al-Badri. Member of the Tagammu' Party and member of parliament. Interview by author, 31 December 1994, Cairo.

al-Fergany, Nader. *Impact of the Proposed Labor Law on Labor Market Flexibility and Social Condition in Egypt: A Preliminary Assessment.* Cairo: Al-Mishkat Center, 1998.

———. "Yes to Pluralism, No to Violence." *Al-Ahram Weekly* (29 December 1994–4 January 1995).

Fisk, Robert. "Egypt Caught Between Islam and the West." *The Independent* (12 October 2001).

Fouad, Khalid. Lawyer and independent Bar Syndicate council candidate. Interview by author, 18 January 2001, Cairo.

Gazzar, Brenda. "The Ballot and the Bullet." *Cairo Times* (2–8 November 2000).

Gerges, Fawaz. "The End of Islamist Insurgency in Egypt? Costs and Prospects." *Middle East Journal* 54, no. 4 (fall 2000): 592–612.

el-Ghobashy, Mona. "Business Unusual." *Cairo Times* (30 May–5 June 2002).

———. "Echoes of Shock." *Cairo Times* (31 May–6 June 2001).

———. "Public Enemy No. 1." *Cairo Times* (22–28 February 2001).

———. "With All Deliberate Speed." *Cairo Times* (6–12 June 2002).

Gillies, David. *Between Principle and Practice: Human Rights in North-South Relations.* Montreal: McGill-Queens University Press, 1996.

Group for Democratic Development newsletter. Cairo, winter 1999.

Habib, Kamal al-Said. Former Al-Jama'a al-Islamiya activist. Interview by author, 19 February 2002, Cairo.

Hassan, Abdalla. "Snatched." *Cairo Times* (27 September–3 October 2001).

———. "Work Rules." *Cairo Times* (10–16 January 2002).

Hatem, M. "Professional Associations in a Developing Country: The Case of the Lawyers and Engineers Syndicates in Egypt." M.A. thesis, American University in Cairo, 1974.

Heikal, Mohammed. *Autumn of Fury: The Assassination of Sadat.* London: Andre Deutsche, 1983.

Henry, Clement, and Robert Springborg. *Globalization and the Politics of Development in the Middle East.* Cambridge: Cambridge University Press, 2001.

Hermet, Guy, Richard Rose, and Alain Rouquie, eds. *Elections Without Choice.* London: Macmillan, 1978.

Hill, Enid. *Mahkama! Studies in the Egyptian Legal System.* London: Ithaca Press, 1979.

———. "Parties, Elections, and the Law." *Cairo Today* (April 1984): 24–27.

Hilmi, Ali. Chairman of the Metal and Steel Industries Company. Interview by author, 14 November 1998, Helwan, Egypt.

Hinnebusch, Raymond A. "Formation of the Contemporary Egyptian State from Nasser and Sadat to Mubarak." In *The Political Economy of Contemporary Egypt,* ed. Ibrahim M. Owciss. Washington, D.C.: Center for Contemporary Arab Studies, Georgetown University, 1990, pp. 188–209.

——. *Syria: Revolution from Above.* London: Routledge, 2001.

Howeidy, Amira. "Destitute but Determined." *Al-Ahram Weekly* (3–9 August 2000).

——. "Registering the Aftershocks." *Al-Ahram Weekly* (16–22 November 2000).

Huntington, Samuel P. *Political Order in Changing Societies.* New Haven, Conn.: Yale University Press, 1968.

Husayn, 'Adil. "Limatha qata'na intakabat 1990? Wa limatha nadakhaliha al-an? Wa masalana al-jabar al-intasar" [Why did we boycott the 1990 elections? And why are we entering them now? And we ask Allah for victory]. *Al-Sha'b* (29 September 1995).

Ibrahim, Saad Eddin. "Democratization in the Arab World." In *Civil Society in the Middle East,* vol. 1, ed. Augustus Richard Norton. New York: E. J. Brill, 1995, pp. 27–54.

——. *Egypt, Islam, and Democracy.* Cairo: American University in Cairo Press, 1996.

Ismail, Mamdoh. Lawyer and former Al-Jihad member. Interview by author, 26 February 2002, Cairo.

Jackson, Robert H., and Carl G. Rosberg. *Personal Rule in Black Africa: Prince, Autocrat, Prophet, Tyrant.* Berkeley: University of California Press, 1982.

al-Kabbani, Nevien. "Behind Walls of Oblivion." *The Program for Amelioration of Prison Conditions.* Cairo: Human Rights Center for the Assistance of Prisoners Press, 2000.

Kafr al-Mikdam villagers and eyewitnesses. Interview by author, 19 May 2001, Cairo.

Kassem, Hisham. Owner of the *Cairo Times.* Interview by author, 7 November 2000, Cairo.

Kassem, Mahmoud. "More Aid Now, Trade Later." *Cairo Times* (13–26 December 2001).

Kassem, Maye. *In the Guise of Democracy: Governance in Contemporary Egypt.* London: Ithaca Press, 1999.

Kepel, Gilles. *Muslim Extremism in Egypt: The Prophet and the Pharaoh.* Trans. John Rothschild. Berkeley: University of California Press, 1984.

Khattab, M. "Constraints of Privatization in the Egyptian Experience." Mediterranean Development Forum, Marrakesh, Morocco, 3–6 September 1998.

Khalil, Ashraf. "Case Closed." *Cairo Times* (23–29 November 2000).

——. "Home Again, with a Warning." *Cairo Times* (11–17 October 2001).

——. "Out of Mind." *Cairo Times* (11–17 October 2001).

Khalil, Nevine. "Setting the Standard." *Al-Ahram Weekly* (16–22 November 2000).

Khir, Abd al-Rahman. Deputy chairman of the Military Production Union, Egyptian Federation of Trade Unions. Interview by author, 19 June 2002, Cairo.

Kienle, Eberhard. *A Grand Delusion: Democracy and Economic Reform in Egypt.* London: I. B. Tauris, 2001.

———. "More Than a Response to Islamism: The Political Deliberalization of Egypt in the 1990s." *Middle East Journal* 52, no. 2 (spring 1998): 219–235.

Korany, Bahgat, Rex Brynen, and Paul Noble, eds. *Political Liberalization and Democratization in the Arab World.* Vol. 2. Boulder: Lynne Rienner, 1998.

Kramer, Gudrun. "The Integration of the Integrists." In *Democracy Without Democrats: The Renewal of Politics in the Muslim World,* ed. Ghassan Salame. London: I. B. Tauris, 1994, pp. 200–226.

Lakah, Ramy. Prominent businessman and member of parliament (2000–2001). Interview by author, 17 November 1998, Cairo.

Lawson, Kay. *The Human Polity.* Boston: Houghton Mifflin, 2000.

Linz, Juan J. *Totalitarian and Authoritarian Regimes.* Boulder: Lynne Rienner, 2000.

Lussier, Annik. "Down and Out?" *Cairo Times* (31 January–6 February 2002).

———. "Striking a Balance?" *Cairo Times* (3–9 April 2003).

MacFarquhar, Neil. "Islamic Jihad, Forged in Egypt, Is Seen as Bin Laden's Backbone." *New York Times* (4 October 2001). www.nytimes.com/2001/10/04/international/04JIHA.html?

el-Mikawy, Noha. *The Building of Consensus in Egypt's Transition Process.* Cairo: American University in Cairo Press, 1999.

Milani, Mohsen M. *The Making of Iran's Islamic Revolution: From Monarchy to Islamic Republic.* Boulder: Westview, 1998.

Military Courts in Egypt: Courts Without Safeguards, Judges Without Immunity, and Defendants Without Rights. Center for Human Rights Legal Aid report, Cairo, September 1995.

al-Mirghani, Hoda. Economist for the Federation of Egyptian Industries. Interview by author, 27 May 1999, Cairo.

Mitchell, Richard P. *The Society of the Muslim Brothers.* Oxford: Oxford University Press, 1969.

Mongy, Mustapha. Deputy chairman of the General Federation of Egyptian Trade Unions. Interview by author, 5 December 1999, Cairo.

Monir, Hazim. "Al-Watani yahasim asmaa' morashiya khalil 48 sa'a: Tinsiq kamal bayn al Togama' wa al-Nasiry" [The National Party names its candidates in the coming 48 hours: Full cooperation between the Tagammu' and the Nasserist parties]. *Al-Ahali* (4 October 1995).

Monshipouri, Mahmood. *Democratization, Liberalization, and Human Rights in the Third World.* Boulder: Lynne Rienner, 1995.

Moussalli, Ahmed. *Moderate and Radical Islamic Fundamentalism: The*

Quest for Modernity, Legitimacy, and the Islamic State. Gainesville: University of Florida Press, 1999.

Mubarak, Hosni. Interview in *Al-Ahram Weekly* (25–31 October 2001).

Mursi, Mohamad. Journalist on Egyptian parliamentary affairs. Interview by author, 10 June 2002, Cairo.

"NGO Law Passed in Full." *Cairo Times* (10–23 June 1999). www.cairo times.com/content/issues/hurights/ngolaw3.html, accessed 13 June 2002.

Nor, Ayman. Independent member of parliament. Interview by author, 28 March 2002, Cairo.

Norton, Augustus Richard, ed. *Civil Society in the Middle East.* Vol. 1. New York: E. J. Brill, 1995.

'Obayd, 'Atef, minister of public enterprises. Speech at NDP election rally, 25 November 1995, Helwan, Egypt.

O'Donnell, Guillermo, and Phillipe Schmitter. *Transitions from Authoritarian Rule: Tentative Conclusions and Uncertain Democracies.* Baltimore: Johns Hopkins University Press, 1986.

O'Donnell, Guillermo, Phillipe C. Schmitter, and Laurence Whitehead. *Transitions from Authoritarian Rule: Comparative Perspectives.* Baltimore: Johns Hopkins University Press, 1986.

Okasha, Saeed. "In With the New." *Cairo Times* (24–30 May 2001).

Ouda, Jihad, Negad el-Borai, and Hafez Abu Saada. *A Door Onto the Desert: Egyptian Legislative Elections of 2000.* Cairo: United Group and Fredich Neumann Foundation, 2001.

Owen, Roger. "Socio-Economic Change and Political Mobilization: The Case of Egypt." In *Democracy Without Democrats: The Renewal of Politics in the Muslim World,* ed. Ghassan Salame. London: I. B. Tauris, 1994, pp. 183–199.

———. *State, Power, and Politics in the Making of the Modern Middle East.* 2nd ed. London: Routledge, 1992.

Perlez, Jane. "A Middle East Choice: Peace or Democracy." *New York Times* (28 November 1999). www.nytimes.com/library/review/112899middle-east-review.html.

Perthes, Volker. "Economic Liberalization and the Prospects of Democratization." In *Democracy Without Democrats: The Renewal of Politics in the Muslim World,* ed. Ghassan Salame. London: I. B. Tauris, 1994, pp. 243–269.

Picard, Elizabeth. "Syria Returns to Democracy: The May 1973 Legislative Elections." In *Elections Without Choice,* eds. Guy Hermet, Richard Rose, and Alain Rouquie. London: Macmillan, 1978, pp. 129–144.

Posusney, Marsha Pripstein. *Labor and the State in Egypt: Workers, Unions, and Economic Restructuring.* New York: Columbia University Press, 1997.

"President Bush Announces New Initiative for Cuba." Washington, D.C., 18 May 2002. www.whitehouse.gov/news/releases/2002/05/200205201.html.

"Presidential Public Address." Ministry of Information and State Information Service, April 1982 and 1 May 1998, Cairo.

Przeworski, Adam. "Problems in the Study of Transition to Democracy." In *Transitions from Authoritarian Rule: Comparative Perspectives,* eds. Guillermo O'Donnell, Phillipe C. Schmitter, and Laurence Whitehead. Baltimore: Johns Hopkins University Press, 1986, pp. 47–63.

"Q&A: Warnings, Past and Present from Mubarak's Egypt." *Washington Post* (21 October 2001).

Radwan, Amany. "Having the Last Laugh." *Time* (21 May 2001).

Radwan, Mohamad, Nagwa Ibrahim, et al. "Evaluation of the People's Assembly's Performance in the Second Plenary of the Seventh Legislative Term 1997." *Group for Democratic Development.* Cairo: Parliament Watch Program, 1998.

Rouleau, Eric. "Egypt's Islamists Caught in a Bind." *LeMonde Diplomatique.* Paris, English ed. January 1998.

Said, Mohamad al-Sayid. "The Roots of Turmoil in the Egyptian Organization for Human Rights Dynamics of Civil Institution-Building in Egypt." *Human Rights: Egypt and the Arab World—Cairo Papers in Social Science,* vol. 17, no. 3. Cairo: American University in Cairo, fall 1994, pp. 65–87.

Salem, Amir. *The Despotism of the Bureaucratic State.* Cairo: Legal Research and Resource Center for Human Rights, n.d.

al-Sayid (al-Sayyed), Hamdi. National Democratic Party candidate. Speech at an electoral gathering, 18 November 1995, Hickstep, Nozha, Egypt.

———. National Democratic Party candidate. Speech at a conference on elections at the Research Center for Human Rights, 25 December 1995, Cairo.

———. National Democratic Party veteran. Interview by author, 1 January 1995, Cairo.

al-Sayid (al-Sayyid, el-Sayed), Mustapha Kamil. "A Civil Society in Egypt?" In *Civil Society in the Middle East,* vol. 1, ed. Richard Augustus Norton. New York: E. J. Brill, 1995, pp. 269–293.

———. "The Islamic Movement in Egypt." In *The Political Economy of Contemporary Egypt,* ed. Ibrahim M. Oweiss. Washington, D.C.: Center for Contemporary Arab Studies, Georgetown University, 1990, pp. 222–239.

———. Professor of political science at Cairo University and the American University in Cairo. Interview by author, 2 October 2000, Cairo.

Schedler, Andreas. "Elections Without Democracy: The Menu of Manipulation." *Journal of Democracy* 13, no. 2 (April 2002): 36–50.

Schemm, Paul. "The Never-Ending Crackdown." *Cairo Times* (31 January–6 February 2002).

———. "NGOs Divided over Resistance to New Law." *Middle East Times* (June 1999).

———. "NGOs' New Big Brother Ready to Help." *Middle East Times* (27 July–2 August 1999).

———. "Rites of Passage." *Cairo Times* (23–29 May 2002).

———. "Terror Tactics." *Cairo Times* (29 November–5 December 2001).

Schiller, Norbert. "Beaten at the Polls." *Cairo Times* (16–22 November 2000).

Senior member of the Muslim Brotherhood. Interview by author, 11 November 1995, Cairo.

Senior state security officer. Interview by author, spring 2001, Cairo.

"Shadow Crackdown." *Cairo Times* (27 December 2001–2 January 2002).

el-Shafei, Omar. "Trade Unions and the State in Egypt." *Cairo Papers in Social Science* 18, no. 2. Cairo: American University in Cairo, 1995.

Shehab, Shaden. "Missing the Point." *Al-Ahram Weekly* (20–26 July 2000).

al-Sheikh, Mursi. "Liberal Lawyers Syndicate Council Candidate Interview." *Middle East Times* (16 June 2000).

Shokar, Abd al-Ghafar. Senior member of the Tagammu' Party. Interview by author, 27 January 1999, Cairo.

Shokar Allah, Rizk Allah. Chairman of the National Metal Industries Company. Interview by author, 18 November 1998, Khanka, Egypt.

Sid 'Ahmad, Mohamad. "Politics Versus Violence." *Al-Ahram Weekly* (14–20 December 1995).

Smith, B. C. *Understanding Third World Politics: Theories of Political Change and Development*. Bloomington: Indiana University Press, 1996.

Soliman Joda. "Al-Jama'yitaraga'un 'an siasa al-'atada 'ala al-akkarin" [Al-Jama'a retreats from its policy of attacking others]. *Al-Wafd* (21 February 2002).

Springborg, Robert. *Mubarak's Egypt: Fragmentation of the Political Order*. Boulder: Westview, 1989.

———. "Patterns of Association in the Egyptian Political Elite." In *Political Elites in the Middle East,* ed. George Lenczowski. Washington, D.C.: American Enterprise Institute for Public Policy Research, 1975, pp. 83–107.

Stacher, Joshua A. "A Democracy with Fangs and Claws and Its Effect on Egyptian Political Culture." *Arab Studies Quarterly* 23, no 3 (summer 2001): 83–99.

———. "Discontent Beyond Discontent: Post-Islamist Rumblings in Egypt?" *Middle East Journal* 56, no. 3 (summer 2002): 415–432.

———. "Moderate Political Islamism as a Possible New Social Movement: The Case of Egypt's Wasat [Center]." M.A. thesis, American University in Cairo, December 2001.

———. "Parties Over? The Demise of Egypt's Opposition Parties." *British Journal of Middle Eastern Studies* (forthcoming 2004).

"Strangling the Press." *Middle East International* (9 June 1995).

Sullivan, Dennis J., and Sana Abed-Kotob. *Islam in Contemporary Egypt: Civil Society vs. the State*. Boulder: Lynne Rienner, 1999.

Sultan, Gamal. Editor-in-chief of *Al-Manar al-Jadid* and former Al-Jama'a al-Islamiya member. Interview by author, 16 February 2002, Cairo.

Sunar, Ilkay, "The Politics of Interventionism in 'Populist' Egypt and Turkey." Research Paper, Bogazici University, Istanbul, 1993.

Tschirgi, Dan. "Marginalized Violent Internal Conflict in the Age of Globalization: Mexico and Egypt." *Arab Studies Quarterly* 21, no. 3 (summer 1999): 13–35.

U.S. Department of State. "Egypt Country Report on Human Rights Practices, 2001." Washington, D.C.: Bureau of Democracy, Human Rights, and Labor, 4 March 2002.

———. "1999 Country Reports on Human Rights Practices: Egypt." Washington, D.C.: Bureau of Democracy, Human Rights, and Labor, 25 February 2000.

Vatikiotis, P. J. *The History of Modern Egypt: From Muhammad Ali to Mubarak.* 4th ed. London: Weidenfeld and Nicolson, 1991.

Wali, Ali. Former chairman of the General Petroleum Company (1958–1966, 1967–1971) and former minister of petroleum (1971–1972). Interview by author, 6 April 2002 and 13 April 2002, Cairo.

Waterbury, John. *The Egypt of Nasser and Sadat: The Political Economy of Two Regimes.* Princeton: Princeton University Press, 1983.

Weaver, Mary Anne. *A Portrait of Egypt: A Journey Through the World of Militant Islam.* New York: Farrar, Straus, and Giroux, 1999.

Zakariya, Farid. "Terrorism: The Roots of Rage." *Newsweek* (14 October 2001).

al-Zayat, Montasir. *Ayman al-Zawahiri: Kama 'Arafitu* [Ayman al-Zawahiri: As I Knew Him]. Cairo: Dar al-Mahrosa, 2002.

———. Al-Jama'a al-Islamiya lawyer and Islamist. Interview by author, 16 February 2002, Cairo.

Zubaida, Sami. *Islam, the People, and the State: Political Ideas and Movements in the Middle East.* London: I. B. Tauris, 1989.

Index

About the Book

Though the regimes of Egyptian presidents Nasser, Sadat, and Mubarak have been decidedly different, the nature of personal authoritarian rule in Egypt has remained virtually unchanged across more than five decades. Maye Kassem traces the shaping of contemporary Egyptian politics, considering why authoritarian rule has been so resilient and assessing the mechanisms that have allowed for its survival.

Kassem begins with the military coup d'etat of July 1952, moving from the single-party system established under Nasser to the current framework in which opposition parties are legal. Along the way, she explores the legacies of Mubarak's predecessors, the functioning of the legislature and judiciary vis-à-vis the president, the roles of political parties and civil society, and the impact of authoritarian rule on the development of extremist Islamic groups. She concludes by reflecting on the long-term effects of authoritarianism on national development, stability, and Egypt's place in the international arena.

Maye Kassem is assistant professor of political science at the American University in Cairo. She is author of *In the Guise of Democracy: Governance in Contemporary Egypt*.